PATH TO THE LIGHT

Kabbalah Centre Publishing is a registered DBA of Kabbalah Centre International, Inc.

For further information:

The Kabbalah Centre
155 E. 48th St., New York, NY 10017
1062 S. Robertson Blvd., Los Angeles, CA 90035

1.800.Kabbalah www.kabbalah.com

Printed in the Canada, September 2021

ISBN: 978-1-952895-11-1

eBook ISBN: 978-1-952895-12-8

Design: HL Design (Hyun Min Lee) www.hldesignco.com

PATH TO THE LIGHT

KABBALAH
CENTRE
PUBLISHING

DECODING THE BIBLE WITH KABBALAH

An Anthology
of Commentary
from Kabbalist
Rav Berg

BOOK OF
BAMIDBAR
Volume 8

Bamidbar
Naso
Beha'alotcha
Shlach Lecha
Korach

TABLE OF CONTENTS

BOOK OF BAMIDBAR:

Portion of Bamidbar

PORTION OF BAMIDBAR

In the portion of Bamidbar we have the revelation of immortality. I bring it up so it will always be available. We have been successful in reversing the aging process with plants, vegetation, and fruits and now know that the same can be applied to people.

Bamidbar was an opportunity for the Israelites to overcome the forces of chaos and evil. By hearing the Torah reading of this portion on Shabbat we can relieve ourselves of some of the chaos. Bamidbar and the next portion of Naso give us a means to be in control while we are in the desert; while we are in this world that feels like a wilderness.

In the Wilderness

Bamidbar, which means "in the wilderness," is the first portion of the fourth Book of Moses. As we have come to understand, the first portion of a Book of the Bible carries the same name as the entire Book. And the etymology of English names used for portions and Books of the Bible often have little to do with the meaning of the Hebrew names. For example, in English, the name of this portion and Book is "Numbers." Yet one might ask the question, what does the concept of numbers have to do with the wilderness? The modern English usage of the term "numbers" might make logical sense because the word numbers can give us an insight into what we can expect from the literal story found in this Book of the Bible— the counting of the Israelites.

The Hebrew language however is an advanced technology, not only a language. In the potent Hebrew language, one code opens up a whole new world, with all its implications, especially if it represents a group of codified letters.

We have a tremendous opening here in this fourth Book of Moses with just this one word—*bamidbar*. All the lessons found in portions of the Book of Numbers are included in the concept of "in the wilderness."

With all that is going on in the world, we might indeed conclude that we live in a wasteland, in a wilderness where the law of the jungle prevails. Personally, we may even be living well, nonetheless there is an element of wasteland. Why do I say this? Because life can be as empty and desolate as a desert. An individual can walk for miles and still be in the middle of nowhere. How much do you feel in control under such circumstances? The desert itself controls us, and this analogy is used to help us understand how little we are in control of our lives.

The Book of Bamidbar exists to reveal to us how we can transform our own wilderness into a fertile land.

The Home of Satan

Bamidbar is probably the most interesting of the five Books of Moses, if only from the point of view of the simple narrative. Whether it be wild or weird, all manner of story can be found in the Book of Bamidbar. It teems with exciting drama. Hollywood need not seek elsewhere when we have every plot right here in this book—chock full of events that defy the imagination. However, we must bear in mind that the negative aspects within this book exist here as an opportunity to reveal the Light.

The word *midbar* means both "wilderness" and "desert." The desert is a place where nothing grows and few things can live. There is emptiness. The Zohar says that *midbar* is the home of Satan. This is where he breeds his offspring of chaos who we have all encountered in one form or another.

For me, personally, this was a great revelation. Now I understand why Bugsy Siegel chose the desert to build his hotel and casino. I do not think he knew the entire implication when he built what has become one of the most popular attractions in the entire world.

What the Zohar is telling us is that we are in Satan's playing field, day and night. As important as we think we are, making decisions, acquiring money, prestige and so on, if we do not have what is available to us in this portion of Bamidbar then the house wins. We are lost and there is no escape.

This portion is telling us that there is little that can bring us as much tranquility as the Book of Bamidbar but this power of peace is concealed. With the technology found in this book we can defeat Satan at his own game, in his own place. Wherever there is Light, we can find him. Satan is like swarms of bugs making an attempt to reach the Light. Satan receives his sustenance from the Light. By travelling through the wilderness, the Israelites experienced the opportunity to overcome the forces of chaos and evil.

It is important to note that the portions of Bamidbar and Naso both represent the same idea. Once we understand what *midbar* (wilderness) is about, we will come to understand what the portion of Naso concerns.

Bamidbar 1:1 And the Lord spoke to Moses in the wilderness of Sinai, in the Tent of Meeting, on the first day of the second month, in the second year after they came out of the land of Egypt, saying: 2 "Take the sum of all the congregation of the children of Israel, by their families, by their fathers' houses, according to the number of names, every male, by their polls; 3 from twenty years old and upward, all that are able to go forth to war in Israel: you shall number them by their hosts, even you and Aaron.

God's Desire to Count the Israelites

The portion of Bamidbar begins with the verse: "And the Lord spoke to Moses…saying: 'Take the sum of all the congregation of the children of Israel….'" The word the Bible uses is *se'u* that is derived from the word *benso'a* in the phrase *vehi benso'a ha'Aron*, which means "when the Ark *traveled* forward." This is sung upon the opening of the Ark in the War Room when we take out the Torah Scroll, before we read from it. The meaning of the word *se'u* combines the two words "travel" and "carry." The Zohar says the word *se'u* does not imply the taking of a census, rather it means to arouse and tap into the awesome Light of the Creator as we do when we open up the Ark to take out the Torah Scroll prior to the reading of it.

The reason the translation infers a census here is because it discusses God's wish to count the Israelites. Why would God want to count the Israelites in the month of Taurus (Iyar), in the second year after the Israelites had left Egypt, and not at some other time? Was it simply to present us with an historical fact? Why do we need to know, today, how many Israelites were in a tribe 3,400 years ago? Nonetheless, this is what we have been reading for millennia.

Every letter, word, and verse in the Bible is a code providing us with important information and technology on how to turn this wilderness, this wasteland, into a land of fruition.

The Zohar provides us with clues as to why we listen to the reading of this portion of Bamidbar on Shabbat. The Zohar explains that the meaning and purpose of the counting of the Israelites is profound and also difficult to explain. It tells us that this episode took place in the second month—the month of Taurus. Incidentally, this portion is read in the month of Taurus every year. The sages organized the Bible into weekly readings for a reason. There is a very specific division of the portions and each division incorporates a different aspect for humankind to transform this wasteland.

According the Zohar, this whole incident with the numbering of the Israelites occurred because the month of Taurus is a biblical revelation. Without the Zohar no one would know that this month embraces the *Ziv* (Light). In addition, Taurus (Iyar) is the only month of the year that signifies *kodesh*, which means "holiness." What is more, where did the Hebrew name Iyar come from? Four thousand years ago, Abraham the patriarch wrote his work, known as the Book of Formation, where he gave each month a name. Abraham did not name the months for the same reason we name a baby. Rather by naming the months as he did, Abraham provided insight into the hidden spiritual essence of each month. The month of Taurus is the month of healing because it is the month of Light.

The Zohar states that, contrary to the accepted opinion in medical circles that there are many diseases and aliments, there is only one disease and that is death. In our time, medicine has become so specialized that there is a doctor for every part of the body.

Yet Rav Shimon says that when an individual is afflicted with an ailment, the real cause is that Satan has found a vulnerability in the body, which permits him to enter.

Satan knows the intimate details of all of our past lifetimes. He knows precisely how each individual needs to leave this world, and what type of death fits into the whole configuration of his or her lifetime, for example whether one is to die of a heart attack or by some other means. Thus when someone is afflicted in any organ or part of the body, the Zohar says it is the one that Satan himself appropriately decided upon. These afflictions are not random, therefore, genetic testing and other research into the causes of various diseases will produce different conclusions. In the final analysis, there will always be exceptions to medical conclusions. The real problem is the exception to the rule.

Kabbalah simplifies matters. The Zohar demonstrates how we can properly deal with ailments. Just as in a darkened room when we turn on the light, the darkness disappears, so, too, in a dark room, when we infuse the space with Light, it removes the darkness. No one can deny this. There is no force that can prevent darkness from disappearing when the lights are turned on. It is a universal law. The Zohar and the Bible provide us with simple clues, in the Month of Ziv—the Month of Light—we can use this time to transform our own personal wilderness. This is how simple it is.

Therefore when the Zohar announces that the month of Taurus is mentioned in this biblical portion, it is because Taurus is the Month of Light. Why this month and not another? At the time of Creation, one month had to be chosen to give humankind an opportunity to flee the wasteland. God gave us this tremendous opportunity in this month. At the time of Creation, He placed within the cosmos a force known as healing. God provided us with the totality of Light that banishes illness and chaos. No matter what its nature, chaos in all its forms can be removed in this month.

The first verse of this portion, says: "In the Sinai desert, in the wilderness, God said to Moses..." indicating what we are able to access in Chodesh Ziv, the Month of Light.

Counting the Israelites

Bamidbar 1:1-2 says, "And the Lord spoke to Moses in the wilderness of Sinai, in the first day of the second month, in the second year... take the sum of all the congregation of the children of Israel." The second month is Taurus, which as was discussed previously, is also named the Month of Ziv. *Ziv* means "Light." This indicates what we can expect to tap into. In the month of Taurus, God decided to count the people, even though He had counted them before. Why count them again? The Hebrew word for counting is also *sefira*. God understood that there was weakness in the consciousness of the people so He infused a new consciousness of Light through the counting. Injecting Light into the universe brings into existence a new kind of information, just as with the invention of the telephone.

The counting, the *sefira*, injects Light into the universe. With this reading, we are infused with the Lightforce so that the darkness, which seems to be ever-present, moves away each and every week with the reading of the Torah scroll.

4 And with you there shall be a man of every tribe, every one head of his fathers' house. 5 And these are the names of the men that shall stand with you: of Reuben, Elizur the son of Shedeur. 6 Of Simeon, Shelumiel the son of Zurishaddai. 7 Of Judah, Nachshon the son of Amminadab. 8 Of Issaschar, Nethanel the son of Zuar. 9 Of Zebulun, Eliab the son of Helon. 10 Of the children of Joseph: of Ephraim, Elishama the son of Ammihud; of Manasseh, Gamaliel the son of Pedahzur. 11 Of Benjamin, Abidan the son of Gideoni. 12 Of Dan, Ahiezer the son of Ammishaddai. 13 Of Asher, Pagiel the son of Ochran. 14 Of Gad, Eliasaph the son of Deuel. 15 Of Naphtali, Ahira the son of Enan." 16 These were the elect of the congregation, the princes of the tribes of their fathers; they were the heads of the thousands of Israel. 17 And Moses and Aaron took these men that are pointed out by name. 18 And they assembled all the congregation together on the first day of the second month, and they declared their pedigrees after their families, by their fathers' houses, according to the number of names, from twenty years old and upward, by their polls. 19 As the Lord commanded Moses, so did he number them in the wilderness of Sinai. 20 And the children of Reuben, Israel's first-born, their generations, by their families, by their fathers' houses, according to the number of names, by their polls, every male from twenty years old and upward, all that were able to go forth to war; 21 those

that were numbered of them, of the tribe of Reuben, were forty-six thousand, five hundred. 22 Of the children of Simeon, their generations, by their families, by their fathers' houses, those that were numbered thereof, according to the number of names, by their polls, every male from twenty years old and upward, all that were able to go forth to war; 23 those that were numbered of them, of the tribe of Simeon, were fifty-nine thousand, three hundred. 24 Of the children of Gad, their generations, by their families, by their fathers' houses, according to the number of names, from twenty years old and upward, all that were able to go forth to war; 25 those that were numbered of them, of the tribe of Gad, were forty-five thousand, six hundred and fifty. 26 Of the children of Judah, their generations, by their families, by their fathers' houses, according to the number of names, from twenty years old and upward, all that were able to go forth to war; 27 those that were numbered of them, of the tribe of Judah, were seventy-four thousand, six hundred. 28 Of the children of Issaschar, their generations, by their families, by their fathers' houses, according to the number of names, from twenty years old and upward, all that were able to go forth to war; 29 those that were numbered of them, of the tribe of Issaschar, were fifty-four thousand, four hundred. 30 Of the children of Zebulun, their generations, by their families, by their fathers' houses, according to the number of names, from twenty years old and upward, all that were able to go forth to war; 31 those that were numbered of them, of the tribe of Zebulun, were fifty-seven thousand, four hundred. 32 Of the children of Joseph, namely, of the children of Ephraim, their generations, by their families, by their fathers' houses, according to the number of names, from twenty years old and upward, all that were able to go forth to war; 33 those that were numbered of them, of the tribe of Ephraim, were forty thousand, five hundred. 34 Of the children of Manasseh, their generations, by their families, by their fathers' houses, according to the number of names, from twenty years old and upward, all that were able to go forth to war; 35 those that were numbered of them, of the tribe of Manasseh, were thirty-two thousand, two hundred. 36 Of the children of Benjamin, their generations, by their families, by their fathers' houses, according to the number of names, from twenty years old and upward, all that were able to go forth to war; 37 those that were numbered of them, of the tribe of Benjamin, were thirty-five thousand, four hundred. 38 Of the children of Dan, their generations, by their families, by their fathers' houses, according to the number of names, from twenty years old and upward, all that were able to go forth to war; 39 those that were numbered of them, of the tribe of Dan, were sixty-two thousand, seven hundred. 40 Of the children of Asher, their generations, by their families, by their fathers' houses, according to the number of names, from twenty years old and upward, all that were able to go forth to war; 41 those that were numbered of them, of the tribe of Asher, were forty-one thousand, five hundred. 42 Of the children of Naphtali, their generations, by their families, by their fathers' houses, according to the number of names, from twenty years old and upward, all that were able to go forth to war; 43 those that were numbered of them, of the tribe of Naphtali, were fifty-three thousand, four hundred.

Transforming Darkness into Light

The names of the heads of the twelve tribes are listed in the beginning of this portion. This information exists to provide us with opportunity and means to control the influences of the twelve signs of the zodiac, which are represented by the twelve tribes. And despite the evidence of the effects of the different months, there are those who do not believe in astrology. In the same manner, the desert in this portion—the wilderness—indicates to us that there is a desert wherever we are. Satan has left his home in the desert to come to our War Room on Shabbat to get Light, and instead we will be transforming his darkness into Light.

As we have said previously, this reading discusses the counting of the people. For some reason we need to know that the tribe of Reuben has 46,500 people, as each and every single tribe is counted. We are told this not for the sake of information but for the connection. As the Zohar tells us, knowledge is the connection. The Bible says that the tribe of Dan had 62,700 people, which indicates that the tribe of Dan rules over Scorpio and that in the Heavens, during the month of Scorpio, the constellation consists of 62,700 stars. The difference in the numbering of each tribe provides us with information about the stars. This knowledge makes our connection to the appropriate technology.

All the months of the year are mentioned in this portion so we have an opportunity, with this reading, to tap into the energy of each month. This is the technology of the Zohar, which relates to specific events mentioned in the Bible and does not ignore the most obscure parts. We capture this enormous energy of the Light by virtue of listening. We allow the Light to feed us, we absorb the Light from all these months, even though they are not all in existence at the same time during the reading. We are beyond time, space, and motion and thus each of us can benefit from all the energy of protection each month has to offer right now.

Bamidbar 2:1 And the Lord spoke to Moses and to Aaron, saying: 2 "The children of Israel shall pitch by their fathers' houses; every man with his own standard, according to the ensigns; a good way off shall they pitch round about the Tent of Meeting.

Creating a Security Shield

Why did each tribe need its own flag? Was it to rally its troops? In the United States of America, we rally around the flag, and everyone around the world recognizes our flag. When it is displayed, we often cover our heart with our right hand and sing the national anthem. Obviously, here in this portion there is something significant about each of the flags of the different tribes. How did each flag look? Whence did the designs on each flag originate? For answers to these questions we resort to the Zohar. The flag for the month of Scorpio is a scorpion. With a little intuition we can know what the flag of Scorpio resembled and what the original flag meant to the people who were in that tribe. The people understood that the manner by which they could bring a particular and necessary dimension of Light was to connect to the flag. Each flag represented and revealed aspects of the stars of the Heavens so that as they went through the wilderness, they would not be affected by outside forces.

We are living in a far more hostile environment than we can imagine. Studying this section is not about knowing how many Israelites existed then or under which flag they were gathered. The purpose of the flag is to be a living instrument offering protection. If we have to pay some of our debts created during this or a previous life, with the help of the energy we receive from the connection to the stars through the flags, the chaos will not be irrevocable, it will be the kind of chaos that comes and goes like the wind, and the suffering or illness will not be of a permanent nature over which we have no control. When we hear about each tribe and their flag, the purpose is to connect us to that particular zodiac sign and the Hebrew letters that govern that particular month. This is to awaken consciousness and to infuse the energy of protection from chaos so as to create a protective shield for ourselves and the world.

3 Now those that pitch on the east side toward the sunrise shall be of the standard of the camp of Judah, according to their hosts; the prince of the children of Judah being Nachshon the son of Amminadab, 4 and his host, and those that were numbered of them, seventy-four thousand, six hundred; 5 and those that pitch next to him shall be the tribe of Issaschar; the prince of the children of Issaschar being Nethanel the son of Zuar, 6 and his host, even those that were numbered thereof, fifty-four thousand, four hundred; 7 and the tribe of Zebulun; the prince of the children of Zebulun, being Eliab, the son of Helon, 8 and his host, and those that were numbered thereof, fifty-seven thousand, four hundred; 9 all that were numbered of the camp of Yehuda being one hundred and eighty-six thousand, four hundred, according to their hosts; they shall set forth first. 10 On the south side shall be the standard of the camp of Reuben according to their hosts; the prince of the children of Reuben being Elizur the son of Shedeur, 11 and his host, and those that were numbered thereof, forty-six thousand, five hundred; 12 and those that pitch next to him shall be the tribe of Simeon; the prince of the children of Simeon being Shelumiel the son of Zurishaddai, 13 and his host, and those that were numbered of them, fifty-nine thousand, three hundred; 14 and the tribe of Gad; the prince of the children of Gad being Eliasaph the son of Reuel, 15 and his host, even those

that were numbered of them, forty-five thousand, six hundred and fifty; 16 all that were numbered of the camp of Reuben being one hundred and fifty one thousand, four hundred and fifty, according to their hosts; and they shall set forth second. 17 Then the Tent of Meeting, with the camp of the Levites, shall set forward in the midst of the camps; as they encamp, so shall they set forward, every man in his place, by their standards. 18 On the west side shall be the standard of the camp of Ephraim according to their hosts; the prince of the children of Ephraim being Elishama the son of Ammihud, 19 and his host, and those that were numbered of them, forty thousand and five hundred; 20 and next to him shall be the tribe of Manasseh; the prince of the children of Manasseh being Gamaliel the son of Pedahzur, 21 and his host, and those that were numbered of them, thirty-two thousand, two hundred; 22 and the tribe of Benjamin; the prince of the children of Benjamin being Abidan the son of Gideoni, 23 and his host, and those that were numbered of them, thirty-five thousand, four hundred; 24 all that were numbered of the camp of Ephraim being one hundred and eight thousand, one hundred, according to their hosts; and they shall set forth third. 25 On the north side shall be the standard of the camp of Dan according to their hosts; the prince of the children of Dan being Ahiezer the son of Ammishaddai, 26 and his host, and those that were numbered of them,

sixty-two thousand, seven hundred; 27 and those that pitch next to him shall be the tribe of Asher; the prince of the children of Asher being Pagiel the son of Ochran, 28 and his host, and those that were numbered of them, forty-one thousand, five hundred; 29 and the tribe of Naphtali; the prince of the children of Naphtali being Ahira the son of Enan, 30 and his host, and those that were numbered of them, fifty-three thousand, four hundred; 31 all that were numbered of the camp of Dan being one hundred and fifty-seven thousand, six hundred; they shall set forth hindmost by their standards." 32 These are them that were numbered of the children of Israel by their fathers' houses; all that were numbered of the camps according to their hosts were six hundred and three thousand, five hundred and fifty. 33 But the Levites were not numbered among the children of Israel; as the Lord commanded Moses. 34 So did the children of Israel: according to all that the Lord commanded Moses, they pitched by their standards, and they set forward, each one according to its families, and according to its fathers' houses.

Astrology, Angels and Positioning of the Tribes

Bamidbar 2:1-2 says: "And the Lord spoke unto Moses and unto Aaron saying, 'The children of Israel shall pitch by their father's houses, every man with his own standard (flag), according to the ensigns. A good way off shall they pitch round about the Tent of Meeting.'" What is the full significance of these verses? This is another demonstration of the corruption of the translation of the Bible, and how the Bible became what we now call religion. The word "religion" for the kabbalist does not carry any weight. The Bible is a cosmic code that is concealed and, therefore, it was left to the Zohar and the kabbalists to decipher and reveal that which is hidden beneath the literal words.

What is the significance of a standard or flag? While we know all countries of the world display them—where did the custom come from and, furthermore, what does it indicate and why is it in this form? This is the first time that flags are mentioned in the Bible, why are we told that each tribe has a flag? What is a flag and why did they need one? Today, we know that a flag has significance, it says who you are. In war, when someone raises their flag over the battlefield it means that they have conquered.

In this same verse, there is a word that follows the mention of the standards that seems to have no meaning whatsoever, the word is *otot*, meaning "signs," followed by *lebeit avotam*, "to your father's house." For someone who is involved in astrology, this phrasing: "signs, to your father's house," will have a great deal of significance. Astrologers understand the connotation of "houses" in an astrological chart, and the "signs" of the zodiac. The word *otot* is also mentioned for the first time in the Bible on the Fourth Day of Genesis I, within the discussion of the sun, the moon, and the *otot*—meaning the signs of the zodiac.

There are very few commentaries on the portion of Bamidbar, thus it was left to the kabbalist, or more specifically to Rav Shimon (Zohar, Bamidbar 3:27-29), to decipher the internal meaning and thereby provide us with further knowledge so we can gain access to the awesome power of the cosmos as we begin to understand all that is around us. With this wisdom we can become master of our own destiny.

The Bible says in Bamidbar 2:3: "Now those that pitch on the east (*mizrach*) side toward the sun rising shall be they of the standard of the camp of Yehuda...." The word *mizrach* means "east." Many people pray in the direction of Mecca or Jerusalem because it is located in the east. Does this precept of praying to the east not apply to those who live north of these cities, should they pray to the south? No. The word *mizrach* does not only refer to a direction of the east, the Zohar deciphers the word *mizrach* as a code referring to the concept of the Central Column, which is represented by the three air signs of the zodiac. When the Bible, in Bamidbar 2:9 says that the camp of Yehuda went first, this was to indicate to us that of the air signs, the tribe of Yehuda is dominant.

When the Bible discusses the tribes, it is neither discussing a gathering of individuals, nor is the Bible concerned with a grouping of people, rather it is, in its entirety, a coded message providing us with information on the formation and nature of the cosmos and the zodiac. Armed with this information, we are no longer subject to the map of our destiny as indicated on an astrological chart, instead by understanding the workings of the cosmos, we can rise above astral influences and become destiny's master.

On a very general basis, everything mentioned in Bamidbar 2 deals specifically with astrology, and what all the zodiac signs offer us as a means of connection to the cosmos.

Concerning Bamidbar 2:2, which says "...every man with his own standard (flag), according to the ensigns..." the Zohar states that the four camps of the congregation of Israel indicate the four Sefirot of Chesed, Gevurah, Tiferet, and Malchut. The reference to the four camps also signifies the four basic elements of the Universe—water, fire, air, and earth. There may be different variations of these four but fundamentally there are only four basic elements in the universe. These four basic elements, originate in the Sefirot, and are manifested as energies. Water, for example, is a physical manifestation of the Sefira of Chesed. When the word "water," is used in the Bible what it is referring to is the Sefira of Chesed, which is a code for the Desire to Share, a positive quality. Water seeks its own level and always seems to expand or spread out because it has a thought energy-intelligence of sharing and expansion. Hence, water is known by its code word Chesed.

Fire manifests the Sefira of Gevurah, which indicates an internal thought energy-intelligence of the Desire to Receive, which is a negative quality—not negative as in bad, negative in terms of an electrical circuit. The code word for the third element, which is air, is sourced in the Sefira of Tiferet. It is the Central Column that acts like the filament in a light bulb. It is only by virtue of the Central Column, the air sign that we can achieve a unified whole. It is like the atom. The atom as a single unified intelligence consisting of three basic aspects: The proton, which is sharing, the thought energy-intelligence of the Sefira of Chesed; the electron, which is receiving and the thought energy-intelligence of the Sefira of Gevurah; and the neutron, which according to Rav Shimon, is the thought energy-intelligence of air and the Sefira of Tiferet. In other words, air is the element that brings together; air is the quality or essence that can create a unified whole of positive and negative.

Those who have studied Talmud Eser Sefirot ("Ten Luminous Emanations") will understand that air is a force of Central Column, and Central Column energy-intelligence is one of resistance. Therefore by nature, anyone who is an air sign has manifested within them the concentrated energy called by its code name, Tiferet. This means that a person who is an air sign is instinctively— this could be for good or bad— one who resists. Air signs love freedom, they cannot be locked in because internally, whether they are conscious of this fact or not, they are always resisting anything that can create a framework around them. The Sefira of Tiferet is the aspect of resistance, indicating to us that all air signs rebel against frameworks but they love to bring together the positive and negative thereby creating their own inclusive framework. Take an air sign and try to put him or her into the framework of fire or water and you will have no success.

The element of *adama* (earth) indicates humankind, meaning the recipient of whatever is flowing from the cosmos. Earth signs are stationary, they love where they are and hate to move; do not upset them. Earth signs are those who, wherever they are, experience everything as fine, as long as you do not pull the rug out from under them. Although where they dwell could be awful, to them it is beautiful.

However, we understand from the Zohar that we can rise above the influence of our astrological signs to the point where none of their negative influences will affect us. I refer to the air sign of Libra only because I am a little more familiar with it—my wife Karen is a Libra. A Libra is one who sees both sides of any issue very clearly but they see it so clearly that they can never make up their mind. This seems to be a little contradictory because if someone can see all sides of any subject—meaning all of the positive and negative qualities at the same time—any decision should be much easier to arrive at because everything is seen. The Libra can see everything from multiple viewpoints, so why can they not make decisions? The two opposing elements—seeing the whole picture yet being unable to make a decision—are known to be the qualities of Libra, and yet, they seem to be irreconcilable.

Astrology, Four Elements, and the Angels

Zohar, Bamidbar 3:27 reveals yet another aspect of astrology, telling us that the four elements are also referred to as Archangels: Michael, Gabriel, Uriel, and Raphael. Michael is Chesed, meaning sharing and the positive pole of the atom and Right Column energy; Gabriel is Gevurah, meaning receiving and the negative pole of the atom and Left Column energy; Uriel is Tiferet, meaning resistance, the neutron of the atom and is the Central Column. Raphael is Malchut, the manifestation of this circuitry and the earth sign.

It is only because of the Zohar that this section of Bamidbar is understood. The Zohar tells us that all of these names and thought energy-intelligences are derived from this portion in the Book of Bamidbar. Rav Shimon says that all of these aspects are represented in the twelve tribes, which are divided up into the four elements. Within each element there are three signs: three air signs, three fire signs, three water signs, and three earth signs. The earth signs are Taurus, Virgo and Capricorn. The air signs are Gemini, Libra, and Aquarius. The water signs are Pisces, Cancer, and Scorpio, and the fire signs are Aries, Leo, and Sagittarius. Moreover within each of the three signs of an element there is an internal aspect, an internal essence of Right, Left, and Central Column energy. For example, within the air signs, which are the Central Column, there is the Right of the Central Column, which is represented by Libra, there is the Left of the Central Column, which is represented by Aquarius, and the Central of the Central Column, which is represented by Gemini. The same applies to every sign of every element.

With the help of the Zohar, we conclude that when the Bible is referring to the twelve tribes and their movements, in essence, it is referring to the four elements and the three components within each one. The Zohar says that when we read that there were three tribes east of the camp, and that the tribe of Yehuda was in the

middle it is to indicate to us that Yehuda is dominant because
he is the Central Column of the Central Column (the air signs).
The Bible says that three tribes camped in each of the four directions
to indicate to us that every sign is considered to be part of the Three
Column System. For example, regarding the three air signs that
camped to the east, there will be an air sign that is predominantly
water and Right Column energy, an air sign that is predominantly
fire, Left Column energy, and an air sign that is predominantly air,
Central Column energy. In kabbalistic astrology, we have three signs
for each of the four elements (earth, air, water, and fire) making up
the twelve zodiac signs of the year. From this we see that the twelve
months of the year are divided into four elements, which the Zohar
explains represents the Tetragrammaton—*Yud*, *Hei*, *Vav*, and *Hei*—
the most powerful channel by which we can control the cosmos.
In fact, it is the only way we can control the cosmos.

When referring to rising above the influences of the planets and
the signs of the zodiac, the Zohar says we must know the structure
of the universe otherwise we cannot connect and control these
energy-intelligences that are there to do our bidding. They exist
for us to influence not the other way around. As the Zohar says
about Genesis 1, nothing moved once it was created, everything
was dormant in a state of suspended animation, the animals did not
move, the Heavens did not move, there was no rain, the sun did
not shine. It was only when Adam appeared that everything began
moving, which indicates to us that humankind is, in truth, the
center of the universe and controls not only its own destiny, which
for most has not been actualized, but also the entire universe.

No one studying conventional astrology knows why Nissan (Aries),
is the first month of the astrological year. The Zohar says Aries is
the month by which the Israelites, upon the exodus from Egypt,
actively began to determine their own destiny. The months that
follow Aries are Taurus and Gemini, and these three months

form a package that is under the influence of the letter *Yud* of the Tetragrammaton. Next comes Cancer, Leo, and Virgo, which are under the influence of the upper *Hei* of the Tetragrammaton, followed by Libra, Scorpio and Sagittarius, which are under the influence of the letter *Vav*, and then Capricorn, Aquarius and Pisces, which are under the influence of the final *Hei* of the Tetragrammaton.

YUD	HEI	VAV	HEI
Aries	Cancer	Libra	Capricorn
Taurus	Leo	Scorpio	Aquarius
Gemini	Virgo	Sagittarius	Pisces

Returning to the original idea that within every sign there are three components, we now know that we have three air signs, which are Libra, Gemini and Aquarius. Gemini is the air sign of the air signs, Central Column of Central Column. We know this because Gemini is in the third position within the package that is under the influence of the *Yud*. Aries is in the Right Column position within the package of the *Yud*, and Taurus is the Left Column within the package of the *Yud* and Gemini is the Central column of the *Yud*. Libra's position in the calendar is stationed in the first position, which is the Right Column and is under the influence of the *Vav*. As the first month in the package of Libra, Scorpio, and Sagittarius, Libra takes on the internal essence that is the Right Column aspect of the Central Column—the sharing aspect. The air sign, Aquarius, is in the position between Capricorn and Pisces, which falls in the packet of energy that is the *Hei*. Its position here makes it the Left Column of the Central Column. This positioning or organization of months is not arbitrary, rather as Bamidbar informs us, it is for us to know the workings of the cosmos so that humanity can pursue its role to control the stars but not be controlled by them.

Why does the Bible tell us where each tribe was located? Does it make any difference to those of us alive today whether Yehuda was on the east side or on the western side? The Zohar says that when we are discussing the positions of Yehuda and where the other two tribes were placed in relation to his tribe, it is to indicate to us which of the tribes were dominant, and which energy-intelligence they represented. Each of these four dominant energy-intelligences became manifested as one of the twelve signs. There were only four flags, each with three tribes: Right, Left, and Central Column. There were three tribes located on each side—north, south, east and west. Each side represented an influence of the four elements: air, fire, water and earth. When the Bible mentions who is located in the west, it is referring to the earth signs. When the Bible is discussing who is located in the north, it is discussing the fire signs; who is in the south refers to the water signs, and in the east refers to the air signs, and each location has three zodiac signs together comprising one unified whole.

Each tribe was placed in its particular position so that we could understand what each sign really consists of. In other words, Taurus is an earth sign and because of its placement, which is located in the second position of the *Yud*, this makes it Gevurah, the Left Column—Desire to Receive. While we have three earth signs under one flag (*degel*), forming one unified whole—Taurus, Virgo, and Capricorn—we know that there is a difference between the three; that each one is represented by another aspect and that each one has its own component.

From a conventional astrological point of view, the signs seem to contradict each other. For instance, Virgo is the air essence of the earth signs, and if earth and air do not go together, how do we reconcile this? Virgos are people who are very meticulous, exacting, and critical because they see things, they focus in on things. Virgo appears as the air essence of the earth signs and because Virgo is so critical, seeing one particular aspect so minutely, they forget everything that surrounds the focused area. Therefore, Virgo is placed in an air sign position because, as we said, air is unlimited. By giving Virgo the benefit of the air essence it helps it not be limited in its scope.

When were these principles first arrived at? Is it really significant when Moses received this commandment from God about the specific tribes? In Bamidbar 1:1, the Bible says, "And the Lord spoke unto Moses in the wilderness of Sinai, in the Tent of the Meeting, on the first day of the second month," meaning this took place in the month of Taurus. Why in the month of Taurus and not in any other month? Taurus is the one sign that Rav Shimon calls Chodesh Ziv (Month of Light)—the month when the most Light appears in the universe and becomes available. Therefore we can understand why the Month of Iyar (Taurus), has always been either a very good month or a very negative period in history. It is so powerful; it is like a live electric wire and it is important that we know how to contain this energy, so we are not harmed.

The significance of Taurus is that it is an earth sign, and earth is Left Column. Taurus is also the second month of the astrological year, meaning it is Gevurah of the three month package organized under the letter *Yud*—there is consistency here. Whereas Virgo is the air element of the earth signs, so there is a conflict. In no other sign do we have such a perfect consistency as we do with Taurus, which is why the Zohar refers to it as Chodesh Ziv. Ziv indicates an uninterrupted flowing of energy. From this explanation we can deduce that we have different code names for the same concept. The Zohar says we cannot take the sign just as it is, we must also look at its position.

Why We Pray to the East and Why Yehuda Travelled First

We have discussed the four directions: north, south, east, and west. We also have the four angels: Michael, Gabriel, Uriel, Raphael, which are code names. The Zohar says the southerly direction is governed by the angel Michael, and Michael is the Right Column of the angels, which is Chesed. In other words, anything that is south has the energy of Chesed. No matter where we stand, the south is where we can tap the energy of Chesed.

<table>
<tr><td></td><td>**NORTH**
Gevurah
Receiving (Negative)
Gabriel
Fire</td><td></td></tr>
<tr><td>**WEST**
Malchut
Manifestation
Raphael
Earth</td><td></td><td>**EAST**
Tiferet
Restriction
Uriel
Air</td></tr>
<tr><td></td><td>**SOUTH**
Chesed
Sharing (Positive)
Michael
Water</td><td></td></tr>
</table>

Why do we pray to the east? Is it because the Holy Temple is in the east? No, from a kabbalistic point of view, no effect ever determines a cause. For example, if the Holy Temple is something physical, it means there must have been another metaphysical thought energy-intelligence that determined why the Holy Temple would be in that location.

Not many question why the sun rises in the east, yet the Zohar does deal with this. The Zohar informs us that the reason the Bible goes into such detail about where the twelve tribes encamped is to teach us the significance of the directions; that directions are energy-intelligences. There is a reason we pray to the east, and this is connected to why the sun rises in the east. The reason all physical manifestations arose the way they did is because of thought energy-intelligences. Just as we do not perform an activity without prior thought, so too, it is with the universe. Before anything became established in corporeal form, there was prior thought energy-intelligence.

While humankind and our environment are unstable, when we look up to the Heavens everything seems to be operating in perfect harmony. There is stability, and there cannot be any stability without prior thought energy-intelligence. Yet we know from our own experience that even at times where there is thought energy-intelligence, we can still render our own situation unstable.

When we see something that has become firmly established, long before we were here, and remains this way long after we will be here, where it seems changeless, there must be prior thought energy-intelligence. What is the prior thought-energy-intelligence known as the four directions? Why are things located where they are? Why is the United States located to the west and Israel in the Middle East? Is it by chance? No. Why are some people drawn to certain areas and not to others? We seem to be so robotic in most things. I believe the psychiatrist is right, by and large, most of us behave in an automatic or unconsciousness manner. Can you imagine that in all of our undertakings like getting married, opening up businesses and so on, we operate with only five percent energy-intelligence? It is frightening. Since most people have not been capable of accessing the remaining 95 percent, maybe this is why there is so much trouble in the world and why we can only learn from experience. But who learns even from experience? Do we not make mistakes over and over again?

The Zohar reveals for us that the angel Michael represents the southerly direction, which has a thought energy-intelligence of sharing. There is a thought energy-intelligence that dictates the nature of each kind of environment. Gabriel represents the northerly direction and has a thought energy-intelligence of Gevurah or receiving and judgment. This is evidenced by the fact that most of the wars in the world occur in the northern hemisphere. Uriel signifies the easterly direction and the thought energy-intelligence of the Central Column. Now we can understand why the Holy Temple is in the east and why Israel is located where it is. The word *mizrach* does not mean "easterly." Do the kabbalists who live in the Galilee pray to the south? Does this mean that those who do not live in the United States pray to the west or the south? No, we always pray to the east because of its significance. The Zohar says the significance is Uriel—the energy-intelligence of the Central Column, which unifies the Right and Left Columns, positive and negative. If there is no unification of positive and negative, then we have chaos, we have fragmentation, we have holocaust, we have separation, we have destruction.

The most important part of the atom is the neutron, which keeps the electron and proton in motion, much as the sun does the planets. These particles get close but never touch, their charge keeps them apart, much the same way as a magnet will repel another magnet. This is the thought energy-intelligence of restriction.

The Zohar says the reason we pray to the east, and why the Holy Temple is located in Jerusalem is because this is where the energy center of the Central Column is located. The physical city of Jerusalem and the physical Holy Temple were located there only as a corporeal channel through which we can connect, not to the east but to the aspect of what it represents—the thought energy-intelligence of the Central Column. Thus when we pray to the east—no matter where we are—we are not truly praying to the east, we are using our prayer to connect Right and Left with the Central Column, thereby creating one unified whole; we are praying to what the east comprises—Central Column, embodied by Tiferet and known by its code name Uriel.

Do we wish to connect to the eternal life-force energy or do we merely wish to connect to temporal energy? The lightbulb is only useful providing it has a circuit of energy. If it does not have a circuit of energy it is useless and sometimes harmful. When we make our connections, we connect to Raphael, meaning we receive, then we connect to the west, to manifestation. After we have established the unification of the three components of the north—Left Column, south—Right Column, and east—Central Column, we can draw on their energy. Then we can behave as the astrological earth signs of the west do with gravitation or Desire to Receive. All of the real goodness in the world, not that which is evanescent, rather, those things that abide, can only be had by exercising the Central Column.

What therefore, does all of this mean to us and our lives? In the portion of Bamidbar, we are presented with the signs of the zodiac and the means by which we can control their influence. What is meant by controlling the signs of the zodiac? The Zohar speaks of "to control" and for what purpose? Each sign of the zodiac contains both positive and negative influences, they do not exist as a unity. Were the positive and negative nature of the signs connected to one another, no problems would arise. Since we come into this world containing these two contradictory aspects—both a positive and a negative nature—we are divided and fragmented beings. The Zohar draws our attention to the fact that in every sign there are three composite entities and if these are not brought into unity then there is no means by which we can achieve dominion over the influence of the signs of the zodiac. We must endeavor to create this unity within ourselves.

When the Bible says that Yehuda traveled first, the Zohar asks why does the Bible tell us how the tribes traveled, when they traveled, and when they stopped? The Zohar goes into great detail describing the manner in which they traveled. The Zohar says the significance of these biblical travels is to draw attention to the journeys of our lives. Therefore when we travel through life we must always begin with Yehuda. We must always begin with the Central Column. If we can draw in the Central Column—the active restriction—into every aspect of living then we have created unity, we have brought positive and negative together. Therefore, when the Bible says that Yehuda was always at the head of these travels it is intended to indicate the way in which we ought to conduct ourselves on the journey and how we can take control of the cosmos. Let us be guided on our path through in life and be led by the Central Column.

When we live life with restriction, then we can bring together—like the filament in a lightbulb—two singular components called positive and negative, and once they are unified we have a circuit of energy. This was the significance of Yehuda traveling first.

The Constellations

When the Bible discusses the tribe of Reuben, represented by the zodiac sign of Aries and the constellation of the Ram, and the month of Taurus by the Ox, it is letting us know what is in the Heavens—the configuration of stars in their various patterns. From a kabbalistic point of view, how many people were in each tribe is not as significant as what they represent, the number of stars that make up the image of a particular constellation of each sign in the Heavens.

Why do we have to know how many people were in each tribe? According to the Zohar, knowledge is our conduit of connection. As it says in the Psalms of King David, "The Heavens declare the glory of God...." (Psalms 19:2) Every month has a particular influence and if we know how to tap into this we can control the various energies. Through observing these great celestial bodies, we can arrive at a sense of clarity. When we hear the verses which deal with the number of people in each tribe, it does not concern a fact that once existed yet no longer does. It exists today. It exists to this day in our ever-increasing knowledge of the sheer scope of this universe. In the heavens year after year, these same number of stars appear to create the configuration of the particular physical celestial bodies by which the influence of the Lightforce is transmitted to this universe to turn this wasteland into paradise.

Knowledge is our only salvation. With knowledge we free ourselves from the ignorance that has persisted for 3,400 years. The Kabbalah Centre is a proponent of knowledge. We know that the Zohar says the stars impel but do not compel. We can be the overseers, we can be the controllers of celestial influences. Kabbalistic astrology does not exist merely to give you information you can find elsewhere, it is an instrument to not only understand the celestial influences and our particular traits, it is also a means to control our destinies and change the influences governing over particular celestial bodies.

The reading of the portion of Bamidbar is so profound because God created the knowledge of every celestial presence in the entire universe before the Israelites even existed. This is what the Talmud meant when it said that Shabbat is a gift. It is not supposed to be a day of rest but rather it is the only day during which we are able to exercise control over every aspect of the universe. Not all of us will be able to comprehend and capture the full complement of energy being offered since it depends on our individual behavior. This is irrefutable truth, and far from easy to accomplish.

With this section, we want to capture the awesome energy of the Light of the month of Taurus, and at the same time, infuse this energy into every other month of the year. It is vital to know the precise number of stars in each constellation since this forms our connection.

Bamidbar and Numbers

The entire Book of Bamidbar is translated into English as the Book of Numbers, but in no way can we connect the word "numbers" to the actual word *bamidbar*, which means "desert"—unless, of course, we could count the grains of sand in the desert. The desert that the Bible is referring to is not the Sahara or the Mojave but rather the desert that surrounds our lives.

The Zohar explains that this portion is named Bamidbar because it refers to the difficulty, the pain and the suffering all of us endure in this physical realm known as the world of Malchut. All of the problems that we could ever imagine are discussed in the Bible as experienced by the Israelites. Throughout the Book of Bamidbar, all manners of suffering are mentioned, including even terrorism. There is nothing new, although we believe these things have come of age in our generation, they have been with us for countless years.

The Zohar says that the reason the Bible tells us how many Israelites were in the tribes has nothing to do with census taking. It has to do with providing us with the understanding that without the Lightforce of God we live in darkness, we exist in the playing field of Satan—the desert.

According to the Zohar, each astrological month has an influence upon this entire planet. By understanding this, we can to tap into that month's particular energy of the Lightforce of God.

Therefore, when the Bible says that the tribe of Dan comprised 62,700 people it is not simply referring to the number of people. What is significant is as King David said in Psalms 19:2: "The Heavens declare the glory of God…." Abraham the patriarch, the first astrologer, explained that the Heavens communicate with us directly and give us an opportunity each and every single month to connect.

What is the significance of the stars? What do they tell us? To help us understand this concept, the Zohar states that there is a difference between the acquisition of information and knowledge. Information is transient, remaining in our minds for but an instant. Knowledge is something that is permanently retained and becomes a part of our lives. Knowledge provides the opportunity to see things as they truly are. The Zohar says that information must be made part of us for it to become knowledge, and it is only when information becomes knowledge that we are able to make the necessary connection.

What is the relationship between the number of people in each tribe and the stars in the Heavens? As mentioned previously, the Zohar explains that when the Bible tells us how many people were in each tribe it is actually telling us how many stars make up each constellation. For example, the month of Aries is represented by a formation of stars resembling a ram. Can any of us number the stars in that constellation? We must know the number of the stars in the constellations because the Bible's intention is for us to make a connection to the astrological influences so we may tap into the energies of each particular month and thus the energy of the Lightforce of God. Therefore, by reading this section we have the ability to connect to all twelve months of the year and all successive years, thereby connecting to the channel that the Zohar and Abraham the patriarch say are the stars. This is how, without a telescope, Abraham could tell us the names of the zodiacal months.

This is also what King David meant by "The Heavens show the glory of God." It is thus clear that we are not discussing a census-taking here but rather acknowledging the fact that we can make a connection to the Lightforce of God energy of each month through each tribe as this section is recited.

With regard to this day and age, Rav Shimon made it clear that we are in *Oy* and *Ashrei*—Woe and Blessed. There will be those who, unfortunately, will have to suffer because they do not have this knowledge. At any given moment, some can exist in Heaven on Earth while those next door to them suffer. This was the case, for example, in Egypt during the Ten Plagues where the Israelites had water and the Egyptians did not. Unfortunately such conditions tend to prevail.

We live in a *midbar*, in a desert, and there is no way out of this desert unless we have the support and assistance of the Lightforce. This is what this portion concerns. The Zohar explains that the portion of Bamidbar gives us an opportunity to connect with the Lightforce of God so that life can become less of a *midbar*, less of a wilderness, and become a land of paradise. I believe in the Zohar. When the Zohar says something I take it at its word. We must be strong and vigilant if we are to save this planet. We, at least, have the instrument of the Zohar, and this instrument most certainly can change the entire world in every respect.

Bamidbar 3:1 Now these are the generations
of Aaron and Moses in the day that the Lord
spoke with Moses in Mount Sinai. 2 And
these are the names of the sons of Aaron:
Nadav the first-born, and Avihu, Elazar, and
Ithamar. 3 These are the names of the sons of
Aaron, the priests that were anointed, whom
he consecrated to minister in the priest's
office. 4 And Nadav and Avihu died before the
Lord, when they offered strange fire before
the Lord, in the wilderness of Sinai, and they
had no children; and Elazar and Ithamar
ministered in the priest's office in the presence of Aaron their father. 5 And the Lord
spoke unto Moses, saying: 6 "Bring the tribe
of Levi near, and set them before Aaron the
priest, that they may minister to him. 7 And
they shall keep his charge, and the charge
of the whole congregation before the Tent of
Meeting, to do the service of the Tabernacle.
8 And they shall keep all the furniture of
the Tent of Meeting, and the charge of the
children of Israel, to do the service of the
Tabernacle. 9 And you shall give the Levites
to Aaron and to his sons; they are wholly
given to him from the children of Israel.
10 And you shall appoint Aaron and his sons
so they may keep their priesthood; and the
common man that draws near shall be put to
death." 11 And the Lord spoke to Moses, saying: 12 "And behold, I have taken the Levites
from among the children of Israel instead of
every first-born that opens the womb among
the children of Israel; and the Levites shall

be Mine; 13 for all the first-born are Mine: on the day that I smote all the first-born in the land of Egypt I hallowed to Me all the first-born in Israel, both man and beast, Mine they shall be: I am the Lord." 14 And the Lord spoke to Moses in the wilderness of Sinai, saying: 15 "Number the children of Levi by their fathers' houses, by their families; every male from a month old and upward shall you number them." 16 And Moses numbered them according to the word of the Lord, as he was commanded. 17 And these were the sons of Levi by their names: Gershon, and Kohath, and Merari. 18 And these are the names of the sons of Gershon by their families: Libni and Shimei. 19 And the sons of Kohath by their families: Amram and Izhar, Hebron and Uzziel. 20 And the sons of Merari by their families: Mahli and Mushi. These are the families of the Levites according to their fathers' houses. 21 Of Gershon was the family of the Libnites, and the family of the Shimeites; these are the families of the Gershonites. 22 Those that were numbered of them, according to the number of all the males, from a month old and upward, even those that were numbered of them were seven thousand and five hundred. 23 The families of the Gershonites were to pitch behind the Tabernacle westward; 24 the prince of the fathers' house of the Gershonites being Eliasaph, the son of Lael, 25 and the charge of the sons of Gershon in the Tent of Meeting, the Tabernacle, and the Tent, the covering thereof, and the screen for the door of the Tent of Meeting, 26 and the hangings of the court, and the screen for the door of the court—which is by the Tabernacle, and by the altar, round about—and the cords of it, even whatsoever pertains to the service thereof. 27 And of Kohath was the family of the Amramites, and the family of the Izharites, and the family of the Hebronites, and the family of the Uzzielites; these are the families of the Kohathites: 28 according to the number of all the males, from a month old and upward, eight thousand and six hundred, keepers of the charge of the Sanctuary. 29 The families of the sons of Kohath were to pitch on the side of the Tabernacle southward; 30 the prince of the fathers' house of the families of the Kohathites being Elizaphan the son of Uzziel, 31 and their charge the Ark, and the table, and the Menorah, and the altars, and the vessels of the sanctuary wherewith the priests minister, and the screen, and all that pertains to the service thereof; 32 Elazar, the son of Aaron the priest being prince of the princes of the Levites, and having the oversight of them that keep the charge of the Sanctuary. 33 Of Merari was the family of the Mahlites, and the family of the Mushites; these are the families of Merari. 34 And those that were numbered of them, according to the number of all the males, from a month old and upward, were six thousand, two hundred; 35 the prince of the fathers' house of the families of Merari being Zuriel the son of Abihail; they were to pitch on the side of the Tabernacle northward; 36 the appointed charge of the sons of Merari being the boards of the Tabernacle, and the bars thereof, and the pillars thereof, and the sockets thereof, and all the instruments thereof, and all that pertains to the service thereof; 37 and the pillars of the court round about, and their sockets, and their pins, and their cords. 38 And those that were to pitch before the Tabernacle eastward, before the Tent of Meeting toward the sunrise, were Moses, and Aaron and his sons, keeping the charge of the Sanctuary, even the charge for the children of Israel; and the common man that drew near was to be put to death. 39 All that were numbered of the Levites, whom Moses and Aaron numbered at the commandment of the Lord, by their families, all the males from a month old and upward, were twenty-two thousand.

Aaron and Control Over Our Lives

In Bamidbar 3:39, there are five dots above the word *ve'Aharon* (and Aaron.) As we know, there are no dots above words in the Torah Scroll except to indicate a unique connection. In this case, Aaron is the chariot for the Sefira of Hod but is also the channel of Chesed because he is the High Priest. The whole concept of taking charge by controlling the four corners of the world and going outside the playing field of Satan is performed through connecting to the Light. Chesed is the force that allows us to connect to the Lightforce that exists far above the realm of Satan. We want the strength of Aaron, the strength of Chesed and the strength of the totality. These five dots connect us to the totality, to total control from Keter to Malchut.

40 And the Lord said to Moses: "Number all the first-born males of the children of Israel from a month old and upward, and take the number of their names. 41 And you shall take the Levites for Me, I am the Lord, instead of all the first-born among the children of Israel; and the cattle of the Levites instead of all the firstlings among the cattle of the children of Israel." 42 And Moses numbered, as the Lord commanded him, all the first-born among the children of Israel. 43 And all the first-born males according to the number of names, from a month old and upward, of those that were numbered of them, were twenty-two thousand two hundred and seventy-three. 44 And the Lord spoke to Moses, saying: 45 "Take the Levites instead of all the first-born among the children of Israel, and the cattle of the Levites instead of their cattle; and the Levites shall be Mine, I am the Lord. 46 And as for the redemption of the two hundred and seventy-three of the first-born of the children of Israel, that are over and above the number of the Levites, 47 you shall take five shekels apiece by the poll; after the shekel of the Sanctuary shall you take them—the shekel is twenty gerahs. 48 And you shall give the money, with which the excess number of them is redeemed, to Aaron and to his sons." 49 And Moses took the redemption money from those that were over and above those that were redeemed by the Levites; 50 from the first-born of the children of Israel he took the money: one

thousand, three hundred and sixty-five shekels, after the shekel of the Sanctuary. 51 And Moses gave the redemption money to Aaron and to his sons, according to the word of the Lord, as the Lord commanded Moses.

Bamidbar4:1 And the Lord spoke to Moses and to Aaron, saying: 2 "Take the sum of the sons of Kohath from among the sons of Levi, by their families, by their fathers' houses, 3 from thirty years old and upward even until fifty years old—all that enter upon the service, to do work in the Tent of Meeting. 4 This is the service of the sons of Kohath in the Tent of Meeting, about the most holy things: 5 when the camp sets forward, Aaron shall go in, and his sons, and they shall take down the veil of the screen, and cover the Ark of the testimony with it; 6 and shall put thereon a covering of badger's skin and shall spread over it a cloth all of blue, and shall set the staves thereof. 7 And upon the table of showbread they shall spread a cloth of blue, and put thereon the dishes, and the pans, and the bowls, and the jars wherewith to pour out; and the continual bread shall remain thereon. 8 And they shall spread upon them a cloth of scarlet, and cover the same with a covering of badger's skin, and shall set the staves thereof. 9 And they shall take a cloth of blue, and cover the Menorah of the light, and its lamps, and its tongs, and its snuff-dishes, and all the oil vessels thereof, wherewith they minister unto it. 10 And they shall put it and all the vessels thereof within a covering of badger's skin, and shall put it upon a bar. 11 And upon the golden altar they shall spread a cloth of blue, and cover it with a covering of badger's skin and shall set the staves thereof. 12 And they shall take all the vessels of ministry, wherewith they minister in the Sanctuary, and put them in a cloth of blue, and cover them with a covering of badger's skin, and shall put them on a bar. 13 And they shall take away the ashes from the altar, and spread a purple cloth thereon. 14 And they shall put upon it all the vessels thereof, wherewith they minister about it, the fire-pans, the flesh-hooks, and the shovels, and the basins, all the vessels of the altar; and they shall spread upon it a covering of sealskin, and set the staves thereof. 15 And when Aaron and his sons have made an end of covering the holy furniture, and all the holy vessels, as the camp is to set forward—after that, the sons of Kohath shall come to bear them; but they shall not touch the holy things, lest they die. These things are the burden of the sons of Kohath in the Tent of Meeting. 16 And the charge of Elazar, the son of Aaron, the priest, shall be the oil for the light, and the sweet incense, and the continual grain offering, and the anointing oil: he shall have the charge of all the Tabernacle, and of all that therein is, whether it be the sanctuary, or the furniture thereof." 17 And the Lord spoke to Moses and to Aaron, saying: 18 "Do not cut off the tribe of the families of the Kohathites

from among the Levites; 19 but so do to them, that they may live, and not die, when they approach to the most holy things: Aaron and his sons shall go in, and appoint them every one to his service and to his burden; 20 but they shall not go in to see the holy things as they are being covered, lest they die."

The Influence of Satan and the Battles of Life

As mentioned previously, the word *bamidbar* means "in the desert" and the desert is the place where the Satan has the most power. The power of the Satan is so great there that it does not leave any space for growth to come in. The portion of Bamidbar begins with the names of all the tribes to show us that no one can avoid the influence of Satan, and this is the reason why the twelve tribes are mentioned. No one in the world can say that Satan has no influence upon them. This portion gives us the opportunity to send Light to all those areas where the Satan thinks he has already established power. This is a huge revelation for us since this portion allows us to act in the appropriate manner.

Before Kabbalah, I thought that the portion of Bamidbar was the most boring of the Torah. Even Rashi has little commentary regarding this portion, and sometimes his comments are repetitious. I want to stress that whenever we find a section of the Bible where there is repetition or even seemingly insignificant information— such as with the Third Meal of Shabbat—we ought to do what I learned from my teacher Rav Brandwein and look more closely at the places that seem less important, where we need to make more effort to connect because in those places the reward is much greater.

Three thousand four hundred years ago, kabbalists understood that this important portion is a mechanism for going on the offensive, and escaping Satan's playing field. Even though we are constantly reminded that we are in Satan's playing field, some of us are in denial. Can anyone tell us we can be guaranteed to live forever, that we will never get sick, and that other problems and difficulties will never arise? The answer is of course not. Why not? Because we are in Satan's playing field and his playing field is the dimension where evil exists. Those unaware that they are on the playing field of Satan are essentially like robots. What is wrong with being a robot? No more hospitals, no more lawyers; we will not need those things we constantly have to depend on to extricate ourselves from our problems. It is only our ego that denies we are machines when the mechanism of the body breaks down, and we do not feel we have control. Suddenly, we realize that the control we thought we had was an illusion. Since we know we are not stupid, how is it possible that we so often do stupid things? Have we not all asked ourselves such questions at one time or another?

When this portion refers to the second month, this is referring to the month of Iyar (Taurus), which is known as the Month of Light. We have at our fingertips the means by which to win this war, the knowledge of the Lightforce of God whereby we may overcome the enemy. This is the only power in the world that can remove us from Satan's playing field. The first verse of the portion of Bamidbar not only tells us how this saga begins—and it is indeed a saga, with so many interesting stories—but also instructions for how to win this war against Satan. There is only one weapon, according to the Zohar, and that is the Lightforce of God.

We have the technology, we have the instruments that have been concealed for 3,400 years. Today, as never before, we have the knowledge of how we can combine these instruments with the firepower. We all go into battle daily; do not ever forget for a moment that everything in life is a battle. If the war does not start today it will tomorrow. It is impossible to avoid battles in one's lifetime. Life is not supposed to be a bed of roses. There is no other way to survive than declaring war on Satan with the firepower supplied by the Light of God. Everything in life is a battle—any situation where we need to influence or convince someone, or need something that someone else has that we wish to have. Any interchange with anything or anyone is a battle. We go into these battles needing something—battles do not only occur between enemies. There could be something we need, something we are missing. Most of us believe that every desire in our lives must be fulfilled, and that it must come from the outside. We are not born fulfilled, our entire life consists of making attempts to be happy. However we think of it, each of us has a different idea of what will fulfill us personally.

I once had a professor who asked what the one thing is that man comes into this world without that every new machine possesses. The answer was an operating manual. Without this, how are we supposed to operate our lives? An intelligent person uses the process of improvisation. Born without tools or instructions, life is necessarily difficult. With the portion of Bamidbar we learn, as the Zohar says, how to go into battle.

Conclusion

The emblems of each tribe are the tools for us to control the twelve signs of the zodiac. Each tribe represents a certain sign of the zodiac, and when we hear the reading concerning the flags it is an opportunity to control any assault from outside forces and to remove any negativity from our lives. The flag includes the idea of the Three Column System of Right, Left, and Central, which is very clearly stated as the order in which these twelve tribes were assembled. It also refers to the four corners of the globe or the four components of existence: man, vegetation, animal and rock. These are the four basic powerhouses of this universe that serve as the tools we are using here: Chesed, Gevurah, Tiferet, and Malchut. These are the forces that will bring us the power of the Lightforce of God. Once we have the Lightforce present there is nothing, according to the Zohar, in the playing field of Satan that can rise up against us.

We have thus learned that the flags (standards) referred to in the Bible are not to be taken literally. The Bible indicates the presence of something significant, yet to discover what that is, we must turn to the Zohar. If we want to achieve miracles and control Satan's playing field we need to think deeply. Using the tools supplied by Kabbalah is the only way in which we can extricate ourselves from the power of Satan and control his playing field. Bringing the power of the Lightforce of God into our lives requires a knowledge of each flag. Can we control what troubles may arise in the future? We can by using the Sefirot. In every conflict we need the Lightforce of God to direct us, we need Chesed, Gevurah, Tiferet, and Malchut. The difficulty is remembering everything that is necessary, but what we must keep in mind is that the energy of the Lightforce of God controls every exchange and confrontation.

BOOK OF BAMIDBAR:

Portion of Naso

PORTION OF NASO

The Revelation of the Zohar

In the Zohar portion of Naso is the Idra Raba section, why should this be? The reason is this section, which deals with the revelation of the Zohar and the Kabbalah is connected to the holiday of Shavuot, when the Torah (Bible) was revealed at Mount Sinai, and always falls around the time the biblical portion of Naso is read on Shabbat.

Why is it that the kabbalists arranged it so that Naso—the longest portion of the Bible with 176 verses—is always read during the week of Shavuot? The reason is that Naso includes all the knowledge of the Zohar and the energy of immortality. This portion includes the complete knowledge of everything written in the Zohar.

When the Temple was in existence, there was peace throughout the world. Only when corruption of the clergy began, as they sold rights to the highest bidder, was the Temple brought down. These clergy are the same group of evil people who keep returning in every generation; they are subject to the laws of reincarnation. Such people are only interested in money and in their position in society. These same people have been, and are still, involved in suppressing the study of the Zohar from generation to generation because they fear its potential to undermine their power.

It is no small achievement that the evil establishment concealed the wisdom of Kabbalah for so long; they are also to blame for creating the world's chaos. I am referring especially to those people who say that humanity at large are not holy enough to study the Zohar.

I share this information because it is crucial that people become aware of what has been happening.

The question: "Where is God when I most need him?" seems to remain unanswered. People look for God in all the wrong places. There are even those who would die or kill to fulfill their idea of a god in Heaven. The violence in schools is impossible to comprehend. The only way we can stop it is for every child to start their day by scanning the Zohar. The only answer is the Zohar, which will bring emancipation to all of humankind. With the Zohar, humankind can connect to the Light without the need of an intermediary. I stress again and again that the only way to bring peace to the world is through the Zohar.

The significance of the portion of Naso is related to the Idra Raba (Greater Assembly) which appears in the section of the Zohar that discusses Naso. When Rav Shimon and his son Rav Elazar came out of the cave after hiding for thirteen years, they brought the teachings of the Zohar and Kabbalah with them; the major part of the Zohar was revealed in Peki'in afterwards, to another eight disciples, who together comprised the Idra Raba. The Bible was divided into 52 sections so that it could accompany the 52 weeks of the year. It was known then that this energy of the revelation of the Zohar would always be needed on Shabbat Naso. This understanding was known even before the Zohar was revealed in printed form.

Chanukah, Idra Raba, and Naso

We find, within the biblical portion of Naso, the sections that are read each day during Chanukah. These verses refer to the tribal chieftains and their individual sacrifices. The sacrifices were important and are included here because each and every one of them addressed a dimension of negative energy that exists in this world, and by having the chieftains of the tribes make these sacrifices, they would vaporize these dimensions of negativity that cause obstructions and the Temple would be able to draw down the Light.

At the Kabbalah Centres, we all know the nature of the Light; the problem is we just do not receive a sufficient amount of this Light. The reason for this is that we have created too many filters, too many veils, curtains between ourselves and the Light. We do not realize that the Light is here and now. The secret that we have access to through the portion of Naso is to draw down the Light. This is why I say The Kabbalah Centre has a War Room where we wage war against those veils that we have created. When we manifest barriers, we give Satan the ability to obstruct the Light from entering.

The Idra Raba, which is by and of itself the power of the whole Zohar, and the power of Shavuot are contained in the portion of Naso. What is the power of Shavuot? To release the full and complete force of the Light to remove the darkness. The revelation of energy at Mount Sinai was of such intensity that together with the connection to the revelation of the Light of Chanukah— the Festival of Lights—also available and read in this portion, culminates with the maximum amount of Light available.

This enormous Light can be revealed because the portion of Naso is read in the month of Gemini (Sivan), which was created and supported by the two letters *Resh* ר and *Zayin* ז that form the word *raz* (secret; רז). "Secret" here does not mean information that is hidden, rather it is referring to the unrevealed Concealed Light— the Or haGanuz, the Light that although we cannot observe, and because of the support of Shavuot—we can receive.

Also in this portion is the concept of *Chanukat haMizbe'ach*, which means "Dedicating or Re-establishing the Altar." The purpose of the Altar during the time of the Holy Temples was to bring Light into the Universe. Whenever we read about the Altar and the performance of the sacrifices, we are re-dedicating ourselves to the war against darkness, the war against our own blockages, and are re-infusing our lives and this room here at The Kabbalah Centre with the energy to be an effective War Room.

The Zohar was first revealed in its written form 1,400 years after it was given orally at Mount Sinai. The anti-kabbalists at the time of the golden calf were also present when the Zohar was revealed. Humankind lacked the ability to draw down Light into the world because they did not have the Zohar. It took Rav Ashlag, the founder of The Kabbalah Centre, known for his translation of the Zohar into Hebrew and commentary on the Zohar, to bring this Light down. It is truly remarkable that it took two thousand years from when the Zohar was first written down for it to be revealed to all humankind. It is amazing how the Hebrew letters have such a lasting potency.

Receiving the Energy of Light

We benefit from the portion of Naso, receiving the full dimension of Light, both the revealed Light of the Written Torah and the Or haGanuz (Concealed Light) within the Torah. We cannot observe the Or haGanuz but we are aware of its existence. It is a force that we can draw on to light up our consciousness and the universe. It is only because of the support of the holiday of Shavuot, which falls at this time, that we can handle the energy of the Light of this portion. Naso provides us with a dimension of the Light that can remove obstacles so that we can draw down the Light of Shavuot. The Zohar says that life is guaranteed for four months from Shavuot to

Rosh Hashanah when we make the appropriate connections to this particular cosmic event.

At Rosh Hashanah, it appears there is a contradiction. One purpose of Rosh Hashanah is to remove the curtain obscuring us from the Light, but then there is another aspect to it. Each of us is endowed with a unique spiritual fingerprint. Thus we each have a certain dimension with which we can receive the Light; we each have a unique capacity for Light with which we are born. During certain times, however, we receive additional support, such as on Shabbat, which only lasts one week, and there is only a slight change. However, at such times we are being infused with Light beyond the capacity of our individual vessel, and we, in effect, make slight transformations to our "fingerprint." When this occurs, we acquire two levels of our soul: Nefesh and Ruach. Ruach is an additional receptacle available to us for receiving energy, even before the reading of the Torah Scroll. This process happens as Rav Shimon recounts in the Zohar. However, Rav Shimon also tells us that we should not believe anything simply because he has said it, if we do not experience it, we should not believe it.

Eliminating Negativity

Shavuot provides the dimension of Light for eliminating every form of negativity, even extreme negativity that can bring an end to one's life. What about those who do not participate in the prayer before the Torah reading—which has an additional benefit? We learned that Rav Shimon has revealed these kabbalistic tools, and that we are one soul. What does this mean? If we are of one consciousness, one soul, there is no separation. If we want to connect, we just need to become associated with another soul, which will enable us to tap into this dimension.

Rav Isaac Luria (the Ari) says that the most important thing we can do is listen to the reading of Torah. Personally, I recommend never missing the Torah reading because of the negative influences surrounding us in the world, as we no longer have the protection of the Temple today.

In the portion of Naso we read that they performed a cleansing with the sacrifices and when we connect to this reading we will have the benefit of this cleansing, which we need to remove the obstacles preventing us from connecting to the Light of the Creator. There is difficulty exposing ourselves to the Light, and if we did not have the different levels of the Sefirot protecting us we would literally burn up. On Shabbat there is such an intensity of this Light.

We know that if we attach a 110 watt appliance to a 220 watt socket, this appliance will burn out. Similarly on Shabbat, we have the ability to build a vessel capable of absorbing a greater capacity of the Light. The creation of such an enlarged and fortified vessel enables the removal of obstacles. From what we have taken in during the Torah reading, to that degree, we have protection from negativity; we simply need to have the consciousness that we want to connect. This is the gift of Shabbat. You do not need to go to one of the great universities, all these things are ours for nothing but we have to be present and listen to the Torah reading.

Woe (Oy) and Blessed (Ashrei)

We are living in a time when the Light is pressing. The Light wants to enter and It will enter. This is the cosmic period of *Oy* (Woe) and *Ashrei* (Blessed/Exalted). We can no longer ask the Light, "Don't put pressure on me now—maybe later." We are now at a place in history where we have to understand that there is no such thing as *I*, as *our selves*. When we say "I know, I think, I do," we are choosing the cassette of Satan, which is from the ego. Anything related to "I" puts us in the cassette of Satan. We have two bodies: the real body and a body with a Desire for Itself Alone that says, "I know and I think, I do." The problem of the ego, is not a problem of the real body. This is Satan speaking. And when we are in this place, we have no free choice. There are two types of cassettes: the cassette of Satan or the cassette of the Light. We do not have the intellectual capacity to decide anything more than which tape to choose; this is our free choice. With the Light there is no "I" whatsoever. Twenty four hours a day, we can choose to be in the cassette of the Light, where it is *not my brain or my intelligence. I have nothing. Everything happens only by means of being connected to the cassette of the Light;* where we are going to be happy, and ultimately more of the Light will enter. Choosing the cassette of Satan connects us to the *Oy.* Thus whenever we hear the voice of Satan, we can say: "Is that you speaking, Satan? I don't want you!"

21 And the Lord spoke to Moses saying:
22 "Take the sum of the sons of Gershon
also, by their fathers' houses, by their families; 23 from thirty years old and upward until fifty years old shall you number them: all
that enter in to wait upon the service, to do
service in the Tent of Meeting. 24 This is the
service of the families of the Gershonites, in
serving and in bearing burdens: 25 they shall
bear the curtains of the Tabernacle, and the
Tent of Meeting, its covering, and the covering of sealskin that is above upon it, and the
screen for the door of the Tent of Meeting;
26 and the hangings of the court, and the
screen for the door of the gate of the court,
which is by the Tabernacle and by the altar
round about, and their cords, and all the instruments of their service, and whatsoever
there may be to do with them, therein shall
they serve. 27 At the commandment of Aaron
and his sons shall be all the service of the
sons of the Gershonites, in all their burden,
and in all their service; and you shall appoint
unto them in charge all their burden. 28 This
is the service of the families of the sons
of the Gershonites in the Tent of Meeting;
and their charge shall be under the hand
of Ithamar, the son of Aaron, the priest.
29 As for the sons of Merari, you shall
number them by their families, by their
fathers' houses; 30 from thirty years old and
upward until fifty years old shall you number
them, everyone that enters upon the service,
to do the work of the Tent of Meeting. 31 And

this is the charge of their burden, according to all their service in the Tent of Meeting: the boards of the Tabernacle, and the bars thereof, and the pillars thereof, and the sockets thereof; 32 and the pillars of the court round about, and their sockets, and their pins, and their cords, even all their appurtenance, and all that pertains to their service; and by name you shall appoint the instruments of the charge of their burden. 33 This is the service of the families of the sons of Merari, according to all their service, in the Tent of Meeting, under the hand of Ithamar, the son of Aaron, the priest.'" 34 And Moses and Aaron and the princes of the congregation numbered the sons of the Kohathites by their families, and by their fathers' houses, 35 from thirty years old and upward until fifty years old, every one that entered upon the service, for service in the Tent of Meeting. 36 And those that were numbered of them by their families were two thousand, seven hundred and fifty. 37 These are they that were numbered of the families of the Kohathites, of all that did serve in the Tent of Meeting, whom Moses and Aaron numbered according to the commandment of the Lord by the hand of Moses. 38 And those that were numbered of the sons of Gershon, by their families, and by their fathers' houses, 39 from thirty years old and upward until fifty years old, every one that entered upon the service, for service in the Tent of Meeting, 40 even those that were numbered of them, by their families, by their fathers' houses, were two thousand, six hundred and thirty. 41 These are they that were numbered of the families of the sons of Gershon, of all that did serve in the Tent of Meeting, whom Moses and Aaron numbered according to the commandment of the Lord. 42 And those that were numbered of the families of the sons of Merari, by their families, by their fathers' houses, 43 from thirty years old and upward until fifty years old, every one that entered upon the service, for service in the Tent of Meeting, 44 even those that were numbered of them by their families, were three thousand, two hundred. 45 These are they that were numbered of the families of the sons of Merari, whom Moses and Aaron numbered according to the commandment of the Lord, by the hand of Moses. 46 All those that were numbered of the Levites, whom Moses and Aaron and the princes of Israel numbered, by their families, and by their fathers' houses, 47 from thirty years old and upward until fifty years old, every one that entered in to do the work of service, and the work of bearing burdens in the Tent of Meeting, 48 even those that were numbered of them, were eight thousand, five hundred and eighty. 49 According to the commandment of the Lord they were appointed by the hand of Moses, everyone to his service, and to his burden; they were also numbered, as the Lord commanded Moses.

The Meaning of the Census

There is another census in the portion of Naso. In the previous
portion of Bamidbar it was a census of all the people of Israel,
and in the portion of Naso it is a census of only the Levites.
This is also connected to the verse we sing when the Ark is opened:
ויהי בנסוע הארון, (*Veyehi binso'a ha'Aron*) which helps us to store the
energy of the Ark. Like with electricity, while we do not activate
anything at the level of the power station, we can turn on the light.
The electricity that is already present is accessed when we flip the switch.

What makes the Levites different? Why is it that they are the
channels for the second Aliyah? The word *pakid* in the Bible has
always been translated as "counting" but it does not mean counting,
rather it refers to the fact that only between the ages of thirty and
fifty did the Levites have the proper energy to be a channel for the
work they were to do. *Pakid* refers to someone who is in charge,
someone who takes responsibility. The Bible provides us with
nothing less than the internal essence that makes up a Levite, so
that we can benefit from it. The whole portion of Naso discusses the
particular internal energy force of the Levite. Rather than a simple
census-taking, the Bible is conveying to us the responsibility and
energy that the Levite represents.

As we have said, each person has a unique set of fingerprints and
in the same way each person has their own particular purpose in
life. What we must remember, and what the Bible is teaching us
here, is that no two people are alike. Each one of us has a different
dimension of internal capability to receive Light. Everyone has their
unique contribution to make, their quality to add to the world, and
not to take for selfish reasons, for example, a doctor who demands
respect by virtue of what he represents without realizing that being
a doctor is simply the means by which he can share in this world.

63

Any war, any conflict anywhere, no matter how far away, affects us all. The Bible here is not addressing the physical world. Wars do not emerge for physical reasons. Each person has a unique contribution to the whole picture and so we each, in turn, influence the world in a unique way. Every one of us holds a great responsibility toward the whole world.

Naso Means "to Elevate"

The idea of census originated in the Bible but we know that the Bible is not discussing a means to count the people who existed at that time. The meaning of *naso* is not "census-taking," *naso* means "to elevate." I will delve into the deeper significance of this.

Found in the portion of Naso in the Zohar we have the teachings of the Idra Raba, the Greater Assembly. This was the first time that the teachings of the Zohar were brought to the public. Some two thousand years ago, Rav Shimon and his son Elazar left the cave in Peki'in after hiding there for thirteen years from the Romans. The two sat down with eight other disciples and for the very first time revealed the wisdom of the Zohar. All of the knowledge that Rav Shimon received was from Moses and Elijah the prophet, although Moses had passed on some 1,400 years before. Both Moses and Elijah came to Rav Shimon and his son twice each day, evening and morning. These were the teachers of Rav Shimon and his son. There is no recording of when this happened but we assume that it took place around the portion of Naso because the Idra Raba, which contains all of the secrets of the universe, is included in this portion within the Zohar. For this to be so significant, there must be a powerful reason.

Tikkun and the Klipa

Our consciousness is familiar and accustomed to symptomatic medicine. For example, when chaos strikes, we perceive only that which is in front of us; and as much as Kabbalah makes an attempt to switch our consciousness, it is still very difficult. We are prone to look at the event before us, meaning the effect not the cause. At the Kabbalah Centres we look to see why that part of the *tikkun* process may be the result of something we did wrong last week, last year, or in a prior lifetime. We make an attempt to remove ourselves from the effect because the effect of things is not the cause. Movement of the hand up and down does not originate with the hand, it originates in the mind, from the metaphysical area of consciousness. It does not originate on a physical level.

For 3,400 years, this has been the way of civilization. But now we are trying to bring about change. Sometimes we want the answers instantaneously but we cannot obtain them because what is required means going back, examining and learning that which we have not yet learned.

This is the revelation of Rav Shimon in the portion of Naso. All these pieces are interconnected and it this the reason Rav Aba, who was the scribe, wrote them down. All these enlightened disciplines and teachings were to be included in Naso because together they provide us with clues.

The beginning of Naso discusses the genealogy of the Levites. From the Levites emerged the Kohens, the Priests—as Aaron the High Priest was also a Levi. The idea with the census of the tribes in the previous portion of Bamidbar and the Levites of Naso is that we are not discussing the human being but rather the energetic influences of life. When we are born, each of us carry a dimension of Light, and this Light has to be expressed on a physical level, and is the reason why we are here. Sometimes the Light within us is so concealed because of violations in prior lifetimes but the ultimate purpose of why we are all here is to release the souls from after the sin of Adam. We are all part of that one unified soul known as Adam and Eve.

We have come into this world, over and over again, to release all of the souls or encapsulations of the Lightforce of God that were overcome and taken by the *klipa* (negative shell) and not released from the darkness and chaos in the world, after the sin of Adam. This is also the purpose of the Kaddish, the prayer we say when a family member passes from this world. In the Kaddish, when we say the *Amen* and *Yistabach*, we are restoring the Lightforce of God into that empty space. But nothing is empty; it is only an indication that where there is space, this is the *klipa*.

Making the Zohar Public

When Rav Shimon revealed the Zohar, what he did with this revelation was add more Light to the world. In essence this is what we do with the *Amen* and the *Yistabach* of the Kaddish. This means that all of the limitations of time, space, and motion are disappearing. I have not found any other reasonable answer as to why the advancement in technology in this century is so phenomenal. No one seems to ask why now? Or what is the cause of this advancement? The past millennia were dark. Look at where we are going and how fast we are getting there. With each year, past technology becomes outmoded. This is because it was in this century that Rav Ashlag brought the Zohar to the world.

Before the work of Rav Ashlag there was no Zohar available. And although Rav Ashlag's commentary and translation of the Zohar was only in Hebrew, it was a foundation for the public to begin to grasp the significance and purpose of this universe. The revelation of the Zohar has brought abundance and the restoration of Light, confirming for us the rule: more Light, less darkness. This is what our prayers and international gatherings are all about, nothing more nothing less. It is not about being religious.

The revelation of the Zohar is meant to assist each of us to be like the Lightforce of God so that we can then get everything. As the Lightforce lacks nothing, if we become an example of the Lightforce, if we behave like the Lightforce, we too will lack nothing. One might think, *I am only a small part, there is no difference.* When Light is expressed, there is no darkness. One only needs a little light to illuminate a room; even in a big stadium, the smallest light on a dark night makes a difference.

Unfortunately, even in our sharing, even in our attempt to improve the world, Satan does not want to let go of his little agenda. In this game of life, I have found you cannot have an agenda. To have a total revelation, our engagement must be without agenda. And this gives us an explanation as to why the portion of Naso is so powerful; it assists us in our attempt to remove every aspect of agenda so that we can experience a pure Desire to Share, with no thought of what will benefit us the moment that we share, and this is not easy.

Why were the same sacrifices brought to the Temple every day? This was to indicate that when the sacrifices were brought, there was no agenda; everything was the same, nothing and no one was better. The Light is smooth, motionless, an instrument of sharing. This is the essence of life, and with that quality of sharing, darkness is removed.

It was Rav Shimon's objective to change our consciousness into one of Sharing-Without-Agenda. When we consciously make the choice to be this way, it is amazing what is revealed. The minute there is a motive we close the door to the Light. There are certain universal laws that cannot be changed, and this is one: we cannot have an agenda.

The Tribes and the Signs of the Zodiac

In this portion, and every time we read about the twelve tribes in the Bible, we are connecting to and achieving control over each sign of the zodiac and the months they represent. Negative and positive energy flows into each and every month. All of this energy is channeled and controlled through two Hebrew letters and the celestial bodies that govern over each month.

Everything we read in the portion of Naso appears to be exactly like the portion of Bamidbar, but with the help of the Zohar we understand that it is not the same. Like everything that exists in this physical world, things must first happen on the level of the Tree of Life, the dimension of truth, the Real Reality, and only then can we draw it to our physical world of Malchut.

Regarding the counting of the tribes, both Rashi and the Talmud ask why the Creator loves to count the Israelites so much. The answer Rashi gives is that the Creator loves the Israelites and therefore counts. What does this mean? We know that Rashi is very deep and we need to understand that what Rashi is discussing is the closeness between the Israelites and the Creator.

The reason there is not an obvious closeness between ourselves and the Creator is because we do not behave like the Creator behaves; moreover, most of us do not think about the Creator unless we are experiencing a problem. This is why we do not think we need to care like the Creator cares. But what about the people who do not have what I have? We—especially those that are studying at the Centres and are connected to the Centres—cannot think that now we have become connected to the Creator that it is only the Creator Who needs to care about others, because we are okay. This way of thinking is a problem.

The Kabbalah Centre can take a person to the well but cannot make anyone drink. There is a lot of knowledge that can be discussed at great length but enough with information, we need to take action. The time has come that we need to make use of this knowledge.

Bamidbar 5:1 And the Lord spoke to Moses, saying: 2 "Command the children of Israel, that they put out of the camp every leper, and every one that has a discharge, and whosoever becomes defiled by the dead; 3 both male and female shall you put outside the camp; that they not defile their camp, in the midst whereof I dwell." 4 And the children of Israel did so, and put them outside the camp; as the Lord spoke to Moses, so did the children of Israel. 5 And the Lord spoke to Moses, saying: 6 "Speak unto the children of Israel: When a man or woman shall commit any sin that men commit in a trespass against the Lord, and that soul is guilty; 7 then he shall confess his sin which he has done; and he shall make restitution for his guilt in full, and add to it one-fifth thereof, and give it to the one whom he has wronged. 8 But if the man have no relative to whom restitution may be made for the guilt, the restitution for guilt which is made shall be the Lord's, even the priest's; in addition to the ram of the atonement, with which atonement shall be made for him. 9 And every heave-offering of all the holy things of the children of Israel, which they present to the priest, shall be his. 10 And every man's hallowed things shall be his: whatsoever any man gives the priest shall be his." 11 And the Lord spoke to Moses, saying: 12 "Speak to the children of Israel, and say to them: 'If any man's wife go astray, and acts unfaithfully towards him, 13 and a man lie with her carnally, and it is hidden from the eyes of her husband, she being defiled secretly, and there are no witness against her, nor was she be caught in the act; 14 and the spirit of jealousy comes upon him, and he is jealous of his wife, and she is defiled; or if the spirit of jealousy comes upon him, and he is jealous of his wife, and she is not defiled; 15 then shall the man bring his wife to the priest, and he shall bring her offering for her, the one-tenth of an ephah of barley meal; he shall pour no oil upon it, nor put frankincense thereon; for it is a grain offering of jealousy, a grain offering of memorial, bringing iniquity to remembrance. 16 And the priest shall bring her near, and set her before the Lord. 17 And the priest shall take holy water in an earthen vessel; and of the dust that is on the floor of the Tabernacle, the priest shall take, and put it into the water. 18 And the priest shall set the woman before the Lord, and let the hair of the woman's head go loose, and put the grain offering of memorial in her hands, which is the grain offering of jealousy; and the priest shall have in his hand the water of bitterness that causes the curse. 19 And the priest shall cause her to swear, and shall say to the woman: 'If no man has lain with you, and if you had not gone astray to uncleanness, being under your husband, be you free from this water of bitterness that causes the curse; 20 but if you have gone astray, being under your husband, and if you are defiled, and some man has lain with you besides your husband, 21 then the priest shall cause the woman to swear with the oath of cursing, and the priest shall say to the woman, 'the Lord make you a curse and an oath among your people, when the Lord makes your thigh to fall away, and your belly swell; 22 and this water that causes the curse shall go into your bowels, and make your belly swell, and your thigh to fall away;' and the woman shall say: 'Amen, Amen.' 23 And the priest shall write these curses in a scroll, and he shall blot them out into the water of bitterness. 24 And he shall make the woman drink the water of bitterness that causes the curse; and the water that causes the curse shall enter into her and become bitter. 25 And the priest shall take the grain offering of jealousy out of the woman's hand, and shall wave the grain offering before the Lord, and bring it to the altar. 26 And the priest shall take a handful of the grain offering, as the memorial-part thereof, and make it smoke upon the altar, and afterward shall make the woman drink the water. 27 And when he has made her drink the water, then it shall come to pass, if she be defiled, and has acted unfaithfully against her husband, that the water that causes the curse shall enter into her and become bitter, and her belly shall swell, and her thigh shall fall away; and the woman shall be a curse among her people. 28 And if the woman is not defiled, but is clean; then she shall be cleared, and shall conceive children. 29 This is the law of jealousy, when a wife, being under her husband, goes aside, and is defiled; 30 or when

the spirit of jealousy comes upon a man, and he is jealous of his wife; then shall he set the woman before the Lord, and the priest shall execute upon her all this law. 31 And the man shall be clear from iniquity, and that woman shall bear her iniquity.' "

Purification of Thoughts

This concept of the unfaithful wife, referred to as the Ritual of the Sotah, discussed in this portion is really describing vessels and Light as it relates to the level of cleanliness and readiness of the vessel.

Rav Ashlag writes in his preface to *Talmud Eser Sefirot* ("Study of Ten Luminous Emanations") that if a vessel is not ready for the Light, it causes greater darkness. If there is a Desire to Receive for Oneself Alone, it causes greater darkness, just like the plague of the Death of Firstborn in Egypt. God did not kill the firstborn sons of Egypt, their death was due to Egypt's Desire to Receive for Itself Alone. As soon as there is a Desire to Receive for Oneself Alone, the influx of more Light causes greater darkness. In the Amidah (Silent Prayer) it is written that "we should not need gifts from flesh and blood," and this is related to our spiritual vessel. Does the Creator need anything? We should strive to be exactly like the Creator so we will not need any favors or gifts.

Why does the adultery discussed in this section concern only women? Is it an indication of the Bible's chauvinism? What is this pre-condition of two witnesses? Who would commit adultery when there were two witnesses? We will not pass over this as many have done for millennia. The Bible says that the water was taken and sanctified, and that dust from the floor of the Tabernacle was gathered, and then this was used to purify the woman. The reason for this procedure, however, was to purify the accusation, to remove the husband's thoughts so he would no longer suspect his wife; essentially, this process took the negative thoughts out of the man. It does not matter whether she did it or not; it is the thought of the man that must be purified because until all doubt was removed from the man's mind, there could not be a union between them again. Here is another example of how when the Bible addresses a situation, it never deals with the obvious.

Today, we can be purified through the process of *teshuvah* even for a transgression like murder or theft. Every violation of the universal laws can be removed by *teshuvah* except for *Lashon Hara* (Evil Speech), which cannot be purified. We cannot say anything about another person out of vengeance or to derive benefit from it, even if it is true. For example, an employee stole from their employer and admitted what they had done and then resigned from the company. If another prospective employer calls this previous employer to ask for a reference, the previous employer cannot say anything negative about their former employee if these comments arise from a place of revenge or anger. He can only state the reason why this person left the company.

Bamidbar 6:1 And the Lord spoke to Moses, saying: 2 "Speak unto the children of Israel, and say to them: 'When either man or woman shall clearly utter a vow of a Nazirite, to consecrate himself to the Lord, 3 he shall abstain from wine and strong drink: he shall drink no vinegar of wine, or vinegar of strong drink, neither shall he drink any liquor of grapes, nor eat fresh or dried grapes. 4 All the days of his Naziriteship he shall eat nothing that is made of the grapevine, from the pressed grapes to the grape seed. 5 All the days of his vow of Naziriteship, no razor shall come upon his head; until the days be fulfilled, in which he consecrates himself to the Lord, he shall be holy, he shall let the locks of the hair of his head grow long. 6 All the days that he consecrates himself to the Lord he shall not come near to a dead body. 7 He shall not make himself unclean for his father, or for his mother, for his brother, or for his sister, when they die; because his consecration to God is upon his head. 8 All the days of his Naziriteship he is holy to the Lord. 9 And if any man dies very suddenly beside him, and he defile his consecrated head, then he shall shave his head in the day of his cleansing, on the seventh day shall he shave it. 10 And on the eighth day he shall bring two turtledoves, or two young pigeons, to the priest, at the door of the Tent of Meeting. 11 And the priest shall prepare one for a sin-offering, and the other for a burnt-offering, and make atonement for him, for he sinned by reason of the dead; and he shall hallow his head that same day. 12 And he shall consecrate to the Lord the days of his Naziriteship, and shall bring a he-lamb of the first year for a guilt-offering; but the former days shall be void, because his consecration was defiled. 13 And this is the law of the Nazirite, when the days of his consecration are fulfilled: he shall bring it to the door of the Tent of Meeting; 14 and he shall present his offering to the Lord, one he-lamb of the first year without blemish for a burnt-offering, and one ewe-lamb of the first year without blemish for a sin-offering, and one ram without blemish for peace offerings, 15 and a basket of unleavened bread, cakes of fine flour mingled with oil, and unleavened wafers spread with oil, and their grain offering, and their drink offerings. 16 And the priest shall bring them before the Lord, and shall offer his sin-offering, and his burnt-offering. 17 And he shall offer the ram for a sacrifice of peace offerings to the Lord, with the basket of unleavened bread; the priest shall offer also the grain offering thereof, and the drink-offering thereof. 18 And the Nazirite shall shave his consecrated head at the door of the Tent of Meeting, and shall take the hair of his consecrated head, and put it on the fire which is under the sacrifice of peace offerings. 19 And the priest shall take the shoulder of the ram when it is sodden, and one unleavened cake out of the basket, and one unleavened wafer, and shall put them upon the hands of the Nazirite, after he has shaven his consecrated head. 20 And the priest shall wave them for a wave-offering before the Lord; this is holy for the priest, together with the breast of waving and the thigh of heaving; and after that the Nazirite may drink wine. 21 This is the law of the Nazirite who vows, and of his offering to the Lord for his Naziriteship, beside that for which his means suffice; according to his vow which he vows, so he must do after the law of his Naziriteship." 22 And the Lord spoke to Moses, saying: 23 "Speak to Aaron and to his sons, saying: This is the way you shall bless the children of Israel; you shall say unto them: 24 'May the Lord bless you, and keep you; 25 May the Lord make His Face to shine upon you, and be gracious unto you; 26 May the Lord lifts up His Countenance upon you, and give you peace.' 27 So shall they put My Name upon the children of Israel, and I will bless them."

The Priestly Blessing

The Priestly Blessing is included in Bamidbar 6:24-27, and encompasses the three *Yuds* (י.י.י) for the purpose of confirming the Resurrection of the Dead. After the sin of the golden calf, by means of the thirteen attributes and the Priestly Blessing, all the people of Israel could once again attain Resurrection of the Dead and immortality. Today, when we connect with this Blessing we are given an opportunity to send Light and healing energy to all the cells of the body where there is illness.

The Priestly Blessing is written in the Bible with particular spaces in the middle of the verses. Spaces normally occur between the different sections but here the spaces are found in the middle of the verse to transfer the energy of healing that the Priest offered two thousand years ago. The energy of this blessing travels through time and is available to us today. It is a powerful connection that combines the Three Column System, helping us to close every opening where chaos may enter. This is achieved through specific combinations of the 72 Names of God. However, without the Temple we receive the Light drop by drop, whereas in the Temple we received it all at once.

Column	Biblical Verse	72 Names of God
Right Column	"May the Lord bless you, and keep you;" —Bamidbar 6:24	*Hei, Hei, Hei* ה.ה.ה *Yud, Hei, Hei* י.ה.ה
Left Column	"May the Lord make His Face to shine upon you, and be gracious unto you," —Bamidbar 6:25	*Yud, Hei, Hei* י.ה.ה *Mem, Nun, Dalet* מ.נ.ד
Central Column (combining the Right and Left columns)	"May the Lord lift up His Countenance upon you, and give you peace," —Bamidbar 6:26	*Yud, Yud, Yud* י.י.י *Hei, Alef, Alef* ה.א.א

These combinations are our delivery system for the consciousness that eliminates space and by combining Right, Left, and Central together we can become like God.

Bamidbar 7:1 And it came to pass on the day that Moses had finished setting up the Tabernacle, and had anointed it and sanctified it, and all the furniture thereof, and the altar and all the vessels thereof, and had anointed them and sanctified them; 2 that the princes of Israel, the heads of their fathers' houses, offered—these were the princes of the tribes, over those that were numbered. 3 And they brought their offering before the Lord, six covered wagons, and twelve oxen: a wagon for every two of the princes, and for each one an ox; and they presented them before the Tabernacle. 4 And the Lord spoke unto Moses, saying: 5 "Accept these from them, so they may be used to do the service of the Tent of Meeting; and you shall give them to the Levites, to every man according to his service." 6 And Moses took the wagons and the oxen, and gave them to the Levites. 7 Two wagons and four oxen he gave to the sons of Gershon, according to their service. 8 And four wagons and eight oxen he gave to the sons of Merari, according unto their service, under the hand of Ithamar, the son of Aaron, the priest. 9 But to the sons of Kohath he gave none, because the service of the holy things belonged to them: they bore them upon their shoulders. 10 And the princes brought the dedication-offering of the altar on the day that it was anointed; even the princes brought their offering before the altar. 11 And the Lord said to Moses: "They

shall present their offering, each prince on his day, for the dedication of the Altar."

Kabbalah and Simplicity

As mentioned previously, in the portion of Naso we have the dedication of the Altar in the Tabernacle, yet the Tabernacle was erected on the first day of Nissan (Aries), not when we traditionally read the portion of Naso. What does the Altar mean? The tradition of altar boys arises from it, but what does it indicate? Everything is very precise; it only means one thing, according to the Zohar— the Altar is Malchut. Rather than a whole dissertation of two thousand pages, Kabbalah uses one word: Malchut. This is the beauty of Kabbalah; it is how we make things so simple.

The difference between science and Kabbalah is captured in one idea—things become simple in Kabbalah, which is not necessarily the case in science where things often become hopelessly complex. Simplicity of consciousness is not so easy. Life should be simple. When it is complicated, we lose sight of what is going on.

Why is this so significant that the Altar is Malchut? This world is full of complexity, and therefore must remain full of chaos. In Kabbalah, we are given codes of the universe, and when we receive these codes, they are meant to open up new dimensions of simplicity. What we have in this, the longest reading of the year, is a portion that will provide us with so much energy surrounding the idea of simplicity. Rav Isaac Luria (the Ari) called the Light: S—I—M—P—L—E. This reading connects us to one thing, simplicity. To get to the truth is our most difficult task. The Ari defines the Light by its simplicity not its complexity.

In one of his letters to me, my teacher, Rav Brandwein, wrote "...you have to go a little further and you will see how simple it is." I did not know then what he was talking about. How on Earth could Kabbalah be simple? It is very difficult to make the transformational change from thinking about the physical to thinking about the immaterial.

The Priestly Blessing of the Kohenim, mentioned in Bamidbar 6:24-27, can be viewed as the ultimate in terms of simplicity. Translated, it literally has almost no meaning except as a blessing. We must, with the support of the Zohar, realize that this Blessing of the Kohenim is a code. Giving the blessing without thinking of it as a code misses the point. It is a code that embraces everything; this is what the portion of Naso is all about. Although it is a long portion, its function is to change our experience from complexity to that which is simple—to extend this Light in its simplicity.

Dedication of the Altar

Is the Dedication (*Chanukat*) of the Altar related to the holiday of Chanukah? People think that the word *chanukat* is derived from the word *chanukah*. Most commentators translate chanukat as "dedication" or "sanctified" but it is actually something entirely different. For example, if someone makes a dedication in the Zohar, this has nothing to do with the holiday of Chanukah. What is an Altar? The word Altar (*Mizbe'ach*) comes from the word *zevachim*, which is the "animal that is sacrificed."

Everything performed regarding the sacrifices and the Altar is connected to the battlefield. Today, the battlefield is our body, where the soul struggles with the essence of the body's nature of the Desire to Receive for Oneself Alone. Most people are occupied with their trivial bodily functions—eating, sleeping, and so on—and the soul needs none of these activities. Body consciousness is also about being preoccupied with what other people have, what other people say and do. All aspects of the ego stem from body consciousness.

The concept of *chanukat* is connected to the word *chinuch* (education,) that is, to educate our Desire to Receive for Ourself. Rav Akiva ended the war with his body. He had educated it to the point that when he ate, he would say to his body, "If you are hungry, please eat. I will watch, as I am not hungry."

This is the connection between the various themes of the portion of Naso, where increased body consciousness is discussed, as well as how to transform this body consciousness into Creator consciousness. There are a number of tools and technologies to be found in this portion, such as the Priestly Blessing and all the 72 Names of God combinations that appear in the portion. There are also all those matters related to being like the Creator, where it states that an individual has all the blessings they need.

12 And he that presented his offering the first day was Nachshon, the son of Amminadab, of the tribe of Judah; 13 and his offering was one silver dish, the weight thereof was a hundred and thirty shekels, one silver basin of seventy shekels, after the shekel of the Sanctuary; both of them full of fine flour mingled with oil for a grain offering; 14 one golden pan of ten shekels, full of incense; 15 one young bullock, one ram, one he-lamb of the first year, for a burnt-offering; 16 one male of the goats for a sin-offering; 17 and for the sacrifice of peace offerings, two oxen, five rams, five he-goats, five he-lambs of the first year. This was the offering of Nachshon, the son of Amminadab. 18 On the second day Nethanel, the son of Zuar, prince of Issaschar, did offer: 19 he presented for his offering one silver dish, the weight thereof was a hundred and thirty shekels, one silver basin of seventy shekels, after the shekel of the Sanctuary; both of them full of fine flour mingled with oil for a grain offering; 20 one golden pan of ten shekels, full of incense; 21 one young bullock, one ram, one he-lamb of the first year, for a burnt-offering; 22 one male of the goats for a sin-offering; 23 and for the sacrifice of peace offerings, two oxen, five rams, five he-goats, five he-lambs of the first year. This was the offering of Nethanel, the son of Zuar. 24 On the third day Eliab, the son of Helon, prince of the children of Zebulun: 25 his offering was one silver dish, the weight thereof was a hundred and thirty shekels,

one silver basin of seventy shekels, after the shekel of the Sanctuary; both of them full of fine flour mingled with oil for a grain offering; 26 one golden pan of ten shekels, full of incense; 27 one young bullock, one ram, one he-lamb of the first year, for a burnt-offering; 28 one male of the goats for a sin-offering; 29 and for the sacrifice of peace offerings, two oxen, five rams, five he-goats, five he-lambs of the first year. This was the offering of Eliab, the son of Helon. 30 On the fourth day Elizur, the son of Shedeur, prince of the children of Reuben: 31 his offering was one silver dish, the weight thereof was a hundred and thirty shekels, one silver basin of seventy shekels, after the shekel of the Sanctuary; both of them full of fine flour mingled with oil for a grain offering; 32 one golden pan of ten shekels, full of incense; 33 one young bullock, one ram, one he-lamb of the first year, for a burnt-offering; 34 one male of the goats for a sin-offering; 35 and for the sacrifice of peace offerings, two oxen, five rams, five he-goats, five he-lambs of the first year. This was the offering of Elizur, the son of Shedeur. 36 On the fifth day Shelumiel, the son of Zurishaddai, prince of the children of Simeon: 37 his offering was one silver dish, the weight thereof was a hundred and thirty shekels, one silver basin of seventy shekels, after the shekel of the Sanctuary; both of them full of fine flour mingled with oil for a grain offering; 38 one golden pan of ten shekels, full of incense; 39 one young bullock, one ram, one he-lamb of the first year, for a burnt-offering; 40 one male of the goats for a sin-offering; 41 and for the sacrifice of peace offerings, two oxen, five rams, five he-goats, five he-lambs of the first year. This was the offering of Shelumiel, the son of Zurishaddai. 42 On the sixth day Eliasaph, the son of Deuel, prince of the children of Gad: 43 his offering was one silver dish, the weight thereof was a hundred and thirty shekels, one silver basin of seventy shekels, after the shekel of the Sanctuary; both of them full of fine flour mingled with oil for a grain offering; 44 one golden pan of ten shekels, full of incense; 45 one young bullock, one ram, one he-lamb of the first year, for a burnt-offering; 46 one male of the goats for a sin-offering; 47 and for the sacrifice of peace offerings, two oxen, five rams, five he-goats, five he-lambs of the first year. This was the offering of Eliasaph, the son of Deuel. 48 On the seventh day Elishama, the son of Ammihud, prince of the children of Ephraim: 49 his offering was one silver dish, the weight thereof was a hundred and thirty shekels, one silver basin of seventy shekels, after the shekel of the Sanctuary; both of them full of fine flour mingled with oil for a grain offering; 50 one golden pan of ten shekels, full of incense; 51 one young bullock, one ram, one he-lamb of the first year, for a burnt-offering; 52 one male of the goats for a sin-offering; 53 and for the sacrifice of peace offerings, two oxen, five rams, five he-goats, five he-lambs of the first year. This was the offering of Elishama, the son of Ammihud. 54 On the eighth day Gamaliel ,the son of Pedahzur, prince of the children of Manasseh: 55 his offering was one silver dish, the weight there-of was a hundred and thirty shekels, one sil-ver basin of seventy shekels, after the shekel of the Sanctuary; both of them full of fine flour mingled with oil for a grain offering; 56 one golden pan of ten shekels, full of in-cense; 57 one young bullock, one ram, one he-lamb of the first year, for a burnt-offer-ing; 58 one male of the goats for a sin-offering; 59 and for the sacrifice of peace offerings, two oxen, five rams, five he-goats, five he-lambs of the first year. This was the offering of Gamaliel, the son of Pedahzur. 60 On the ninth day Abidan, the son of Gideoni, prince of the children of Benjamin: 61 his offering was one silver dish, the weight thereof was a hundred and thirty shekels, one silver basin of seventy shekels, after the shekel of the Sanctuary; both of them full of fine flour mingled with oil for a grain offering; 62 one golden pan of ten shekels, full of incense; 63 one young bullock, one ram, one he-lamb of the first year, for a burnt-offering; 64 one male of the goats for a sin-offering; 65 and for the sacrifice of peace offerings, two oxen, five rams, five he-goats, five he-lambs of the first year. This was the offering of Abidan, the son of Gideoni. 66 On the tenth day Ahiezer, the son of Ammishaddai, prince of

the children of Dan: 67 his offering was one
silver dish, the weight thereof was a hundred
and thirty shekels, one silver basin of seventy
shekels, after the shekel of the Sanctuary;
both of them full of fine flour mingled with
oil for a grain offering; 68 one golden pan of
ten shekels, full of incense; 69 one young
bullock, one ram, one he-lamb of the first
year, for a burnt-offering; 70 one male of the
goats for a sin-offering; 71 and for the sacrifice of peace offerings, two oxen, five rams,
five he-goats, five he-lambs of the first year.
This was the offering of Ahiezer, the son of
Ammishaddai. 72 On the eleventh day Pagiel,
the son of Ochran, prince of the children of
Asher: 73 his offering was one silver dish, the
weight thereof was a hundred and thirty
shekels, one silver basin of seventy shekels,
after the shekel of the Sanctuary; both of
them full of fine flour mingled with oil for a
grain offering; 74 one golden pan of ten shekels, full of incense; 75 one young bullock, one
ram, one he-lamb of the first year, for a
burnt-offering; 76 one male of the goats for a
sin-offering; 77 and for the sacrifice of peace
offerings, two oxen, five rams, five he-goats,
five he-lambs of the first year. This was the
offering of Pagiel, the son of Ochran. 78 On
the twelfth day Ahira, the son of Enan, prince
of the children of Naphtali: 79 his offering
was one silver dish, the weight thereof was a
hundred and thirty shekels, one silver basin
of seventy shekels, after the shekel of the
Sanctuary; both of them full of fine flour

mingled with oil for a grain offering; 80 one golden pan of ten shekels, full of incense; 81 one young bullock, one ram, one he-lamb of the first year, for a burnt-offering; 82 one male of the goats for a sin-offering; 83 and for the sacrifice of peace offerings, two oxen, five rams, five he-goats, five he-lambs of the first year. This was the offering of Ahira, the son of Enan. 84 This was the dedication-offering of the altar, in the day when it was anointed, at the hands of the princes of Israel: twelve silver dishes, twelve silver basins, twelve golden pans; 85 each silver dish weighing one hundred and thirty shekels, and each basin seventy; all the silver of the vessels two thousand, four hundred shekels, after the shekel of the Sanctuary; 86 twelve golden pans, full of incense, weighing ten shekels apiece, after the shekel of the sanctuary; all the gold of the pans a hundred and twenty shekels; 87 all the oxen for the burnt-offering twelve bullocks, the rams twelve, the he-lambs of the first year twelve, and their grain offering; and the males of the goats for a sin-offering twelve; 88 and all the oxen for the sacrifice of peace offerings twenty and four bullocks, the rams sixty, the he-goats sixty, the he-lambs of the first year sixty. This was the dedication-offering of the altar, after that it was anointed. 89 And when Moses went into the Tent of Meeting that He might speak with him, then he heard the Voice speaking unto him from above the ark-cover that was upon the ark of the testimony, from

between the two cherubim; and He spoke unto him.

The Zohar and the Restoration of Immortality

In the discussion of Naso found in the Zohar, Moses speaks to Rav Shimon and tells him that through the reading of the Zohar, through the scanning of the Zohar, through the wisdom of the Zohar, through the secrets of the Zohar, will we have the ability to eliminate chaos from our lives. In connection with the Zohar, Rav Shimon explains that it is as simple as when we turn on the Light and the chaos disappears. When that Light makes its presence felt under any conditions, darkness, otherwise known as chaos, must and will disappear. But here we are not referring to physical light, electric light or candlelight, we are referring to the Lightforce of God.

In the biblical portion of Naso, we have all the verses that are read on each of the eight days of Chanukah, the Festival of Lights. Contrary to popular belief, Chanukah is not about lighting the candles, lighting the oil, or celebrating a victory. Tradition is not what the kabbalists were telling us would reappear thousands of years later. Instead, what they are referring to is a condition where the Lightforce makes its presence felt and known; however this condition is not present every day. Even if we make an attempt, most of what we do during the week merely staves off the effects of darkness thus lessening the brutality of chaos. But there is no chance of eliminating chaos during the week. It is written in Genesis, "…there was evening and there was morning." This means that every day there is a test.

The Zohar tells us that it means we cannot eliminate the darkness. We can eliminate the effect of darkness upon our personal lives but we cannot dispense with it entirely. The essential force that creates chaos in our lives remains present during the week. Only on Shabbat and the holidays do we have the opportunity to tap into the Lightforce without an admixture of darkness. On these days, when we administer the right *kavanot* (meditations), we gain the power to eliminate darkness, to eliminate those aspects of darkness that can, God forbid, come upon us at any given time.

This portion of Bible deals with the Light. There are other sections that do not deal with the Light but rather deal with the Satan, the golden calf, the presence of chaos. The golden calf brought an end to what happened on Mount Sinai, on Shavuot. It brought an end to what would have become a permanent fixture in the form of revelation—immortality. All that was necessary was the physical connection. But the Israelites could not wait the forty days, they missed it by six hours. They had no patience, even though Aaron said that Moses would come down and return with the instrument that would make immortality a permanent part of the physical landscape of humanity. So immortality disappeared.

Now, we are constantly searching for how we can restore immortality. Once we make our connection to Shavuot, there is no question that we are taking with us that force that will not permit the Angel of Death, the real cause of every death, to have any dominion over us. Yes, we can blow this too, as one blows out a candle. This is why it is important to learn the rules of the technology. They are not difficult to understand, but they are difficult to put into practice.

Human Dignity

The one thing that can ruin our chances of immortality, as happened with the golden calf, is to treat another human being with anything less than human dignity. The Zohar says that it is because there is a lack of understanding of the concept of treating every human being with human dignity that we need all the volumes of Zohar to explain it to us. There is no justification for the disregard of human dignity, even if someone has hurt you or you disagree with them. Affording someone human dignity does not mean you have to agree with everything they say, it does not mean you do not take them to task. You simply cannot abuse that individual or make them suffer. Although there are several times during the year when we can restore immortality to the world, each time we treat another with less than human dignity we lose our capacity for immortality. We have this opportunity because God, in His infinite wisdom, knows how difficult it is for us to maintain this consciousness.

The Zohar, the physical book itself, demonstrates this power. Take a moment—not when you are in distress, not when you are having a difficult time—and put your hand over the Zohar. Do this for more than one minute; it may take a few minutes. Eventually, you will unquestionably, on a tangible level, feel the power of the Zohar. After this, you will regard the Zohar in its connection with the Lightforce of God, which you cannot feel.

While Naso is a long section, it is like a bank vault that is open for us to take our fill. Everyone would love it to be open all day. This is the same approach to have with the portion of Naso; the longer the portion, the longer we stay with it. Sometimes we get tired, and it is an effort. There are conditions that manifest themselves when we possess the right tools. When we participate, as we do here, in an experiential that provides us with a tremendous amount of energy by use of whatever tool we are applying in that moment, we feel something, not only on an intellectual level but we begin to feel something shift, this is why we all come back year after year.

Naso, the Idra Raba and Shavuot

We are given an opportunity to take in the energy that is available by merging the many tools we are given in the portion of Naso. We have the connection to the Light of Chanukah (the Festival of Lights, as well as the letters *Resh* ר and *Zayin* ז, which together have a numerical value of 207, which is the same numerical value as the Hebrew word for Light, *Or* אור. This is what Shavuot really concerns; it is about the Light. It is all about trying to contain and absorb as much Light as we possibly can. With the portion of Naso we have the singular opportunity to have the largest vessel to compliment the Light of Shavuot, which is the greatest amount of Light that was ever revealed at any given time.

Rashi and all the commentators say that the word *naso*, which means "to elevate" is generally associated with *nesiah* (travels), but here the word *naso* means "count." In Hebrew there is a better word than *naso* to be used for counting. And as we have learned, the first verse of each portion gives us an overview of what we are to expect and to receive, as well as help us delve into the benefits of the reading. In the portion of Naso, the word *lifkod* (count) is also found, but neither *lifkod* nor *naso* is really connected to counting. Moreover we have the connection to the princes of each tribe, each of whom brought an offering. Is it pure coincidence that the word *nasi* (prince) is derived from the root of the word naso?

Also, the Priestly Blessing is found in the portion of Naso, and what, in fact, is a blessing? Is a blessing something we receive by asking for it from a kabbalist or is a blessing from the Creator? If we were the Creator, why would we need a blessing? Does the Creator ask for a blessing from anyone? Therefore this must be a sign that when we ask for a blessing, we are invested in our Desire to Receive for Oneself Alone and are not connected to our inner Creator.

The portion of Naso is always read after Shavuot, and the Idra Raba (Greater Assembly) section is discussed in the Zohar of this portion. Rav Aba, who wrote down the words of Rav Shimon, could have placed this discussion anywhere in the Zohar, not necessarily in the section that deals with the biblical portion of Naso. At the time of the Idra Raba there was such a revelation of the Light that three of the participants died. Angels bore them upward, and then Elijah appeared and asked, "What happened?" He was told that the three had completed their *tikkun*, their spiritual correction. Then Rav Shimon asked Elijah the Prophet where he had been; for Elijah was supposed to have been one of the ten, the quorum of the Idra. Elijah the Prophet apologized and said that he had been working on liberating Rav Hamnuna Saba, who had been imprisoned. Elijah the Prophet explained that he had to break down the walls of the prison to free Rav Hamnuna Saba and his companions, which is why he did not arrive. This reflects the tremendous revelation of the Light that took place at the time of the Idra Raba. It is also related to the tremendous revelation of Light on Shavuot, which continues for seven days afterwards and is similar to an aftershock of an earthquake. This is why Naso is always read after Shavuot.

Power of Naso and the Twelve Tribes

The portion of Naso is so powerful that through it we receive control over the entire year. This occurs through the princes of each tribe, and since the Desire to Receive for Oneself Alone accompanies us in every month, we must gain control over it. The reason for this very extensive reading is because Naso typically follows Shavuot when so much energy is released. Consequently, the manifestation that we are fortunate to receive with the portion of Naso takes in every area, not just one particular area but all of the places in which chaos could develop.

Power of Naso and the Tribes

What seems very trivial is the idea of the *nesi'im*, the chieftains of each tribe, who each brought their particular sacrifice. We have learned that the sacrifices for each of the twelve tribes was simply part of the festivity that was joined in at the time the Tabernacle was completed, as it is stated in this week's reading.

The Zohar says:

> "And the Lord said to Moses, '...each prince [chieftain] on his day.'" (Bamidbar 7:11). HE ASKS: "What is the meaning of 'on his day'?" Rav Yehuda said: "These are the days above that were prepared to be blessed, which are the twelve boundaries, MEANING CHESED, GEVURAH, TIFERET AND MALCHUT; EACH ONE CONTAINING THREE COLUMNS, WHICH IS THE SECRET OF THE TWELVE BOUNDARIES that are divided. Each one is constructed and inaugurated with blessing through these PRINCES below, SINCE EACH PRINCE ESTABLISHED ONE DAY. We have learned that all are blessed for the Altar Above, WHICH IS BINAH, and even the Lower WORLD and even the nations of the world are blessed."
>
> We have learned that Rav Shimon said: "If these twelve princes would not have brought their offerings, the world could not have prevailed before the twelve princes of Ishmael, as is written: '...twelve princes [chieftains] according to their tribes.' (Beresheet 25:16) When those TWELVE PRINCES of Israel had brought their offerings, the dominion was taken away from all of them. Therefore, it is written: '...each prince on his day.' (Bamidbar 7:11)"
> —Zohar, Naso 23:197-198

We have also learned that each tribe represents a sign of the zodiac. The reason for each tribe presenting their sacrifice—which does not mean a sacrifice in only the literal sense—was that it was technology that acted like nano-robots reaching into the influence of each sign of the zodiac, which is not of a material nature.

Kabbalah helps us to understand that the Bible is only addressing matters of a non-physical nature—which is where all things begin. Every activity has its origin in the mind. The person who acts without thinking is viewed to be foolish—literally thoughtless. When we discuss the control over anything, such as the zodiac, we are clearly dealing with control at the level of the Upper Worlds, which again refers to only to consciousness.

Each chieftain or head of a tribe brought the sacrifice. Was he designated because he was the leader and representative? After all, if 147,000 people all brought their individual sacrifices, it would take who knows how long for each tribe. Clearly this is not the reason. To eliminate any form of chaos, no matter how it becomes manifested, we have to treat that instability at its root or seed—which is of course of immaterial origin.

The Bible wants to teach us that it is the head, the beginning that we must be concerned with. The position of chieftain was not a mere formality or honor. If we want to eliminate any form of instability, no matter where or how it is manifested, we must treat it at the root level.

An economist will predict where the country is supposedly headed financially, based on past trends. Yet we all know many things may happen in the future, obliterating such predictions. Thus, how can such economists be relied upon? Alternatively, consider a surgeon who has just operated and removed a cancerous tumor. What has been removed? Where does the cause for that tumor originate? Doctors do not think like this. The cancer may have gone undetected for thirty or forty years, so where did the tumor come from? It developed from an immaterial state.

We have to re-condition our way of thinking from merely dealing with it, to instead, going back to the cause. And the cause can only be what we may have done to create this instability. No one else can ever be the cause for the instability that exists in our lives. This is what it means to take responsibility. I am not saying here that you must come to this conclusion but nonetheless, this is what the wisdom of Kabbalah teaches: all instability, including the first atom of instability, began on this terrain by Adam. Let us stress again that all forms of instability that result in chaos have a point of origin. Therefore when we discuss the chieftains bringing the sacrifices, the Bible is telling us that if we want control over any sign of the zodiac throughout the year, we do so by controlling the root level. Consequences must be addressed at their source. Thus the chieftains were the ones to bring the sacrifices.

In the portion of Naso we also have the beautiful blessing of the High Priests—the blessing that we hear recited time and again. In its brevity, it is so complex, not that it is difficult to understand but that it takes in the complexity of this entire universe. We learn in Kabbalah that what is more is less and what is less is more, down to the nano level where we can no longer see it, smell it, hear it or touch it. It is mind boggling. As a direct result of our teaching Kabbalah, this change was brought about in the world. We were alone, in addressing things in the realm of the unseen, the immaterial realm—spirituality. Today, science is establishing that the kabbalists 4,000 years ago knew what they were talking about.

This does not mean everyone must experience this instability simply because today we are aware of its all-pervasive nature. What we find in the portion of Naso is literally the dissemination, the diffusion, and the infusion into this universe of all the energy that was released. How do we make this connection? We simply listen to the reading and receive the energy. How do we make this energy become manifest in our own lives? All of us may find that as we pass through the four months from Shavuot to Rosh Hashanah we are assured that neither death nor any serious accident can befall us. We are assured of it if we were present, participated, and conformed to the technology that Rav Isaac Luria (the Ari) and the Zohar have provided us so that we can capture that maximum amount of Light that emanated on the night of Shavuot. This is a truly incredible source of energy. May we all take full advantage of this enormous, profound Light that was shared with us on this night.

The Three Column System

Let us not forget the concept of the Central Column that is only taught at the Kabbalah Centres. It is a concept that, unfortunately the world, including the scientific community, does not understand. The Central Column of the Three Column System is the crux of what we do at the Centres and it is what is taught in our classes at the very beginning of your journey into the wisdom of Kabbalah.

According to Kabbalah, this Central Column force provides us with immortality—be it only for four months or only for one year. There is a force that brings about death, as it has done for the past 5,700 odd years. The force of death, which mankind has never been able to overcome, with the exception of a few kabbalists like Rav Shimon and his companions, comes into a manifestation during this period. What is this essential force and why do we speak about the Central Column? We are told in the Bible that all this takes place in the third month, the month of Sivan (Gemini) because it represents Central Column. What is the Central Column? Science has completely ignored the purpose of the neutron. Without the neutron there would be total chaos in the atom because the neutron represents Central Column. Central Column is restriction or resistance.

When we speak of becoming like God, we are discussing one who has attained such a state as to be without ego. If we have everything can we be humiliated? Humiliation only happens when someone touches a chord, awakening the sense that we are not what we think we are because of lack.

Along comes the Central Column and does the job that creates stability. It merges the Left Column with the Right Column and the Left Column becomes subject to the Right Column. Remember, we must always have a Left Column, just as we must always have a sharing and receiving element, to have circuitry.

The only problem we have in the removal of chaos in any form is that the Left Column runs amok. The electron is always in motion. As I have said over the past year, until we change the word "electronics" we are guiding the entire civilization into the idea of Receiving for the Self Alone. We have to have the component of sharing.

The manifestation of the Light here is to give us the consciousness to exercise restriction in our daily life. When we react, we are in the "electronic business" again. But when we resist, when we reject, when we restrict, we provide a climate whereby this electron becomes subject to the power of the Right Column—which is to share—and with that, the electron assumes a Desire to Receive for the Sake of Sharing.

Without restriction, our connection here is for no reason. If this message does not register for us, we will not be able to connect to the only source given to us to remove every form of chaos—even to the extent of immortality. If we think we have arrived because we have just restricted, we need to know that before we can achieve the removal of every form of chaos, there may be areas that each of us, depending on our own requirements of reincarnations has to cover. It comes with suffering.

Each opportunity where we did not exercise restriction is a missed opportunity of the manifestation of the awesome Light that was revealed on Shavuot. The portion of Naso is long, 176 verses to be very precise. In fact, dividing 176 by 4 is 44, which is the numerical value of the word *dam*, which means blood. Naso is the lifeblood of everything.

BOOK OF BAMIDBAR:

Portion of Beha'alotcha

PORTION OF BEHA'ALOTCHA

The Light and the Encampment

The biblical portion of Beha'alotcha begins with the lighting of the Menorah; Aaron the High Priest lit the "lamps" or candles. What is the meaning of the lighting of candles and what did it symbolize? The Light was ready, everything was ready to go; the physical Tabernacle was established. The Bible then details the encampment of the tribes, the significance of which we have already covered in the portion of Bamidbar. What is the Bible teaching us here? It appears to be a trifling incident not worthy of attention, and without the assistance of the Zohar it would be virtually incomprehensible. The Zohar finds the encampment of the tribes so important that Rav Shimon devotes more ink to this part than any other within Beha'alotcha which, as we shall see, deals largely with the drawing of energy.

Bamidbar 8:1 And the Lord spoke to Moses, saying: 2 "Speak to Aaron, and say to him: When you light the lamps, the seven lamps shall give light in front of the Menorah." 3 And Aaron did so: he lit the lamps so as to give light in front of the Menorah, as the Lord commanded Moses. 4 And this was the work of the Menorah, beaten work of gold; from the base to the flowers, it was beaten work; according to the pattern which the Lord had shown Moses, so he made the Menorah.

The Lightforce and Doubt

In synagogues an eternal lamp is lit but what does it signify? It is written that the Menorah was constructed as one solid piece of metal, and that Moses was not able to construct it successfully until the Creator showed him how. In speaking about the Menorah, we are referring to the tool that brought the Lightforce. This is why it is written that it was one piece—one wholeness of uninterrupted Light—free from chaos or disease. It is not the same as electric current, where when you turn off the light, the current stops.

The portion of Beha'alotcha concerns how to leave Satan behind, how to eliminate doubt. The Torah reminds us that the only enemy of the nation of Israel, from generation to generation, is Amalek. As we have learned, the *gematria* (numerical value) of the world *amalek* equals the same numerical value as the word "doubt". (ספק = עֲמָלֵק). The power of Satan is doubt, this is his weapon. His main instrument of war is not the ego, whereby his negative force lowers our defenses. The real battle is with doubt, and as we have seen, everyone must constantly fight to destroy it. It is important to come to come to the realization that when we experience doubt, this is coming from Satan.

Therefore, when we recite, "David blessed the Lord (וַיְבָרֶךְ דּוִד אֶת יְקוָק)," the first letters of which spell certainty (וד'אי), we should make contact with the power of certainty. We are truly fortunate to have this revelation so that we may connect to the Lightforce in this manner. It is said if anyone is in doubt, this is all Satan needs to cause confusion, this is how he enters.

Moses and the Menorah (Candelabra)

Why does the Bible say, "Speak to Aaron" at the beginning of the portion and then state again, "and say to him"? Would it not suffice to say it once? Why was the Menorah made in such a demanding manner—from one solid piece of metal? Why was it so difficult for Moses to make it? Would it not have been better to get a craftsman to make it or to have it made out of parts that could be joined, as is done today?

According to the Zohar, this portion is more powerful and more important than the Giving of the Torah on Mount Sinai because it contains a greater revelation of the Light than any other portion in the Bible. The Ten Utterances were the seed but here, in this portion, is the revelation of all the power that came about through Aaron. In the Zohar that explains the biblical portion of Beha'alotcha, it is written that the Bible itself should not be taken literally. It would be foolish to read the simple stories and think one understands. For two thousand years, the authorities have been trying to tell us: just accept things as they are; do not attempt understanding; and do not ask questions. This is the exact opposite of what the Bible truly wants from us. Unfortunately, there is no synagogue in the world where these questions are being asked.

There are so many transformative occurrences in this portion. There is a great revelation of Light, and when there are such occurrences, there are rapid changes, in every moment, in all spheres of life; as has been the case in the last few centuries compared to the last few thousand years.

The Zohar explains that the biblical text does not say *light* the candles, rather it uses a verb that denotes *raising up*, connecting to the superhighway, the direct path to the Light of the Creator. Here, we are not discussing Aaron lighting candles to create a special ambiance but that with this very lighting, Aaron elevated the children of Israel to a higher level. This Shabbat is the Shabbat of Lights, the lighting of the Menorah and our protection shield. We can tap into this energy of Light simply by lighting the candles as we do on Chanukah.

Moses could not understand the creation of the Menorah in the Temple, and this section says Moses needed special directions from God to explain how to create it. The difficult part for Moses was how to create the Menorah in one piece. Thus Moses asked God to give him a vision, and he was shown how to construct the menorah as a whole structure, not as separate sections molded together. For over a millennia, until the revelations of Kabbalah and the Zohar, whenever this section of the Bible was read, the challenge was in understanding how to construct the Menorah out of one piece.

The Zohar and the kabbalists help us to understand the deeper significance of this section and what it can teach us about our own lives. The only thing that can sustain us in every aspect of our lives is the Lightforce of God, which indicates that we must make a connection to the Flawless Universe. Since we are unfamiliar with this concept, chaos reigns supreme in every aspect of the physical realm. There is no aspect of physicality that does not experience chaos in some form, be it through death, decay, and other means.

Moses, therefore, in his question regarding the Menorah, indicates for us today the difficulty of connecting to the totality of the Lightforce of God in the physical realm, which is ruled by limitation. It was not so much the difficulty of how to create a Menorah as one piece but rather how to create unity between ourselves and the Creator. This is what the Zohar tells us is the deeper significance of what God and Moses were discussing.

Issues concerning the contemplation of the totality resembles the situation in medicine today. If you have something wrong with your arm, you go to an arm doctor, if you have something wrong with your finger, then a finger specialist. It is difficult to find a general practitioner. There is no longer a connection to the totality. What the Zohar teaches us is that we must examine the whole body. We need to connect to the whole. This is what holistic medicine is about, a comprehension of the unification of the whole so that we may connect to the Lightforce of God, which is complete. Using the example of the Menorah, we are learning in this portion that there must be a totality of connection; it cannot be broken or fragmented. This is a very deep lesson.

We can acquire this kind of knowledge from the Zohar and transform our consciousness. Before we can demand that we live in a totally Flawless Universe we have to be whole in the connection itself. We have to have unity within ourselves. We should work to remove that which creates division within ourselves as well as towards others. The purpose here is to not only create a unified system but also to be an un-fragmented person dwelling within it. We have to strive to create the unity within, which then creates unification between the realms of the Tree of Life and the Tree of Knowledge. However, this does not mean that we ignore the physical. We are discussing a state of consciousness by which the physical reality does not influence our decisions, as unfortunately, most of us are prey to. We have the power within to override these influences and elevate ourselves to the point where, no matter how heavily the physical world weighs upon us, we can still rise above. This is what we are trying to achieve.

At any time, when the challenges of the physical world become the deciding factor, we distance ourselves from the Flawless Universe. For those of us who permit our physical body, environment or existence to control the real self, in this portion we can receive—through the concept of the Menorah—the knowledge of how to be whole. The important thing to understand is that if we have difficulties on the physical level it is because in our consciousness we still permit the physical realm to dominate us. For example, when you are involved with your business, do not allow your business to dominate your life, always remember your higher consciousness.

Rashi (Rav Shlomo Yitzchaki, 1020–1105) tells us that the real Menorah is not seven branches. The real candelabra is in fact eight branches, connecting to the consciousness of Binah. Moses could not grasp it because he was connected to the consciousness of Binah. If you are in the consciousness where you are elevated, expressing unconditional love and sharing, not feeling your own lack, you cannot get or be involved in anything that is less. Betzalel was involved in the physical world, and therefore could get it. Moses could not understand what this emptiness, darkness was because he was so connected to the Light.

Although Moses was verbally instructed on how to create the Menorah, God had to show him the design, which was created from Light and appears to us in the shape of a Candelabra. This is the basis for how all Light comes to this world. When we listen to the reading of this section, we can literally go back in time, be present, and embrace the warmth and power of the Light. This is the only method by which we can travel backward in time and be immersed with contentment and fulfillment in the essence of the Light.

If we connected to this reading for no other reason, this would
be sufficient.

The Light of Shavuot

There is, in fact, no other section in the entire Torah that addresses
the lighting of the candles in this way. It is no coincidence that
there are 136 verses in this portion, making it one of the longest in
the Bible. Why, we may ask, did the sages not distribute the verses
equally? The wisdom of Kabbalah makes us aware that a certain part
of the Torah is necessary to remove the chaos revealing itself at that
particular time of year. Let us not forget that this is the fundamental
reason why we come to the Kabbalah Centres on Shabbat. For
3,400 years, perhaps this has not been the primary reason but those
who know Kabbalah understand that we read the Torah to remove
chaos from our lives. We also know that Kabbalah always raises
questions, for without the raising of questions there is no possible
chance of receiving answers.

This reading on the Shabbat that follows Shavuot is evidence that it
is a good time to re-energize our lives with the Lightforce of God.
The full implications of Shavuot can be felt thirty days after the
event, which has the added benefit of taking place in the month of
Gemini (Sivan) with its letters of *Resh* (ר) and the *Zayin* (ז), which
make up the Hebrew word *Raz* (רז; Light). We have filled our
lives with such intense Light during Shavuot, yet because we are
afflicted with short memories we are inclined to forget that what we
captured can be activated in a time of chaos. How many forget that
we have the Light of God always with us that can banish all chaos
and darkness? The curse of forgetfulness has always been one of
Satan's greatest weapons.

In lighting the candles, Aaron the High Priest was not merely lighting them 3,400 years ago, his action remains relevant and appropriate each and every year since. There could be no more important time than now to experience this, as we are in the midst of the battle of Armageddon, and this planet is completely infested with chaos. We are under constant threat from things that can destroy our bodies, the earth, the economy, and everything else. Here, we have the opportunity to draw down all the mechanisms that sustain not just our lives here, but the very planet itself, from its economy to its environment.

The internet is full of information, and if we were to read it all, we would find it exceedingly difficult to live any kind of ordinary life. The importance of this portion is that it provides us with the energy to improve our lives; it gives us the Light that removes darkness. It is one of the basic principles of this universe that when we turn on the Light, the darkness must disappear. It is impossible to over-emphasize the power of this portion.

Most of us believe we are so educated, having perhaps received graduate and post-graduate degrees, yet it comes as a great surprise that we never learned something as simple as what is revealed here. Not until I had started studying Kabbalah did the importance of the questions Rav Shimon asked about this section become apparent. Herein is discussed the Light of *Ein Sof* (Endless World), that all-inclusive, all-embracing, all-powerful Force without which nothing in this world could move, operate or perform in any way. Aaron is told to light the seven lights of the Menorah. All the commentators ask why there are seven lights. All things become manifested in this world by seven stages, seven degrees, seven Sefirot.

5 And the Lord spoke to Moses, saying:
6 "Take the Levites from among the children
of Israel, and cleanse them. 7 And so shall
you do to them, to cleanse them: Sprinkle
the water of purification upon them, and let
them cause a razor to pass over all their flesh,
and let them wash their clothes, and cleanse
themselves. 8 Then let them take a young bullock, and its grain offering, fine flour mingled
with oil, and another young bullock shall you
take for a sin-offering. 9 And you shall present
the Levites before the Tent of Meeting; and
you shall assemble the whole congregation of
the children of Israel. 10 And you shall present the Levites before the Lord; and the children of Israel shall lay their hands upon the
Levites. 11 And Aaron shall offer the Levites
before the Lord for a wave-offering from the
children of Israel that they may do the service of the Lord. 12 And the Levites shall lay
their hands upon the heads of the bullocks;
and offer you the one for a sin-offering, and
the other for a burnt-offering, to the Lord, to
make atonement for the Levites. 13 And you
shall set the Levites before Aaron, and before
his sons, and offer them for a wave-offering to the Lord. 14 So shall you separate the
Levites from among the children of Israel;
and the Levites shall be Mine. 15 And after
that the Levites shall go in to do the service
of the Tent of Meeting; and you shall cleanse
them, and offer them for a wave-offering.
16 For they are wholly given unto Me from
among the children of Israel; instead of all

that opens the womb, even the first-born of all the children of Israel, have I taken them unto Me. 17 For all the first-born among the children of Israel are Mine, both man and beast; on the day that I smote all the first-born in the land of Egypt I sanctified them for Myself. 18 And I have taken the Levites instead of all the first-born among the children of Israel. 19 And I have given the Levites— they are given to Aaron and to his sons from among the children of Israel, to do the service of the children of Israel in the Tent of Meeting, and to make atonement for the children of Israel, that there be no plague among the children of Israel, through the children of Israel coming near to the Sanctuary."

Purification

In this section, we are presented with the process of cleansing the nation of Israel, which is not a discussion about bathing. We are dealing with all of the forces within that urge us toward negativity in its manifold forms; this portion can help cleanse us of such negative inclinations. The Zohar presents an entire discourse on this most vital of procedures. As we have learned, the words of the Bible are necessary integral components that comprise a very complex machine. The Lightforce energy is not only a force or instrument to make things happen, it also acts as a vehicle or medium.

20 So did Moses, and Aaron, and all the congregation of the children of Israel, to the Levites; according to all that the Lord commanded Moses touching the Levites, so did the children of Israel to them. 21 And the Levites purified themselves, and they washed their clothes; and Aaron offered them for a sacred gift before the Lord; and Aaron made atonement for them to cleanse them. 22 And after that the Levites went in to do their service in the Tent of Meeting before Aaron, and before his sons; as the Lord had commanded Moses concerning the Levites, so did they do to them. 23 And the Lord spoke to Moses, saying: 24 "This pertains to the Levites: from twenty-five years old and upward they shall go in to perform the service in the work of the Tent of Meeting; 25 and from the age of fifty years they shall return from the service of the work, and shall serve no more; but shall minister with their brethren in the Tent of Meeting, to keep the charge, but they shall do no manner of service. So shall you do to the Levites regarding their duties."

The Tabernacle and the Levites

Again, we read about the Levites and the arrangement of the Tabernacle, and all of the material that was already mentioned before. We know that the Tabernacle was the most powerful power station, and that it still exists today, even though we cannot see it, dominated as we are by the physical realm. Therefore, the blessing of being able to see the Light, to see the presence of people who have long departed this world, and to communicate with them is what we will be receiving when we connect to the portion of Beha'alotcha.

Why were the Levites and the priests so designated, what of the rest of the Israelites? Why would they become second class citizens, not as important as the priestly family? The Zohar explains that it is because of what happened at the time of the golden calf. The Levites did not participate in the building of the golden calf. At that time there were no Kohens (Priests), there were only Levites. Today we have Kohens and Levities. It was only after Aaron was designated to be a Priest that we have Kohens. Aaron was a Levite to begin with and then he was elevated to the status of Priest. These are all very important parts that make up the Israelites.

Bamidbar 9:1 And the Lord spoke to Moses in the wilderness of Sinai, in the first month of the second year, after they came out of the land of Egypt, saying: 2 "Let the children of Israel keep the Passover in its appointed season. 3 In the fourteenth day of this month, at dusk, you shall keep it in its appointed season; according to all the statutes of it, and according to all the ordinances thereof, shall you keep it." 4 And Moses spoke to the children of Israel, that they should keep the Passover. 5 And they kept the Passover in the first month, on the fourteenth day of the month, at dusk, in the wilderness of Sinai; according to all that the Lord commanded Moses, so did the children of Israel. 6 But there were certain men, who were unclean by the dead body of a man, so they could not keep the Passover on that day; and they came before Moses and before Aaron on that day. 7 And those men said to him: "We are unclean by the dead body of a man; why are we kept from bringing the offering of the Lord in its appointed season among the children of Israel?" 8 And Moses said to them: "Stay you that I may hear what the Lord will command concerning you." 9 And the Lord spoke to Moses, saying: 10 "Speak to the children of Israel, saying: 'If any man of you or of your generations shall be unclean by reason of a dead body or be in a journey afar, yet he shall keep the Passover to the Lord;

Eliminating Satan, the Power of the Dot above the Word *Rechokah*

In Bamidbar 9:10, there is a dot above the letter *Hei* in the word *rechokah*, which means "afar" or "distance." The reason for this is very simple, it is to eliminate Satan. When we distance ourselves from Satan, this is how we neutralize him.

What Kabbalah knew four thousand years ago scientists are just discovering: what is less is more. In the past, a cable across the Atlantic could only handle one hundred phone calls per wire. These are now obsolete, it seems that the thinner the cables are today, the more calls are able to be made. Does the idea of "less is more" also mean that the less money we have, the richer we will be? In mathematics or economics, the position of a single dot can mean the difference between a thousand dollars and a million dollars. If you spent a million dollars a day, you could not spend a billion dollars in a year. How do you lose fifty billion in less than one year? The dynamic atomic activity was missing from the money, which is why so much could be lost in such a short time. With this dot we have the opportunity to reveal so much Light with the least amount of physicality.

The Power of the Dot

As mentioned previously, there is a dot above the letter *Hei* in the word *rechokah*, and we know whenever there is a dot—unusual in the Torah scroll—it represents the material world, but in its most infinite state of physicality. How small is a dot? Infinitely small. We know that these dots, only present in ten places throughout the entire Torah, are another opportunity for us to eliminate physicality. Does it mean we need to get rid of the body? No, it means that our consciousness is totally divorced from physicality. Should we

116

pay no attention to the physical? No, we are talking about a state of consciousness by which the physical reality does not make our decisions, as unfortunately, most of us succumb to.

Why does the Bible say here, "of your generations"? Why does it not say for the next generations? It is because we are not talking about physical distance. When we pray the Amidah (Silent Prayer) on Shabbat or during the week, it is so long that the mind can wander. There is a parable depicting this truth: When the Baal Shem Tov came to the place where his students would make their prayer connections he said, *Shalom alechem* (an expression used to welcome back one who has returned from traveling) to one individual, even though neither this person nor any of his relatives had left town. The student asked the Baal Shem Tov why he would always greet him with *Shalom alechem*. The Baal Shem Tov replied, "It's very simple. For 30 years you have not been here. Your body is here, but you have not been here." We need to be aware of where we are when we are praying and make an effort to be present with our consciousness.

We can override the body and elevate ourselves to the point where, no matter how heavily the body weighs upon us, we can still be like Rav Akiva, who, when food was served to him, said to his body, "Okay, go ahead, you can eat it. But me personally, I do not even want food." This does not indicate that we should refrain from eating altogether, it simply stresses how Rav Akiva was able to separate the two realms of being—and this is what we are trying to achieve here. As has been stated already, where the body dominates our consciousness, we distance ourselves from the Flawless Universe. Those of us who permit our physical body or environment to control our true self can receive in this portion—through the wholeness of the Menorah—the ability of how to be whole. Despite the aches and pains of the body, know the rule of mind over matter, and then the body cannot be in control.

The important aspect is to understand that if we have difficulties on the physical level, it is because in our consciousness we still permit the physical realm to dominate us. The mainstream deals with the physical reality. Should we thus ignore it? No, we must, of course, eat, and so on, yet while doing so, strive to not be connected to the physical realm. It is the same with our work or business, when you are at work, do not permit your work to become your master.

11 in the second month on the fourteenth day at dusk they shall keep it; they shall eat it with unleavened bread and bitter herbs; 12 they shall leave none of it to the morning, or break one of its bones; according to all the statutes of the Passover they shall keep it. 13 But the man that is clean, and is not on a journey, and ceases to keep the Passover, that soul shall be cut off from his people; because he did not bring the offering of the Lord in its appointed season that man shall bear his sin. 14 And if a stranger shall dwell among you, and will keep the Passover to the Lord: according to the statute of the Passover, and according to its ordinance, so shall he do; you shall have one statute, both for the stranger, and for him that is born in the land."

A Chance for the Energy of Pesach (Passover)

Following the discussion of Pesach, the evening of the 14th day of Nissan (Aries), the Bible states that those people who could not be present, who were unclean and unprepared for the 14th day of Nissan, could receive a diminished version of Pesach called Pesach Sheni on the 14th day of Iyar (Taurus), the month of healing. It was not as powerful, nor as strong but the unprepared people did not have the receptacle to contain all the awesome energy available on the night of Passover. There is a discourse concerning what should be done on the evening of 14th day of Iyar, and the answer is the same actions, however, the energy is not the same. One may have the same vessel but this does not mean that the vessel becomes filled up as it did on the first night of Pesach. Today, on Pesach Sheni we participate in the eating of *matzah*. And with this reading, those who could not make the connection the 14th or 15th day of Nissan are given another chance to make the connection to the awesome Light of Pesach.

The Zohar asks, "If the final end of chaos came about on the night of Pesach, why would they be celebrating a month later?" Rav Shimon reveals that an event as powerful as Passover, which literally brought an end to chaos, continued uninterruptedly. He says that the effect of this event, the metaphysical aspects of Light continue for thirty days. Rav Shimon explains that this is what brought about the end of chaos, so that on the 30th day, Malchut, we are given another opportunity to connect to the Light of Pesach, which, for a moment, creates that division between the Tree of Life and the Tree of Knowledge universe.

This concept is so profound that we could continue to discuss it for thirty years, and maybe then we could fully appreciate this gift of being constantly connected to the Light. What the Torah Scroll does for us is that we can go back to this cosmic event that gives us unlimited Light. We forget because it comes easily, it does not take much effort to get to the Centre. However, the only way to keep what we receive when we hear the reading on Shabbat is to appreciate the gift we have received.

What does the account of Pesach have to do with the lights of the Menorah? As we have learned, experiencing a kabbalistic Pesach is vastly different from any other Passover we may have experienced before studying Kabbalah. It is a journey into self-perfection.

15 And on the day that the Tabernacle was reared up, the cloud covered the Tabernacle, even the Tent of the Testimony; and in the evening there was the appearance of fire on the Tabernacle, until morning. 16 So it was always: the cloud covered it, and the appearance of fire by night.

The Ark and the Cloud

When the Tabernacle was established, a cloud covered the Ark. As we already know, the significance of the Ark was that it was the antenna and receptacle on a physical corporeal level for the most awesome power of the universe. By the virtue of the power of the Ark, the Israelites as they roamed in the wilderness never feared being overtaken by the other nations. Therefore, the cloud was not merely a cloud, it also represented a direct connection to the Lightforce of God. In the Centre, we generally refer to meditation as a process of making connections, whether it is to the Hebrew alphabet or the words of the Siddur (Prayer Book). During the biblical period there was no necessity for any of these connections, the connections were automatic by virtue of the cloud.

The cloud was a physical representation of all metaphysical connections, therefore the Israelites were able to be powerful and without fear. One would think that if they had no fear then they ought not have had any troubles because essentially the only problem that people face in this terrestrial realm are fears related to tomorrow, fear that they will not have enough, fear of the unknown. The Israelites then, were provided with such a connection to the awesome power, which we call certainty; there was nothing that was left to doubt. Nevertheless, as we have discovered in this portion, for whatever reason, this was not enough to make the Israelites feel content, not even the Ark could provide all the necessities of life.

17 And whenever the cloud was taken up from over the Tent, then after that the children of Israel journeyed; and in the place where the cloud settled, there the children of Israel encamped. 18 At the commandment of the Lord the children of Israel journeyed; and at the commandment of the Lord they encamped: as long as the cloud settled upon the Tabernacle they remained encamped. 19 And when the cloud tarried upon the Tabernacle many days, then the children of Israel kept the charge of the Lord, and journeyed not. 20 And sometimes the cloud was a few days upon the Tabernacle; according to the commandment of the Lord they remained encamped, and according to the commandment of the Lord they journeyed. 21 And sometimes the cloud was from evening until morning; and when the cloud was taken up in the morning, they journeyed; or if it continued by day and by night, when the cloud was taken up, they journeyed. 22 Whether it were two days, or a month, or a year, that the cloud tarried upon the Tabernacle, abiding on it, the children of Israel remained encamped, and journeyed not; but when it was taken up, they journeyed. 23 At the commandment of the Lord they encamped, and at the commandment of the Lord they journeyed; they kept the charge of the Lord, at the commandment of the Lord, by the hand of Moses.

Bamidbar 10:1 And the Lord spoke unto Moses, saying: 2 "Make you two trumpets of silver; of beaten work shall you make them; and they shall be to you for the calling of the congregation, and for causing the camps to set forward. 3 And when they shall blow with them, all the congregation shall gather themselves to you at the door of the Tent of Meeting. 4 And if they blow only once, then the princes, the heads of the thousands of Israel, shall gather themselves to you. 5 And when you blow an alarm, the camps that lie on the east side shall take their journey. 6 And when you blow an alarm the second time, the camps that lie on the south side shall set forward; they shall blow an alarm for their journeys. 7 But when the assembly is to be gathered together, you shall blow, but you shall not sound an alarm. 8 And the sons of Aaron, the priests, shall blow with the trumpets; and they shall be to you for a statute forever throughout your generations. 9 And when you go to war in your land against the adversary that oppresses you, then you shall sound an alarm with the trumpets; and you shall be remembered before the Lord, your God, and you shall be saved from your enemies. 10 Also in the day of your gladness, and in your appointed seasons, and in your new moons, you shall blow with the trumpets over your burnt offerings and over the sacrifices of your peace offerings; and they shall be to you for a memorial before your God: I am the Lord, your God." 11 And it came to pass in the second year, in the second month, on the twentieth day of the month, the cloud was taken up from over the Tabernacle of the Testimony. 12 And the children of Israel set forward by their stages out of the wilderness of Sinai; and the cloud settled in the wilderness of Paran. 13 And they took their first journey, according to the commandment of the Lord by the hand of Moses. 14 And in the first place the standard of the camp of the children of Judah set forward according to their hosts; and over his host was Nachshon, the son of Amminadab. 15 And over the host of the tribe of the children of Issaschar was Nethanel, the son of Zuar. 16 And over the host of the tribe of the children of Zebulun was Eliab, the son of Helon. 17 And the Tabernacle was taken down; and the sons of Gershon and the sons of Merari, who bore the Tabernacle, set forward. 18 And the standard of the camp of Reuben set forward according to their hosts; and over his host was Elizur, the son of Shedeur. 19 And over the host of the tribe of the children of Simeon was Shelumiel, the son of Zurishaddai. 20 And over the host of the tribe of the children of Gad was Eliasaph, the son of Deuel. 21 And the Kohathites, the bearers of the Sanctuary, set forward, that the Tabernacle might be set up against their coming. 22 And the standard of the camp of the children of Ephraim set forward according to their hosts; and over his host was Elishama, the son of Ammihud.

23 And over the host of the tribe of the children of Manasseh was Gamaliel, the son of Pedahzur. 24 And over the host of the tribe of the children of Benjamin was Abidan, the son of Gideoni. 25 And the standard of the camp of the children of Dan, the rear-guard of all the camps, set forward according to their hosts; and over his host was Ahiezer, the son of Ammishaddai. 26 And over the host of the tribe of the children of Asher was Pagiel, the son of Ochran. 27 And over the host of the tribe of the children of Naphtali was Ahira, the son of Enan. 28 Thus were the journeys of the children of Israel according to their hosts. And they set forward.

Encampment of the Twelve Tribes, Poverty, Life and Death

This section deals with the encampment of the twelve tribes, and therefore their astral influences, mentioned previously in the portion of Bamidbar. There was the tribe of Yehuda in the east and the tribe of Reuben in the west; both of these tribes were accompanied by two other tribes each. The leader of the north was the tribe of Dan and the leader of the south was the tribe of Ephraim. Naturally this raises the question, what was the purpose of informing us about how these Israelites sat around when they were not doing anything, and in what position they were? Why does the Bible have to report on the way the Israelites rested between their travels? As the Zohar asks, of what importance is it where they were encamped? We discussed previously just one aspect of the flags and that was the flag of the tribe of Yehuda. Why the repetition? For the straightforward answer and to make our proper connection, we turn to the Zohar to understand on various levels precisely what the cosmic code, the Bible, is implying.

Concerning Bamidbar 9:15, the Zohar says:

> "And on the day that the Tabernacle was erected..." Rav Chiya opened the discussion saying: "He has distributed freely, he has given to the poor; his righteousness endures forever; his horn shall be exalted with honor." (Psalms 112:9) and asks "what is the meaning of 'distributed freely and has given to the poor?'" He answers "It is as you say, 'there is one who gives freely, and yet increases.' (Proverbs 11:24) We can also say that it is true for everyone who distributed freely. As soon as one gives freely to the poor, the giver becomes worthy. What is the meaning of '... and yet increases?' It means in everything. He increases in wealth and increases in life."
> —Beha'alotcha 17:95

The establishment of the Tabernacle provided not only the Israelites but all of humankind with whatever their necessities might be. Through the Tabernacle, which ultimately was brought into a greater fruition by virtue of the Holy Temple, the poor would be totally provided for. Poor does not necessarily mean someone who is lacking monetarily but it also means poor in whatever respect one might find oneself lacking. The Zohar interprets this verse as the Tabernacle took care of all of the needs of the people.

What more do we require if all our needs are totally provided for? What could possibly be wanting if the moment we think of something we lack it is instantly provided for? What does the word *venosaf* (more) mean in this context? It indicates that there was still one other aspect of lack, the fear of death. Of course, death is not the first thing that comes to our minds. For most people, the fear of uncertainty comes first. Although young people die as

127

well, it is only really when old age arrives that most people begin to understand there could be a possibility of another fear. Therefore, Rav Chiya clarified that the Tabernacle was going to provide eternal life.

Rav Chiya explains that anyone who gives charity to the poor, meaning the truly poor, arouses the Tree of Life, which is Zeir Anpin, and therefore the giver provides life to Malchut, which is our terrestrial realm where death exists; death does not exist on any other level. The Zohar says that Moses did not die, he simply no longer existed within our realm. Death is an illusion, and the Tree of Life stands over the one who gives charity and shields them in a time of need and removes death from their midst.

From this verse in the Bible, we understand that charity (*tzedaka*) is an aspect of bringing life. Someone's ulterior motive could be that they are giving charity because they want to remain alive. Yet if the intention behind someone giving to charity is to be saved from death, is this charity then given with an ulterior motive?

The Talmud relates that Jeremiah pleaded and implored for the mercy of God when he saw the imminent destruction of the Temple. He asked the Creator to please send a true poor man because if God could send that true poor man then all of the people would be saved by permitting them to give charity to him. Jeremiah was seeking out a poor man so that the principle of *tzedaka yatzil memavet* (charity saves one from death) could be actualized. In other words, if there is an opportunity of giving charity to a poor man, even with an ulterior motive, nonetheless it will save a life.

The question is, why? Both the Gomorrah and the Zohar say because a true poor man is considered a dead man for various reasons. First of all, from a poor man you never hear wisdom. He could be the wisest in the world but because he is poor he is not heard, it is almost as though he does not exist. For this reason, when someone gives him charity, it takes him out of that frame of death and into a state of being of having his needs fulfilled. He feels no lack. He feels complete, and at that moment death becomes nullified. This is what is meant by the verse that the Ark provided the Israelites with all of their necessities, and by virtue of providing them with all of their necessities, life becomes established and death becomes nullified; the aspect of the poor man becomes nullified. Therefore, when a person has no needs a person is alive. It is the uncertainty of our needs and wants that brings death.

However, the Zohar also explains that the establishment of the Tabernacle is not enough to remove death. The verse goes onto explain how they were encamped. Why is this repeated? Because as was stated previously, the encampment is the control of the astral influences. So while we can make connections with life, nevertheless this does not preclude that the stars impel. The stars may not compel but they still impel. They do not constrain us but they do provide a strong force for us to overcome. Therefore, although we can seek a certain connection or we can give charity, maybe we do so at the wrong time, as with the months of Tevet (Capricorn), Av (Leo), or Tammuz (Cancer) where there are astral influences that, despite giving charity, despite the presence of the Tabernacle, by and within itself this was not sufficient to create life. In other words, the Ark could act as a channel but it was not enough. There is a system by which to make the connections.

To control astral influences, we pray to the east. However, there have been many throughout the centuries that have prayed eastward and still calamities were not prevented for all of humankind. It is similar to the giving of charity. It is not enough.

Central, Right and Left Columns

The Zohar says we should pray eastward. This does not mean pray in an easterly direction. The concept of east is referring to the Central Column that combines Right and Left Column, like in the lightbulb. It is also known as the force of compassion. The Central Column acts like a filament creating a circuit of energy. Once a circuit of energy is established there is nothing that can affect us in any way. The discussion in Beha'alotcha is not about where they sat or where they encamped. These encampments formed the codes we use to control our destiny today. These codes help us to understand how to direct energies towards the astral influences that are prevalent.

Within every month there are positive and negative astral influences, with the exception of the three months Tammuz (Cancer), Av (Leo), and Tevet (Capricorn), which the Zohar tells us are completely negative. In these three months we do not begin anything new. Nonetheless, all of the other months have both positive and negative influences and it is those negative influences that we want to be certain will not affect us. The verses about the encampment tell us how to control the twelve astral influences. On each of the four sides there were three tribes, indicating the twelve astral influences.

The tribe of Yehuda sat with the other two tribes of Issaschar and Zebulun. In the month of Tammuz we want the support of the tribe of Yehuda, we want the support of the Angel Michael so that we can counteract the negative energy-intelligence that impels, though it does not compel.

The second flag, is the flag of the tribe of Reuben. It deals with enlisting the celestial hosts of war. This is where astrology becomes very confusing. The Zohar says that the Angel Uriel is one of the codes for drawing positive energy for the aspect of the south. The flag of the tribe of Reuben was to the south. The south represents Chesed—this never changes. Chesed means positive energy, Right Column energy, which fits with Reuben because he was the firstborn. Reuben rules over Aries because Aries is the first month and the Right Column of the first three months. Yet, we just finished discussing that Yehuda was Central Column, so what does he have to do with the Right Column? Only through the Central Column does the Right Column become a force. How do we get electricity? The negative pole draws the energy that ultimately becomes manifest through the right pole. The Central Column does not make it manifest, rather the Central Column acts as a centrifugal force that, like the filament, creates the condition by which the Right Column provides us with an abundance of Light. But what was the cause of it? The Central Column.

With regard to the zodiac signs that deal with Reuben, Shimon, and Gad, how can we connect with positive energy of these months when it is their time to rule in the cosmos? The Zohar tells us that even if we have the Ark, which is the most powerful instrument of connection to the power of the cosmos, we still need to know about the encampments. What does this mean? It means that we can have the greatest equipment but if we lack the knowledge of how to make use of it, it will not serve us.

We may have all the tools of connection, like the lost Ark itself but how do we implore its energy? The Amidah Prayer too, is the strongest channel but what do we do with it? It is not enough to say: "God told me to pray." There is also the Ana Beko'ach that deals specifically with the cosmos. The Light is ready and everything is established but the Zohar deals with drawing this energy.

Therefore, I return to the discussion of the second flag and the tribe of Reuben, which is the Right Column, the energy of Chesed.

What is the difference between the tribe of Yehuda and the tribe of Reuben? As stated previously, the tribe of Reuben is in the south and the south is the Right Column energy of the first three months. Yehuda also represented the essence of Right Column energy as he rules over the month of Cancer (Tammuz), which is the first month of the second quarter of the year. The Zohar asks what the difference is between Yehuda and Reuben, and then explains that although the tribes of Yehuda and Reuben consist of both qualities: Central Column and Right Column energy, they are not the same. The tribe of Yehuda has the distinction. While Yehuda encompasses both the Central and Right Columns, the dominant factor within him is the Central Column. And because the dominant energy-intelligence of Yehuda is Central Column, he encamped in the east as east is symbolic of restriction. The idea of restriction is to have the strength not to grab everything that comes our way; that is what is meant by Central Column.

When we pray to the east, we concentrate on Central Column energy-intelligence, not on the direction. With all our connections, it is important to know what we are doing. The Central Column makes manifest the Right Column without the worry of drawing energy. As we understand from *Talmud Eser Sefirot* ("Study of Ten Luminous Emanations"), if we put out the energy of restriction we will be amazed how the energy comes back. Push it away, it comes back. It is a paradox.

The Tribes of Yehuda and Reuben

Within Yehuda there is the support of the Angel Michael, which is all Right Column. Michael is the Angel, who if you call him, he comes. If you do not call him, he will not come. Therefore, if we are concentrating on Mercy we have to concentrate on the Angel Michael. If we mention the name Michael but are not conscious of what we want from him, he will come and he will ask us, "What do you want?" The problem is that we may not hear him. We will feel that he did not come because we did not do what was necessary. Without actively calling the Angel Michael nothing will happen. Without dialing the number nothing will happen despite the fact that we have all the right equipment.

In the case of Reuben, his intrinsic dominating energy-intelligence is Right Column, therefore the Zohar says he was encamped in the south. We are not talking about where they went, where they camped, where they moved, rather we are talking about how they drew that awesome power of the cosmos. Therefore, the intrinsic and essential energy-intelligence of Reuben is Right Column. Yehuda's intrinsic energy-intelligence is Central Column, and the Central Column brings energy to the Right Column as well as some energy to the Left Column. Herein lies the secret of why the tribes of Reuben and Yehuda are not exactly alike. If they were exactly alike, there would be no reason for both of them to exist. They are both inclusive; they are both Right Column and Left Column.

The Zohar, Beha'alotcha 18:101-102 says:

> A wind of the four winds IS ROBED in four compartments and four sides in the brilliance that was created that supports the illuminated faces. Therefore, they are like the appearance of the Living Creatures, which are the four corners UPON WHICH the standards were unfurled, THAT ARE REFERRED TO AS Lion, Eagle, Ox, and Man. These comprise the Four Dominating Angels—WHO ARE MICHAEL, GABRIEL, URIEL, AND RAPHAEL— and include everything, SINCE THESE FOUR ANGELS COMPRISE ALL THE HEAVENLY HOSTS.

The first standard is an armed camp THAT IS THE SECRET OF THOSE ABLE TO GO TO WAR FROM THE AGE OF TWENTY AND HIGHER. ITS LIVING CREATURE IS a Lion. THE ANGEL IS Michael, recorded in the unfurled standard that is spread to the Right Side, AND ITS WIND IS the east—that is, the rising of the sun that travels with its light.

Here, the Zohar mentions the Four Holy Beasts. What do the Four Holy Beasts stand for? There is the Lion, the Ox, the Eagle, and Man who is the recipient of the three basic energies. The Eagle is Central Column, the Lion is Right Column, and the Ox is Left Column.

One would imagine that because Reuben is to the south and the first of the three months—the month of Aries that he is under the influence of sharing. However, that is not all there is in Reuben because the Right Column, by and within itself, does not permit us to connect and master the positive energy of this month. It is not enough. Sharing is not enough. Many people become frustrated after sharing, thinking, *I gave too much or it wasn't worth it.* I can give you a thousand reasons why, after sharing, a person has second thoughts about what they did. Why? Because by and within itself sharing is not enough; it does not take into account every situation that may arise in the month of Aries, since there is a negative quality in Aries as well.

When we understand the essence of the Eagle, there is a clue as to how to control this negative quality. The Eagle is a code for another type of energy; the Eagle is the Central Column energy of the Four Holy Beasts. The energy of the Eagle brings the manifestation of Central Column. This is why Reuben is considered to also have the Central Column aspect of the Eagle. It is for our benefit. There are negative aspects to Right Column energy, like giving too much. The

Sun can give too much. A parent can give too much and smother a child with too much sharing. There can be too much Sun even if it gives life. Too much can be harmful. In other words, even in the sharing we have to have balance, we have to restrict and apply the Central Column. In the case of the Sun, the Central Column says, "Stop."

We can understand this better if we examine the movement of the sun. According to the Zohar, the mid-day sun is in the south. Why is it midday in the south? The sun could move very quickly and be in the west. Does the sun move faster in the morning and slower in the afternoon? How come it works out that high noon, mid-day, should be Central Column? This is because when it begins to move towards the left direction; it begins from the east, which is the Right Column. What's the right side of south? The right side of south is east and the sun begins to go in a westerly direction. The reason for that is to provide energy to the Left Column as well, not because Left Column energy is the sun's intrinsic characteristic. The sun is shining even while it is waning. Once it wanes, it is indicative of only Left Column energy.

An article in Newsweek said, that all over the world, most crimes are committed between the hours of 5:00 pm and 7:00 pm but, in fact, this phenomenon is in the entire universe as well. Why between the hours of 5:00 pm and 7:00 pm? They don't know. However, we know that between 5:00 pm and 7:00 pm, the sun is just about setting. Yet at 12:00 noon, it continues to shine, to provide a balance between the Right and the Left Columns. High noon, mid-day, is in the south so that the sun can provide for the east as well as the west, and in this way the Left Column also receives energy. So, in effect, while the sun's intrinsic characteristic is not Central Column, it also makes manifest Central Column energy.

Therefore, if you would like to avoid Left Column or Judgment energy, do not begin something in the afternoon. If you would like to start a new business or if you want to get married, do not do it in the afternoon. Afternoon weddings are not a good idea because the sun is waning. And why is the sun waning? Why does it begin to descend? The sun itself is only matter. There is a force that tells the sun, "You have power but there is a time when that power has to begin to become diminished." The power of negativity says, "I want to rule." The sun begins to descend because at 12:00 noon the power of negativity steps in.

However, the sun does not completely disappear, as it does on the 16th day of the Hebrew month. It is also advisable not to get married on the 16th day of a Hebrew month because the moon is waning. Why is the moon diminishing? The Zohar says, for a very specific reason; but suffice it to say that on the 15th day of the Hebrew month the moon does not shine anymore. Yet we may look up and see that on the 16th day of the Hebrew month the moon shines but is it giving energy? The Zohar tells us no. So how do we explain that there is still light? Until the 15th day of a Hebrew month there is complete revelation and this is why there is a full moon, meaning complete revelation. On the 16th day, we may think it is in fact is simply going down a little, like the sun, but the Zohar says there is no more energy. Why then does the moon still seem to have life? The Zohar likens it to a chicken; when a chicken is killed by chopping off its head and it still continues to move. There is no energy there. What is taking place afterwards is not energy—like the chicken, although there is no life energy anymore, there is still movement.

Furthermore, what are the clues here? As discussed previously concerning the Four Holy Beasts, which are all a code for energy, the Eagle is Central Column. It brings the manifestation of Central Column energy. And like the high noon that permits energy to continue from the sun to the Left Side, it is not completely balancing the energy but it at least provides the Left Side with energy also. Meaning there is somewhat of a balance; we still have a continuity of the energy. It is not like the moon, which is completely cut off from any kind of energy. If an individual sat down to discuss going into a new business, and for whatever reason, the meeting continues past 12:00 noon, should they cancel the meeting? No, because you can access the Eagle (Central Column energy) after 12:00 noon.

Reuben was considered to also have the aspect of the Eagle (Central Column energy) because although there are some negative aspects to the Right Column energy, as we illustrated previously with the example of giving too much, like the sun at midday, the Central Column says, "Stop giving; you have to balance the giving." Even in the sharing, to whatever extent, we have to have a balance, we have to restrict.

Therefore with the tribe of Reuben, we have the Angel Uriel, who is also Central Column because here, we need two aspects of Central Column energy. With Yehuda, he by himself was enough for Central Column because his intrinsic characteristic is Central Column energy.

The Tribe of Dan

The Zohar discusses the third flag, the flag of the tribe of Dan; and the tribes of Asher and Naphtali are included in this encampment. The Zohar explains that the flag of the tribe of Dan is supported by the energy of the Ox, one of the Four Holy Beasts. These three tribes were encamped in the north, which has the energy-intelligence of Gevurah, Left Column, and is connected to the Angel Gabriel who is also from the Left Column. Here we see a complete departure from the other two groups of Yehuda and Reuben. Now, from every aspect, there is the Left Column energy of Gevurah and the Ox rules with its energy of Judgment. It is almost unfair; why did the Creator not permit a little more balance into this aspect of the Ox?

Nevertheless, we are discussing the period of absolute night, meaning after midnight, which is already another clue for these three months. The west is partially evening or night, but it always contains something of the daytime, from a physical point of view. The north, unless you are in the northern part of Norway, Alaska or Canada can have a little light coming from both sides but these are not populous locations. In fact, the reason many people are not located there is because they could not withstand it physically. We have the Ox, which is the Left Column of the Four Holy Beasts and the Angel Gabriel who is also the Left Column of the Archangels manifesting in the North, which is Gevurah and also Left Column.

Taurus (Iyar), with its astrological representation of an Ox, has all of this surrounding influence of Light because it is called Chodesh Ziv (Month of Light). No other month is called the Month of Light, except Taurus. Therefore, there is something in Taurus that cannot be all negative despite the fact that it is commonly thought of as such. For this reason, it does not need support to maintain its balance.

Understanding Positive and Negative Energy

The Zohar says that when there is the most intense negativity, is when the *tzadik* (righteous person) or the kabbalist will rise to study. The kabbalist wakes for this purpose after midnight. In almost all parts of the world, especially in the north during the summertime, midnight represents complete darkness. We have learned that where there is complete darkness there is the greatest opportunity of drawing down more energy; that is, if we know how to take advantage of it. The reason the *tzadik* and the kabbalist rise after midnight is because at this time there is the highest intensity of negative energy, and when there is the most intense negative energy is exactly where we have the greatest ability to draw power. This is when we have the greatest opportunity for balance, which is what the *tzadik* desires.

There is an incredible concentration of negative energy at this hour. Why do most people feel too tired to get up in the middle of the night? Why does everyone feel more tired at night and not so much during the day? Is it because we worked hard during the day and that is why we feel tired at night? The Zohar says no, that this time is reserved for the *tzadikim*. Because it is a time with such an intensity of negative energy—Left Column energy—it is the opportunity for the greatest amount of energy to be drawn down. The *tzadikim* and kabbalists draw this energy with whatever prayers and *kavanot* (meditations) are required.

Therefore, it is not surprising that suddenly we find here that the tribe of Dan is in the north, where there is total darkness—both from the point of view of the north, which is Gevurah and Left Column, and the angel Gabriel who is Left Column, as well as the Ox, which is the Left Column of the Four Holy Beasts.

Should we therefore commence a business after midnight? Is this why the kabbalists recommend marriages under the stars? We now understand that it is because at this time there is so much negative energy, which means so much opportunity. Many marriages wind up in divorce because of this cosmic condition. Because this opportunity of drawing down the most negative energy is present during the nighttime there are tools provided to support us to handle this energy. This is what the Seven Blessings, recited at a wedding, are about. With the help of these blessings we can take advantage of this kind of Left Column energy that becomes manifest only at night. When we have the greatest amount of negative energy, we then have the greatest potential for drawing down the greatest amount of Light, however, there is also a risk of great disaster.

Consider this example: if we have a two billion watt circuit in a building and there is a short, this would create a devastating fire in the building, whereas were it a five watt bulb that short-circuited, nothing would happen. Of course, there is nothing wrong with getting married in the daytime, one can get married in the morning, but know that you are settling for less. This is why I have said there is a possibility that business deals or other things should be consummated at night, but then one is running a risk, whereas in the morning one runs no risk. The morning is heavily laden with positive energy.

Positive energy means the sharing concept, negative energy means drawing to oneself. When we draw energy to ourselves, this is not a circuit of energy; the light in the lightbulb ultimately comes from the positive pole. This means that one must have negativity and the greatest negativity must involve sharing. Positive means sharing, negative means receiving. Sharing extends out, it embraces more around us; it embraces almost the entire universe. When we receive for ourselves alone, it is a negative action, and we close everything out; we close out the whole world. In Kabbalah, we have another word for negative: Desire to Receive for Oneself Alone.

The Tribe of Ephraim

The fourth flag and tribe of Ephraim is referred to in Bamidbar 10:22. Included in this group are the tribes of Ephraim, Manasseh and Benjamin, who are encamped in the west. Other than the direction where the sun sets, what does west mean? The Zohar explains that the west is referred to as *Adam* (Man) and draws the energy of the three other Holy Beasts. Does *Adam* mean a person? Intrinsically, the characteristic that humankind is born with is the Desire to Receive for Oneself Alone. When the baby comes out of the mother's womb, the first thing the doctor will do is open the clenched fists and see if they revert back to their original position, and if the baby comes out with its arms crossed over its chest, the physician will separate the arms and if they immediately fold back, then this indicates that the baby is normal. The Zohar says that innately we are of self-centered energy-intelligence, we draw everything to ourselves.

Adam, Malchut, Archangel Raphael, and the West

The difference between *Adam* (Man) and the tribe of Dan is Malchut. The tribe of Ephraim is Malchut, the west is Malchut, and Malchut is not an energy-intelligence, it is the recipient of whatever is around us. It is whatever we say we would like because everything around us wants to come into us. It is the vessel, so to speak, it is not an energy-intelligence. There are only three energy-intelligences, as it is with the atom: Right, Left, and Central Column. Energy-intelligence is not the effect but rather the cause. There is a cause of energy referred to as positive energy. What makes one want to share? It is the infusion of positive Right Column energy. What causes one to want to receive? The negative Left Column energy. What permits one to have a thought that the primary purpose of the existence of humankind is to apply resistance? The Central Column energy.

Now, what is *Adam*? What is man? Man can make use of these energies, although Man by and within himself is only the recipient of them. If he makes use of these three, this is what he will get. If he makes use of only one, he will receive only a portion. He is only the recipient. Negative energy is the vehicle by which we make movement. The effect is not a cause. *Adam* indicates the effect. If you share, you will get something, you will be the effect of that action. If you restrict, you will be the effect of that action. If we are completely tuned only into the Desire to Receive for Oneself Alone, we will receive the result of that kind of energy-intelligence. Therefore, there are only three Holy Beasts, and Man is the recipient. *Adam* is the recipient of whatever action is taking place, of whatever energy-intelligence is performing.

The angel that rules the west is Raphael, which is represented by Malchut. There are four basic Sefirot: Chesed, Gevurah, Tiferet, and Malchut. Malchut refers to the western side of the universe, the recipient of everything. Why is the west associated with healing and the Angel Raphael? There are four Archangels: Michael, Gabriel, Uriel, and Raphael. Raphael is the angel connected with healing, and is who deals with those three influences referred to as Ephraim, Manasseh, and Benjamin, and we know that Taurus is the month of healing. As far as *Adam* (Man) is concerned, Taurus is negative because the effect is also a form of negativity, the effect is receiving; it is not an energy-intelligence. This is very subtle. What is the difference between Gevurah and Malchut? Gevurah is the pure energy-intelligence of desire, which does not make Gevurah bad. We must have a Left Column pole in an atom just as we must have a Left Column pole in a lightbulb because this is part of any circuitry. The result of this circuitry is called Malchut, it is the desire for the result of energy.

Some people would rather just be a sharing kind of person; they never want to receive anything in return. Their satisfaction comes from sharing. On the other hand, negativity happens when we perform a certain action and this action will permit that which we seek to become a reality. Where is the root of Malchut? Malchut is the recipient, whether it is an active recipient or the result of receiving. In other words, having a home is the result of negative energy, the home itself was not the negative energy. I need a home, therefore, the fact that I need a home creates activity within me, either I have to go work or I have to do something by which I shall be able to have a home.

There is no guarantee that just because someone opens a business that it will provide everything they desire. Using of the negative energy-intelligence of desire will not necessarily result in us achieving *Adam*, which is what we seek. Where does the Angel Raphael fit in? We want the goal but do we want to do the work necessary to achieve it? By work I am not referring to working for a pastime, to keep busy for the sake of being busy. What is being discussed is making use of time to achieve an objective. Embarking on a financial venture to buy a house requires activity. However, that activity may not necessarily obtain the desired outcome. Therefore, the Creator has put the energy-intelligence of the Angel Raphael into this concept, which is connected with Taurus. Taurus is the negative energy, this is how it begins. As we have learned, Taurus is the month of healing, of restoring our lives to their original state.

A person who is healthy does not need a cure. However when the system is thrown off balance, a cure is necessary to restore it. A cure does not create something new, rather it restores the body into a position of balance. The Creator has given us the Angel Raphael, who is the angel of the west, so that we may connect to any part of our intended goal. The Angel Raphael is in the west because the sun is our only physical energy source; without the sun we cannot exist and the sun sets in the west. Where does all the energy of the day's labor go? It goes to the west. Let us say someone's objective is to buy a home, the energy involved goes to the west. This is the place where all desires are ultimately directed. Therefore, the west refers to receiving. Malchut originates from a Desire to Receive, and without this Desire to Receive there can be no effect. In other words, when we share, this does not necessarily mean that we receive pleasure from this action. One may have a desire and want to achieve it; but not every desire will achieve its goal. The Angel Raphael comes to balance, to stabilize things so that even though I could be completely wrong in what I think I will receive, hopefully the effort that I have infused will produce the result that I really need. The Zohar provides us with these tools because although there is desire, there are no guarantees.

29 And Moses said to Hobab, the son of Reuel, the Midianite, Moses' father-in-law: "We are journeying to the place that the Lord said: 'I will give it you; come you with us, and we will do you good; for the Lord has spoken good concerning Israel.'" 30 And he said unto him: "I will not go; but I will depart to mine own land, and to my kindred." 31 And he said: "Leave us not, I pray you; forasmuch as you know how we are to encamp in the wilderness, and you shall be to us instead of eyes. 32 And it shall be, if you go with us, yes, it shall be, that what good the Lord shall do to us, the same will we do to you."

Seeing and Consciousness

Moses entreated Jethro to come with the people and be their eyes, but Jethro refused. Why did Moses, who had reached the level of Zeir Anpin, need Jethro? Could Moses not see? Jethro saw the Light, which is why he came to Moses in the first place. For us, it is very hard to see. We have barriers, which is why we so often malign other people and obtain more *klipot* (negative shells). Of course, Moses saw more than Jethro but here Beha'alotcha is teaching us about consciousness because we need higher consciousness. This is the power of *beha'alotcha* (elevating) and only in this way will we be able to see more.

Moses took the daughter of Jethro, a Midianite, to marry. Moses told his father-in-law that they would be traveling to the place that God had provided for them. He invited Jethro to come with them, assuring him that the experience would bring only good. What did Jethro reply? Moses told him that God had promised Moses all the good in the world would accrue to him. What more assurance could anyone need? Through this story of Jethro, the Bible is not suggesting that we intermarry but rather that we should understand that we need to connect to the Light more fully to understand what the portion is saying and not take it for granted. Imagine if Moses approached you and said that if you come with him, all difficulties would be over. I do not think there is one person who would say they would prefer to hang onto their past. We would welcome being relieved of our difficulties, no matter whence they spring. Yet Jethro instead refused the offer, saying he would prefer to return to his birthplace.

Moses did not want to give up on the idea that Jethro be the eyes of the whole nation. Consider this, Jethro, a Midianite, was told by Moses, the man who spoke directly with God, that he, Jethro, would be the eyes of the Israelites. Why did Moses need eyes when he spoke to God mouth to mouth? Moses repeated the offer to Jethro a second time, as if Jethro was deaf. Then the conversation is concluded and the Bible continues with the Israelites embarking on a journey. Did Jethro ignore Moses? Did he change his mind? The answer to this dialogue is difficult to understand. How does one become the eyes of a nation?

Power of a Ba'al Teshuvah

Rashi and all the commentators struggled with this section. Sometimes between one section and another, the Bible includes either a letter *Pei* or *Samech* followed by a space to signify the end of a conversation. Here there is no conclusion to the conversation; it simply ends with Moses pleading a second time with no response from Jethro. Jethro's name is not even mentioned thereafter, the Bible just continues with how the Israelites traveled for another three days.

What did Moses want from Jethro? What could Jethro possibly offer more than Moses could do himself? According to the Zohar, a *Ba'al Teshuvah* (someone who returns to the Light), is one who truly repents, not simply with an outwardly apparent change, we know it requires a little more than that. This is why The Kabbalah Centre is a little difficult because we constantly hound ourselves on becoming better people. The Centre is an informal place, where how we dress does not determine who we are. We do not want to be seen as the group of people who always wear white. We do not always wear white because doing so would make us a conforming group and we do not want to be that. Every individual needs to have an opportunity to exercise free will. No one has the right or the authority to command what one can and cannot do.

The Zohar says *Ba'al Teshuvah* is when a person begins to change on a profound level, when their physical consciousness transforms itself into one of sharing more with his fellow man. Even someone guilty of murder can truly repent and transform their internal nature. The changes take place within us, and scanning the Zohar can create such a change. It says in the Zohar that even a *tzadik* cannot match one who has conducted *teshuvah*; someone who has been in the abyss of the physical world, who may have even committed every crime under the sun, and now has transformed. Other conventional norms of religion do not apply. Refraining from eating certain foods does not make one a great kabbalist. Religion is simply a matter of cultural upbringing.

What does the Bible want to teach us when it says that Moses asked Jethro to join them? The Zohar explains that Moses knew that Jethro, as the High Priest of Midian, was at the highest degree of negativity on an immaterial level, which is why Moses said Jethro could lead them. Jethro had become a *Ba'al Teshuvah*, he had tasted the Other Side. The Zohar explains that the intensity of Light in someone who has done evil or indulged oneself tremendously and then returns to a path of the Light, is so great that a *tzadik* could not take his place. This is why Moses said to Jethro, "You be our eyes."

33 And they set forward from the mount of the Lord three days' journey; and the Ark of the Covenant of the Lord went before them three days' journey, to seek out a resting place for them. 34 And the cloud of the Lord was over them by day, when they set forward from the camp. 35 And it came to pass, when the Ark set forward, that Moses said: "Rise up, Lord, and let Your enemies be scattered; and let them that hate You flee before You." 36 And when it rested, he said: "Return, Lord, to the ten thousands of the families of Israel."

The Traveling of the Ark and the Two Inverted Nuns

There are the two inverted letter *Nuns*, one before and one after the verse: "Rise up, Lord, and let Your enemies be scattered; and let them that hate You flee before You. And when it rested, he said: 'Return, Lord, to the ten thousands of the families of Israel.'"

נ וַיְהִי בִּנְסֹעַ הָאָרֹן וַיֹּאמֶר מֹשֶׁה קוּמָה יְהֹוָה וְיָפֻצוּ אֹיְבֶיךָ וְיָנֻסוּ מְשַׂנְאֶיךָ מִפָּנֶיךָ נ

["...'Rise up, Lord, and let Your enemies be scattered; and let them that hate You flee before You." is recited in Hebrew before we immerse in the Mikveh] Those of us who go to the Mikveh (spiritual cleansing immersion) might ask ourselves, why should I not spiritually cleanse in my own bathtub, it is probably much cleaner? Rav Ashlag stated that one should never let more than three days go by without going to the Mikveh.

The Zohar explains that the letter *Nun* indicates *nefila*, which means "falling," and that an inverted *Nun* is the opposite of falling. We have an opportunity with the two inverted *Nuns* to transform any spiritual falling, and change our character and physical behavior. Before the section of the two *Nuns*, Moses begs Jethro to come with them into the desert. At the end of the conversation, Jethro refuses. What was the point of the conversation Moses had with Jethro? What can we learn from it? Jethro was on the outside, he could see the big picture, unlike the rest of the people. He did not have the uncleanness that everyone else attained with all their disagreements. This is why Moses asked that he come with them and be like eyes for them. Yet Jethro refused when he saw how great the people's problems were and all of their failings.

One of the most important verses in the Torah and in life in general is the verse: "...and it was when the Ark traveled." Why did the Ark need to travel? It has been explained that the Ark is a vessel for the Light, not the Torah scroll. It is dismaying to find that many people believe that there must be an Ark in the synagogue because we no longer live wandering in the desert, therefore the Ark has no need to travel. This is nonsense, it is utterly baseless. When the Ark traveled, there was a connection to the Light, and therefore when we read the section about the travelling of the Ark there is an opening for us to connect to the most sublime Upper Worlds. The Zohar says that the Torah scroll is like a battery inside the Ark, the Ark is Binah and the Torah scroll is Zeir Anpin. This is why it does not speak about carrying the Ark [it certainly does elsewhere] or the journey of the Ark but rather about the connection with the Light. Getting rid of Satan is the power of the Ark's traveling.

After this, the verse says: "...return," which implies that after the discovery of the great Light, the Light must be retained so it does not escape. It is not enough to discover the Light, one must also be concerned that this Light is retained, hence the reason for the second verse.

This entire portion completely focuses on eliminating Satan. We must understand that Satan's greatest power is doubt. If a person is in doubt, even if they appear to be right, they will not go far because doubt has no place beside the Light. The Light does not work through uncertainty but rather through certainty. Therefore, someone who connects to separateness cannot continue with the Light even if they are in the right.

When we open the Ark, we recite, *Vayehi binso'ah ha'Aron Vayomer Moshe...* which can be translated literally as, "when the Ark traveled, Moses said...." What does this mean for us today? We are not carrying the Ark anywhere. Again, we cannot take the Bible at face value, rather it is the configuration of the Hebrew letters, words, and phrases that arouses the Lightforce. The Ark is a channel of the Lightforce and assists us in raising our consciousness. Through the reading of the Bible, we can tap into this energy and connect to the real world, the world without chaos. This very unusual configuration connects us to the Ark that traveled with the Israelites in the wilderness.

The Inverted Nuns

It was not until I began studying the Zohar and Kabbalah that I was even aware of the existence of the two inverted letter *Nuns*. King David, the author of the Ashrei Prayer, intentionally left out the letter *Nun*. We connect to the Ashrei to establish order in our lives through the letters of the Hebrew Alef-Bet. Why is the letter *Nun* missing? The Zohar says that before the world was created, each of the letters of the Hebrew Alef-Bet went before the Creator to plead its case to be the letter that begins Creation. The *Nun* was not chosen because it represents the energy intelligence of "falling." This is also the reason why it is omitted from the Ashrei as it would be an impediment to structure and order.

What other system is thousands of years old and still functioning in the modern age other than Kabbalah? There are so many great new systems and new revelations. Kabbalah, however, has a life of its own. The only hope for the removal of chaos in our lives is the reading and scanning of the Zohar.

There is nothing I would like better than to sleep in on Shabbat morning rather than come to our War Room to pray and read the Torah but the Torah reading is our means by which to tap into the Tree of Life and remove chaos. As long as there is chaos in any part of the world, it affects us individually and collectively. Until chaos is removed, I cannot rest. I would rather be in our War Room for a few hours than spend weeks in a hospital. I care about me, I know that what goes on out there affects me. Quantum physics helps us understand that everything affects us, when there is pain and suffering in some part of the globe it affects us. For this reason, we come to the Kabbalah Centre War Rooms. Any negativity anywhere should be of concern to us. There is only one motivation and that is the Desire to Receive for the Oneself Alone. I never heard this before Kabbalah, we all think we are *tzadikim* (righteous people).

Most of us know of the Five Books of Moses but the kabbalists teach us that there are in fact seven books. These two verses within the Book of Bamidbar comprise book five. The verses that appear after these two verses in the rest of the Book of Bamidbar are book number six and then the full Book of Devarim is book seven. Only because we have been blessed in our study of Kabbalah can we learn the power and the importance of these two *Nuns*. The *Nun* is the energy of *nefila*, which is "falling"—falling into all forms of chaos, falling out from those positives states—physically, mentally, and emotionally.

Because of this knowledge of Kabbalah, King David, wrote the famous Ashrei Prayer, which brings order, which brings a modicum of sanity into our lives. For most of us, chaos seems to be the order of the day. The letter *Nun* is left out of the Ashrei Prayer because it represents the epitome of chaos, which is the opposite of structure. We look around and see how people have fallen from their early innocence, and that is the energy-intelligence of the letter *Nun*.

What is so powerful about this portion, and something with which the Light is most concerned, is that the letter *Nun* is reversed. *Nun* represents every aspect of chaos that we fear as inevitable. Chaos is always there not because we seek it, rather the Zohar says it is impossible to avoid it. An animal sees a fire and it runs away, a man sees a fire and may even rush into it.

Our environment is so hostile that we cannot avoid the importance of connecting to the Ark and these two inverted *Nuns*. The Ark is where the Light is revealed, thus as we listen to the reading of this biblical portion, we can capture that Light. *Vayehi benso'a ha'Aron, vayomer Moshe....* When we open the Ark, we arouse the Light that needs to be revealed. Beha'alotcha also contains the returning of the Ark, the *Shuva...* verse that is recited when we return the Torah back into the Ark. This is not a physical process. How does one return Light? If in our consciousness we can accept the idea of mind over matter, that our mind is Light, then we can understand this concept.

There is no word known as *Nun* in the Torah. Every component of the Torah is a word, whether a two letter, three, eight or ten letter word. But the letter *Nun* by and of itself does not have a meaning. We do not even pronounce it. We will not even utter the letter *Nun*. The reader, as he reads this verse, will not say *Nun* or "nn" or use any other means to indicate there is a letter there. Therefore, when we raise the Torah, at least in the Kabbalah Centres, we understand that it is imperative that we capture this energy because we are all able to gather around the Torah at that moment to scan that letter. The only opportunity we have is when the Torah is raised. If we did not scan it, we did not receive what was intended for us. Furthermore, for 3,400 years, those of us who were not readers did not know that these letter *Nuns* were present in the Torah, only those who read are familiar with these anomalies.

The Hebrew word *beha'alotcha* means "elevation." If we allow ourselves, each one of us will receive a completely elevated consciousness with this portion. If you had the consciousness to see, you would see a beam of energy streaming from the Torah. This portion connects to the Sefira of Binah, elevation to a place where the complete Light of the Creator can be revealed.

It is said that during Chanukah we reveal the highest elevation of Light that exists. According to the Zohar, it is a concealed portion of Light, reserved for the righteous in the World to Come, the Or haGanuz (Concealed Light). The Zohar allows us to touch this Light, the most powerful Light that can be revealed, the Light that is with us through all the pains, challenges, and the systematic work through which our transformation takes us.

The Zohar says that what we have discussed here can only take place in Beha'alotcha because this portion is not as concealed as it is at Chanukah. Even though this took place at a later date, we know it was first manifested at the time of Creation. There is really no such thing as yesterday and tomorrow. In life, whenever we are confronted with something we feel we do not understand, when we do not know what is or is not going to happen, it brings us terrible fear and anxiety.

Those of us who are making the connection are always reminded by the Zohar during the week or on Shabbat that the letter *Nun* is omitted in the Psalm of Ashrei, which is structured according to the Hebrew Alef-Bet. King David included the Ashrei in his Book of Psalms to provide us with the tool with which we can reinforce structure in our lives. And as was previously discussed, the reason, says the Zohar, why the *Nun* is omitted is because the letter *Nun* represents the energy of *nefila* (falling). Falling is a very precise word that kabbalists have always used for the purpose of defining chaos. Chaos, in a word, is falling. Any form of chaos refers to the idea of falling from a state that was. Yesterday a person was healthy, today he falls from health. Every form of chaos that exists is the result of falling. Therefore, in this most appropriate time, when we take out the Torah we must understand that it is going to raise us up and arouse the Lightforce of God. We recite *Vayehi binso'a ha'Aron* when we take out the Torah scroll from the Ark on Monday, Thursday, Shabbat or any holiday.

Here, in this portion, we have the actual encapsulation of all the Lightforce energy that comes to us by virtue of the verse *Vayehi binso'a ha'Aron* found in the biblical text to provide us with a state of certainty removed from fear, and also with the removal of chaos. This is the reason the *Nuns* are back to front. The *Nuns* are inverted and they face away because this position is the opposite of their usual nature and is therefore the opposite of falling, it is that simple. The Light that is aroused by this verse will spread throughout the world, and remain for us as an instrument. In this way, the letter *Nun* escapes its purpose of falling, and on this Shabbat we actually energize this *Nun* to serve us always in every case of chaos so that we will be fulfilled with the Lightforce of God.

There is much commentary in the Zohar on the purpose of these two *Nuns* that were inserted. It is another demonstration of the force of the Bible, and how it is a vital instrument in establishing that Lightforce in our lives. Everything is so calculated to perfection to give us that energy we so sorely need.

Bamidbar 11:1 And the people were complaining, speaking evil in the ears of the Lord; and when the Lord heard it, His anger was kindled; and the fire of the Lord burnt among them, and devoured in the uttermost part of the camp. 2 And the people cried to Moses; and Moses prayed to the Lord, and the fire abated. 3 And the name of that place was called Taberah, because the fire of the Lord burnt among them. 4 And the mixed multitude, who were among them, yielded to intense craving and the children of Israel also wept and said: "Would that we were given meat to eat! 5 We remember the fish, which we ate freely of in Egypt; the cucumbers, and the melons, and the leeks, and the onions, and the garlic; 6 but now our soul is dried away; there is nothing at all; we have nothing except this manna to look to." 7 Now the manna was like coriander seed, and had the color of the color of bdellium. 8 The people went about, and gathered it, and ground it in mills, or beat it in mortars, and seethed it in pots, and made cakes of it; and the taste of it was as the taste of a cake baked with oil. 9 And when the dew fell upon the camp in the night, the manna fell upon it. 10 And Moses heard the people weeping, family by family, every man at the door of his tent; and the anger of the Lord was kindled greatly; and Moses was displeased. 11 And Moses said to the Lord: 'Why have You dealt ill with Your servant? And why have I not found favor in Your Sight, that You lay the burden of all

this people upon me? 12 Have I conceived all
this people? Have I brought them forth, that
You should say to me: 'Carry them in your
bosom, as a nursing-father carries the suck-
ing child, to the land which You did swear to
their fathers?' 13 When should I have meat
to give to all this people? For they trouble me
with their weeping, saying: 'Give us meat,
that we may eat.' 14 I am not able to bear
all this people alone, because it is too heavy
for me. 15 And if You deal so with me, kill
me, I pray You, out of hand, if I have found
favor in Your sight; and let me not look upon
my wretchedness." 16 And the Lord said to
Moses: "Gather to Me seventy men of the
elders of Israel, whom you know to be the
elders of the people, and officers over them;
and bring them to the Tent of Meeting, so
they may stand there with you. 17 And I will
come down and speak with you there; and I
will take of the spirit which is upon you, and
will put it upon them; and they shall bear
the burden of the people with you, that you
bear it not alone. 18 And say to the people:
'Sanctify yourselves for tomorrow, and you
shall eat meat; for you have wept in the ears
of the Lord, saying: Would that we were given
meat to eat for it was well with us in Egypt;'
therefore the Lord will give you meat, and
you shall eat. 19 You shall not eat one day,
nor two days, nor five days, neither ten days,
nor twenty days; 20 but a whole month, until
it come out at your nostrils, and it be loath-
some to you; because you have rejected the

Lord Who is among you, and have troubled Him with weeping, saying: 'Why, now, came we forth out of Egypt?'" 21 And Moses said: 'The people, among whom I am, are six hundred thousand men on foot; and yet You have said: 'I will give them meat, that they may eat a whole month! 22 If flocks and herds be slain for them, will they suffice them or if all the fish of the sea be gathered together for them, will they suffice them?' 23 And the Lord said to Moses: "Is the Lord's Hand waxed short? Now you shall see whether My Word shall come to pass unto you or not." 24 And Moses went out, and told the people the words of the Lord; and he gathered seventy men of the elders of the people, and set them round about the Tent. 25 And the Lord came down in the cloud, and spoke to him, and took of the spirit that was upon him, and put it upon the seventy elders; and it came to pass, that, when the spirit rested upon them, they prophesied, but they did so no more. 26 But there remained two men in the camp, the name of the one was Eldad, and the name of the other Medad; and the spirit rested upon them; and they were of them that were recorded, but had not gone out to the Tent; and they prophesied in the camp. 27 And there ran a young man, and told Moses, and said: 'Eldad and Medad are prophesying in the camp.' 28 And Joshua, the son of Nun, the minister of Moses from his youth, answered and said: "My lord Moses, shut them in." 29 And Moses said to him: "Are you zealous for my sake? Would that all the Lord's people were prophets, that the Lord would put His spirit upon them!" 30 And Moses withdrew into the camp, he and the elders of Israel. 31 And there went forth a wind from the Lord, and brought across quails from the sea, and let them fall by the camp, about a day's journey on this side, and a day's journey on the other side, round about the camp, and about two cubits above the face of the earth. 32 And the people rose up all that day, and all the night, and all the next day, and gathered the quails; he that gathered least gathered ten heaps; and they spread them all abroad for themselves round about the camp. 33 While the flesh was yet between their teeth, ere it was chewed, the anger of the Lord was kindled against the people, and the Lord smote the people with a very great plague. 34 And the name of that place was called Kibroth-Hattaavah, because there they buried the people that lusted. 35 From Kibroth-Hattaavah the people journeyed to Hazeroth; and they camped at Hazeroth.

The Nature of Desire, Manna

The manna had the quality that it could taste like whatever one desired. In this section, the Israelites were complaining, which is the reason why Jethro left. Then Moses prayed to God, and God set the edge of the camp on fire. The Bible mentions some of the things about which the people were complaining. It is human nature and especially the nature of the Israelites to never be content with what they have. Yet after so many people died, the Israelites started praying to God. How do we behave toward our fellow man when we are in a state of suffering? When someone falls in any way, they want things to be restored to where they were, and when things are restored, then usually the person is not grateful, they simply want more. The fire of God devoured part of the people, so when the flame abated, the people that survived thanked God. Nonetheless, even after this event, the people returned to their old ways. This portion tells us how the Israelites reminisced about their good life in Egypt—the fish, the meat—and that they wanted to return. They did not consider the conditions they were liberated from, they were only concerned with returning to their comforts. We desire all those things we once had.

Many people live their lives looking forward to retirement, be it a life of golfing or swimming in Florida. Did Moses complain that this was not what he expected for his retirement? He cried to God, declaring that his life be taken away, that the burden given to him to transform and lead these people was too heavy. Moses tried to transform the people; he was not only their spiritual leader, he experienced many difficulties.

There are many burial sites mentioned in this portion, and toward the end it says they called the place Kibroth-Hatta'avah for all those people who died and were buried there.

Bamidbar 12:1 And Miriam and Aaron spoke against Moses because of the Kushite woman whom he had married; for he had married a Kushite woman. 2 And they said: "Has the Lord indeed spoken only with Moses? Has He not spoken also with us?' And the Lord heard it. 3 Now the man Moses was very meek, above all the men upon the face of the earth. 4 And the Lord spoke suddenly to Moses, and to Aaron, and to Miriam: "Come out you three to the Tent of Meeting." And they three came out. 5 And the Lord came down in a pillar of cloud, and stood at the door of the Tent, and called Aaron and Miriam; and they both came forth. 6 And He said: "Hear now My Words: if there is a prophet among you, I the Lord do make Myself known to him in a vision, I do speak with him in a dream. 7 My servant Moses is not so; he is trusted in all My House; 8 with him do I speak mouth to mouth, even manifestly, and not in dark speeches; and the similitude of the Lord does he behold; why then were you not afraid to speak against My servant, against Moses?" 9 And the anger of the Lord was kindled against them; and He departed. 10 And when the cloud was removed from over the Tent, behold, Miriam was leprous, as white as snow; and Aaron looked upon Miriam; and, behold, she was leprous. 11 And Aaron said to Moses: "My lord, lay not, I pray you, sin upon us, because we have behaved foolishly, and for that we have sinned. 12 Let her not, I pray, be as one dead, of whom the flesh

is half consumed when he comes out of his mother's womb." 13 And Moses cried to the Lord, saying: "Heal her now, God, I beseech You." 14 And the Lord said to Moses: "If her father had but spit in her face, should she not hide in shame seven days? Let her be shut up outside the camp seven days, and after that she shall be brought in again." 15 And Miriam was shut up outside the camp seven days; and the people journeyed not till Miriam was brought in again. 16 And afterward the people journeyed from Hazeroth, and pitched in the wilderness of Paran.

Miriam and Aaron's Lashon Hara

Miriam and Aaron spoke against Moses and the Kushite woman whom he had married. However, the Zohar and as well as Rashi say that the word *kushite* means "beautiful," and that they stated that Moses' wife was very beautiful. In the next verse, the Bible also adds that Miriam and Aaron also asked the question, had the Lord indeed spoken only with Moses? Had he not spoken also with us, and the Lord heard it? The Bible also states that Moses was very humble, there was no greater humility in any living individual. Why then, did they speak *lashon hara* (evil speech) about Moses for marrying a Kushite? Did they not know that Moses was profoundly connected to God? Bamidbar 12:6 says, "… 'Hear now My words, if there is a prophet among you, I the Lord do make Myself known to him in vision… My servant Moses is not so, he is trusted in all My house. With him I speak mouth-to-mouth…'" What does all this mean? Is the Lord trying to impress Miriam and Aaron about the greatness of their brother? They were not speaking about a stranger.

Furthermore, when the cloud was removed from over the Tent of Meeting, Miriam became leprous.

The Zohar, Beha'altocha 12:61-62 says:

> Come and behold: There is a dress that is visible to everyone. The fools, when they see a person dressed beautifully, WHO APPEARS TO THEM DISTINGUISHED BY HIS CLOTHING, do not observe any further. THEY JUDGE HIM ACCORDING TO HIS DISTINGUISHED APPAREL and consider the dress as the body OF MAN, and the OF THE PERSON LIKE his soul.
>
> Similar to this is the Torah. It has a body, which is composed of the commandments of the Torah that are called the "body of the Torah." This body is clothed with garments, which are stories of this world. The ignorant look only at that dress, which is the story in the Torah, and are not aware of anything more. They do not look at what lies beneath that dress. Those who know more do not look at the dress, but rather at the body beneath that dress. The wise, the sages, the servants of the Loftiest King, those that stood at Mount Sinai, look only at the soul OF THE TORAH, which is the essence of everything, the real Torah. In the time to come, they will look at the soul, the soul of the Torah.

The Zohar here explains *beha'alotcha*, and very clearly says that if anyone believes that the stories of the Bible are nothing more than narrations and history, they are a fool because the stories are complete secrets. The Zohar also states here that the Bible is a cosmic code and because of this, we must make use of the Kabbalah. Why does the Zohar stress that the Bible's meaning is a secret?

Also, why did only Miriam receive the brunt of the wrath of the Lord for the *lashon hara*? What about Aaron? Moses pleaded for Miriam in the profound and often used verse for healing, Bamidbar 12:13: *El Na Refa Na La* (Please God please heal her.) There are several questions concerning what occurs here. Why did it bother them that Moses was married to a Kushite? Why did Miriam and Aaron wait so long if Moses married Tziporah many years before, why did they not speak to Moses about their concern before the marriage? This is Miriam that we are discussing, so it is very difficult to explain what really happened. What she received for this was leprosy, and Moses prayed for her: "Please God please heal her" אל נא רפא נא לה, which is comprised of eleven Hebrew letters. The Zohar says that these letters are connected to the eleven herbs and species that made up the incense used in the Holy Temple to exhaust the power of Satan.

As you may recall, we said that the Third Meal of Shabbat is the connection to the body's immune system, and that we sing the song Yedid Nefesh at the end point of the Third Meal, which includes this verse of *El Na Refa Na La* that has the power of healing.

Why would Aaron the High Priest and Miriam the Prophetess speak badly about Moses when they truly loved him? It is also written, "...concerning the Kushite woman whom he took, for he had taken a Kushite woman." Why is this phrase repeated? Following this, the Creator said, "And the man Moses was very humble." What connection is there between the Kushite woman and the fact that Moses was humble? What does it mean when the Bible says, "suddenly"? Since when does the Creator do things suddenly?

In Bamidbar12:10, where it is written, "And behold, Miriam was leprous as white as snow, and Aaron turned to Miriam, and behold, she was leprous." Does this imply that Aaron did not believe? Also, why does the verse repeat the word "leprous" twice? It is unlikely

that people on such a high level would malign Moses. They were
also his family, and if they were unhappy about his choice of bride
then they should have said something at Moses' marriage, rather
than fifty years later.

The entire purpose of this is to make us conscious of refraining from
slander. Nevertheless, it is important to understand that if someone
comes to ask us about a person's character, we are still obliged to tell
the truth. If that person is, for example, a thief, we must impart that
information upon inquiry. Slander originates from the desire to hurt
someone or where the motivation is revenge or anger. If, however,
the purpose is to help, the situation is different, and one has to tell
the truth about that person.

Concerning this portion, we have focused on the verse where Moses
pleaded for Miriam to be healed. It is a line found in the song Yedid
Nefesh that we sing during the Third Meal of Shabbat connection.
It is also found in this Bible reading. The letter *Pei* is in the middle
of this verse, and the *Pei* (פ) is also one of the letters that created the
month of Taurus, Iyar (פו).

One does wonder how Moses could marry a non-Israelite woman,
and how it is that he could not find a suitable and attractive Israelite
woman. Aaron and Miriam were Moses' blood relatives, very high
souls, a Prophetess and a High Priest, who produced the miracle
of the Red Sea, how could they question Moses in such a manner?
They were at the highest level of spirituality, how could they speak
lashon hara about him?

As a result of the *lashon hara*, Miriam became afflicted with leprosy
and was placed outside of the camp. The Zohar says that it would
never have entered Miriam's consciousness to speak evil tongue
and that we can never treat anything in the Bible literally, therefore
we conclude that the Bible is teaching us about the consequences

of evil tongue. This story exists to have a positive impact on the cosmos and to teach us how to maintain control over our lives.

As previously mentioned, this is the Shabbat of Healing as it contains the verse: *El Na Refa Na La*. In this story, God was very angry with the Israelites, and in fact He was so angry that He took the cloud that hovered over the nation of Israel away and Miriam became a leper. It is beyond comprehension that Miriam and Aaron, Moses' sister and brother, could speak *lashon hara* about him. Aaron grieved for his sister, and Moses prayed to God saying those famous five words: *El Na Refa Na La*, "Please God please heal her." Aaron and Miriam spoke out against Moses so that we could benefit today from reading these five words that carry the power of healing.

Next, the three of them stepped out of the Tabernacle and God began to tell Miriam and Aaron of the greatness of Moses, as if until now his leadership was in question, even with the splitting of the Red Sea. God said "…but only to Moses did I speak mouth-to-mouth, why did you not fear to speak about my servant Moses…" Moses pleaded to God and his prayer *El Na Refa Na La* became the prayer that we use to strengthen our immune system. We do not have to fight against darkness and disease because these entities have always been with us. Science is trying to fight each battle one by one but the superior way of healing is to strengthen the immune system.

Nanotechnology and the Hebrew Letters

We have been hearing a great deal about nanotechnology, and perhaps it seems as if we are changing some of the concepts that the Bible wants to teach us. But as Rav Ashlag said about revelation, we never do away with that which has already been stated or that which has already been revealed. What we do is add to what has already been said.

This portion can only be explained with nanotechnology. If you recall, the Israelites had been enjoying manna in the desert, yet in Bamidbar 11:5 they were complaining again. The manna from Heaven would be a steak, if they wanted a steak for example. The manna had the extraordinary ability to be any delicacy. The raw, naked energy of manna could turn itself into anything the consciousness of the recipient desired. Yet, the Israelites, of course, were not satisfied, demanding real meat instead, reminding Moses of the fish they ate in Egypt. The Israelites said, "Our souls are dry, we have nothing but this manna in the wilderness." What did Moses respond to all this? "I cannot handle these people anymore. This is too heavy for me." One can only imagine how onerous a burden the Israelites had become to Moses that he could beg God to release him from the heavy obligation of leading them.

The Bible then goes on to say that at Jethro's suggestion, Moses gathered the seventy elders so that they might help carry the burden; he would not be alone. After this conversation between Moses and the Israelites, we have another interesting incident concerning Jethro, Moses' father-in-law. "And Moses said to his father-in-law, we are traveling to a place that God said I will give unto you." And Moses begged his father-in-law, and there is some debate as to whether he had converted or not because, as we know, Jethro was not an Israelite. And when Moses asked his father-in-law to join them in the land that God had promised them, Jethro refused and said that he was returning to his homeland. Moses pleaded with Jethro, saying that he was needed to be the eyes of the people. Moses assured his father-in-law, promising him a share in all the good that God intended for them. There was no response from Jethro. In fact, within this same paragraph the verse goes on to discuss another idea.

What is truly taking place in this section? Why would Jethro be considered to be the eyes of Moses? There was nothing that Moses could not handle, he had the gift of prophecy but the burden of his task was becoming ever greater.

I think each and every single year that we pass this section, I raise the same question. Sometimes I have an answer; sometimes I am not satisfied. I was thinking this time that there must be another kind of answer. The answer must be connected to some new concepts that are permeating from this Kabbalah Centre. We know the power of nanotechnology. We know we can move information, and not necessarily over the Internet where information is transferred instantaneously.

What did Jethro see on a deeper level that he would not go along with Moses and the rest of the people? Would he not want to be with his grandchildren, his daughter? Why would Moses even say to Jethro: "You would be our eyes"? What we learn here, and what Moses understood when Jethro refused, is that Jethro saw and knew the difficulties that Moses was undergoing with the Israelites. Scripture makes it so clear. The Israelites wanted the fish they tasted in Egypt, the meat the chefs prepared for them in Egypt. And we thought they were slaves? There was a system; there was a culture of resting where things are good. Why fix a good thing? What was the good thing? That they had steaks, freedom, everything they wanted in Egypt. Why change that?

In fact, as we read throughout the Book of Bamidbar, all the Israelites did was complain about Moses. "Why did you take us out of our comfort zone?" And when Moses assured Jethro he could have their comfort zone and it would be good, that was what God promised, Jethro did not opt for that. When Moses said to Jethro, "You would be our eyes," this was Moses telling all of us, giving us the message that he was actually receiving from Jethro that nothing will come of the comfort zone that we are involved with. "They will come into this world and they will disappear from this world as they came into it." Is this the purpose? How could the accumulation of material comforts be the purpose of life when we come into this world with nothing and we disappear from this world with nothing? Moses and Jethro both saw that these Israelites were not going to make it.

As we shall soon see, in the next portion of Shlach Lecha, the Israelites lost it all. When the spies came back and the Israelites heard disturbing reports, who was right, the spies or God? This is true in our life as well. Sometimes God seems to be on vacation, how much can we depend on His Presence? Maybe God really means for us to fend for ourselves.

Moses was saying that Jethro had eyes; he saw what the Israelites did not see. He saw that there was a purpose in coming into this world and in leaving this world a great deal better than the way we found it. In this context, *seeing* means *understanding*. When we say, "I see it now," we are not talking about physical vision, we are talking about insight. Does this mean we are more spiritual, therefore will leave this world better than when we entered? No.

The reason nanotechnology will never work in the ultimate removal of chaos, which is what science says and thinks at the present time, is because of the idea of consciousness. It is not a question of morality or spirituality that we should consider leaving this world better than when we entered but rather it is the only route, the only technology that can bring us to a point where we can eliminate our own chaos. To eliminate our own chaos is a personal matter; it is not about being good to other people. If you want to benefit yourself, there is only one road you can take and that is to consider others.

If scientists are thinking of a Nobel prize and not what will benefit humankind, if they do not have the consciousness that it is not for themselves alone but rather what they can do for humankind, there is no way, even with all the nanotechnology, that will emerge quicker than they can imagine, that we can remove chaos. Physical nanotechnology is not the be-all-and-end-all. It is not the answer to the removal of chaos. There is only one answer: the nano-robots, which are the Hebrew letters, and the combinations that we already have.

What has been lacking since the days of the Israelites in the wilderness is to consider leaving the comfort zone, which might bring them far more pleasure, satisfaction, fulfillment, than it would if they were seeking the comfort zone. When you do not seek the comfort zone, is when you can have it. It is a paradox. Before you can breathe in, you have to breathe out. One does not go without the other.

With this interpretation of what scripture has to teach us, we can then understand the last section about Miriam and Aaron speaking *lashon hara* (evil tongue) about Tzipora, the wife of Moses. These three people: Aaron, Moses, Miriam, as the Zohar constantly reminds us, were truly brothers and sisters. They were close and it could never enter the minds of Miriam and Aaron to speak evil tongue on their brother or listen to evil tongue.

So what happened there? This teaches us the connection between the disease of cancer and evil tongue. It teaches us about airborne diseases. There are lots of things we can learn from this portion. But more importantly, Miriam and Aaron both knew that ordinary people could not easily reach their high level of consciousness, and therefore to have the most powerful eleven letters that we use on Shabbat for healing—*El Na Refa Na La*—as well as in the Yedid Nefesh, would never have emerged had Miriam and Aaron not spoken *lashon hara*. They knew this was their sacrifice to provide us, the future generations, with a combination of nanotechnology, the most important energy for healing.

For that, they were prepared to even give up their lives, to suffer the consequences of leprosy. This was the way this technology would and did emerge. By this means, scripture brought about these eleven letters of the *El Na Refa Na La*. These righteous people were prepared to share far more with the world than they ever received for themselves. With this reading we have an opportunity to eliminate the *erev rav* (Mixed Multitude), the anti-kabbalists.

Conclusion

Beha'alotcha speaks about the Light. This portion truly belongs to Rav Shimon, since to rule over Satan one must rule over all the aspects where he is to be found. For this reason, one must connect to great currents of energy that lead to the Lightforce of God. It is written that the Creator showed Moses the way to construct the Menorah. Moses knew that the Menorah was the vehicle for connecting to the Light, even though he was not aware of how it was supposed to function.

In this portion we again have a further naming of the tribes, each of which is connected to a different constellation. Without this understanding of the cosmos we cannot be in control of our lives at all, which has been the case now for more than two thousand years.

As we have already noted, in Bamidbar 10:34, we have something that is found nowhere else in the entire Bible, the two inverted letter *Nuns* at the beginning and end of the verse we recite when opening the Ark. This verse is the way the Light is to be revealed, it contains everything. The Ark contains all the Light that has been revealed in our War Rooms, which is not like a bank where the money is constantly vanishing. At the Kabbalah Centres, the energy does not disappear, it is constantly present in the Ark. The letter *Nun* represents the totality of Satan's power, which causes people to fall. This letter exists to cause chaos, earthquakes, disease, and so on, which is why it has a place in our world, it provides us with the opportunity to attain the Light.

We think chaos is an act of God but this is not so. The reason the letter *Nuns* are inverted is because we do not want Satan to be present when we open the Ark, at that moment when we become saturated with the Light. As we are always saying here, when we turn on the Light, darkness disappears, and if we turn off the Light, then it is dark again. In this world, Light and dark cannot exist simultaneously, yet we cannot eliminate the darkness, since it is so potent and intelligent. No one can eliminate it, except when we are in a place where we can raise our consciousness to a supreme connection to the Lightforce. Thus by this process, the darkness cannot and does not exist when we turn on the Light.

When we talk about cancer and undergoing chemotherapy, we are supposedly removing and eliminating the malignancy. Today, medicine claims that it is possible to remove 99.9 percent of the cancer cells. It is indeed a great achievement, yet we cannot destroy Satan. When we destroy cancerous cells, we are making room for Satan, which is why we should restore the cells with Light instead, and draw down this connection to the Lightforce of God into the body.

Did you know that a fetus has the most cancer cells in its body? How is it that they do not manifest? It is because a fetus is immersed in water. This is the power of the Mikveh. It can restore the cells but under no circumstances are they to be eliminated.

The reason for the inverted *Nuns* is so that we can overturn, not eliminate, the power of Satan. The portion of Beha'alotcha provides us with a direct connection to the Light. This is what we should focus on during the Torah reading. People often come for Shavuot and go to the Mikveh and then get sick. Then they ask, how can this be? Satan waits for this question. As we explained earlier, his power lies in doubt.

People frequently come to the Kabbalah Centres asking for advice and we tell them they must follow their own free will and that all the answers are in the Holy Ark. In Bamidbar 11:1 it says that the people complained to God, and then they came to Moses and said that they longed for the fish they used to freely eat in Egypt. Why does the Bible say "for free"? It does not seem relevant. The Israelites received manna daily as a gift from God, and it tasted like whatever they wanted it to taste like. They ate the manna, and if they wanted it to taste like fish, it tasted like fish. Nevertheless, they were still missing something. Receiving everything, they did not appreciate it, instead they focused on their appetite for meat. This is the problem, when we have everything, we do not appreciate anything.

There was a crime lord with a history of murder, robbery, in short, a serious record. After he died, he got to a receiving station and saw two lines. One of them towards Paradise, the other one towards Hell, and there were angels along the way directing traffic so that everyone reached the destination they deserved. This crime lord decided to get on the line going to Paradise. To his surprise no one said a word to him and he got a ticket to Paradise. He entered, and an angel received him and asked him what he wanted. He thought for a minute and then said, "I liked women in our world." The angel, with a snap of his finger, immediately brought him women. The angel then asked, "What else do you want?" The man replied, "Italian food." With another snap of his fingers the angel brought him his desired food. Anything he desired he received immediately.

After a little while, the crime lord said to the angel, "You know, I used to rob banks. Do you think you can arrange something like that for me over here?" The angel said, "Yes, of course!" and arranged a bank for him. The crime lord went into the bank, took the money and left. No one put up a fight. He said to the angel, "Isn't there any action? Isn't there some guard I can shoot? Isn't there any resistance? Something?" The angel replied, "Sorry. That is something we cannot do here!" Then, the crime lord said, "You know what? I would prefer being in Hell." At that point, a Divine voice called out, "Where do you think you are?"

BOOK OF BAMIDBAR:

Portion of Shlach Lecha

PORTION OF SHLACH LECHA

Bamidbar 13:1 And the Lord spoke to Moses, saying: 2 "Send men to spy out the land of Canaan, which I give to the children of Israel; from each tribe of their fathers you shall send a man, every one a prince among them." 3 And Moses sent them from the wilderness of Paran according to the commandment of the Lord; all of them men who were heads of the children of Israel. 4 And these were their names: of the tribe of Reuben, Shammua, the son of Zaccur. 5 Of the tribe of Simeon, Shaphat, the son of Hori. 6 Of the tribe of Judah, Caleb, the son of Jephunneh. 7 Of the tribe of Issaschar, Igal, the son of Joseph. 8 Of the tribe of Ephraim, Hoshea, the son of Nun. 9 Of the tribe of Benjamin, Palti, the son of Raphu. 10 Of the tribe of Zebulun, Gaddiel, the son of Sodi. 11 Of the tribe of Joseph, namely, of the tribe of Manasseh, Gaddi, the son of Susi. 12 Of the tribe of Dan, Ammiel, the son of Gemalli. 13 Of the tribe of Asher, Sethur, the son of Michael. 14 Of the tribe of Naphtali, Nahbi, the son of Vophsi. 15 Of the tribe of Gad, Geuel, the son of Machi. 16 These are the names of the men that Moses sent to spy out the land. And Moses called Hoshea, the son of Nun, Joshua. 17 And Moses sent them to spy out the land of Canaan, and said to them: "Go up here into the South, and go up into the mountains; 18 and see what the land is like; and whether the people that dwell there are strong or weak, whether they are few or many; 19 and whether the land that they dwell in is good or bad; and whether cities they dwell in are camps or strongholds; 20 and whether the land is fat or lean, whether there are forests there or not. Be of good courage, and bring of the fruit of the land." Now was the time of the first-ripe grapes. 21 So they went up and spied out the land from the wilderness of Zin unto Rehob, at the entrance to Hamath. 22 And they went up into the South, and came unto Hebron; and Ahiman, Sheshai, and Talmai, the children of Anak, were there. Now Hebron was built seven years before Zoan in Egypt. 23 And they came to the valley of Eshcol and cut down from there a branch with one cluster of grapes, and they bore it upon a pole between two; they also took of the pomegranates and of the figs. 24 That place was called the valley of Eshcol, because of the cluster which the children of Israel cut down from there. 25 And they returned from spying out the land at the end of forty days. 26 And they went and came to Moses and to Aaron, and to all the congregation of the children of Israel, to the wilderness of Paran, to Kadesh; and brought back word to them, and to all the congregation, and showed them the fruit of the land. 27 And they told him, and said: "We came to the land where you sent us, and surely it flows with milk and honey; and this is the fruit of it. 28 Nevertheless the people that dwell in the land are fierce, and the cities are fortified, and very great; and moreover we saw the children of Anak there. 29 Amalek dwells in the land of the Negev; and the Hittite, and the Jebusite, and the Amorite, dwell in the mountains; and the Canaanite dwells by the sea, and along by the side of the Jordan." 30 And Caleb stilled the people toward Moses, and said: "We should go up at once and possess it; for we are well able to overcome it." 31 And the men that went up with him said: "We are not able to go up against the people; for they are stronger than us." 32 And they spread an evil report of the land which they had spied out to the children of Israel, saying: "The land through which we have passed to spy it out, is a land that eats up its inhabitants; and all the people that we saw in it are men of great stature. 33 And there we saw the Nephilim, the sons of Anak, who come of the Nephilim; and we were like grasshoppers in our own sight, and so we were in their sight."

Bamidbar 14:1 And all the congregation lifted up their voice, and cried; and the people wept that night. 2 And all the children of Israel murmured against Moses and against Aaron; and the whole congregation said to them: "Would that we had died in the land of Egypt! Or would we had died in this wilderness! 3 And why does the Lord bring us to this land, to fall by the sword? Our wives and our little ones will be a prey; were it not better for us to return into Egypt?" 4 And they said one to

another: "Let us make a captain, and let us return into Egypt."

The Promised Land

In the first verse of Shlach Lecha it says: "And God says to Moses, send you…." All the commentators are in agreement that this was for Moses' benefit. There is no reference to Moses having made a request of God or from the people, rather this was God's idea for Moses to designate these people to explore the land to see if it was the promised land of milk and honey.

On the surface it appears that this is a section to teach us about Israel, yet before the Israelites could leave the wilderness to enter into the Promised Land, Moses preferred that they investigate to see if it was appropriate for habitation. From the event at Mount Sinai until the present day, there have been difficulties throughout the land of Israel. Israel been a thorn in the side of many nations of the world, as it never permits any peace in that region, going back to the time when this land was promised by God to Abraham.

At this point in the narrative, Moses indicates that the Israelites should survey the Promised Land before rushing in, so it seemed as if he had some doubts. Could this be the motivation behind Moses' desire to send twelve people—one from each tribe—to spy out the land? Moses wished them to ascertain whether the land was good or bad, and to find out the strength of the nation now occupying it, as well as if there were many trees growing there. This is the translation in a very superficial, literal sense. How could Moses not know whether or not there were trees in the land? God had already told Moses that this is the land of milk and honey. Certainly Moses did not question God about the nature of the land, yet he asked the scouts to bring back information. When they returned, the scouts had varying reports—two praised the land, while the rest felt that an invasion would be disastrous.

As we have always emphasized, the Bible is only a code and therefore, according to Rav Shimon, we cannot treat it as a history of the Jewish people. Even this so-called little incident concerning the spies, according to Rav Shimon, has a true and deeper meaning, and only appears to be a minor occurrence on the surface. It is stated in this portion that when the scouts returned with the report, the entire nation wept because they knew that henceforth, destruction would be a fundamental part of their world. The day that the spies came back with this report was Tisha B'Av, the ninth day of Av (Leo). On this day throughout history there was devastation: the destruction of the First and Second Temples took place on this day, and as well as many other disasters that befell the Jewish people: Bar Kokhba's revolt, the expulsion of the Jews from Spain during the Spanish Inquisition, as well as the formal approval of the Final Solution which resulted in the Holocaust.

We must turn to the Zohar to uncover this portion's true meaning, which certainly is still relevant for us today and is the only purpose of this story. The Zohar says regarding the verse:

> "Whether there is a tree in it, or not..." (Bamidbar 13:20) Rav Chiya said: "Did Moses not know that there are a variety of trees there, different one from the other? Isn't he the one who praised the land several times WITH ITS OLIVES, GRAPES, POMEGRANATES, and was satisfied with it. Didn't the Holy One, blessed be He, tell Moses originally that this was a land flowing with milk and honey?" Rav Yosi said the friends already noted that it is written: "There was a man in the land of Utz, whose name was Job." (Job 1:1), MEANING THAT HE WISHED TO INQUIRE OF

THEM WHETHER JOB WAS THERE TO PROTECT
THEM. AND TREE (*ETZ*) IS LIKE *UTZ*.
—Zohar, Shlach Lecha 6:35

According to the Zohar, Moses was not really inquiring about trees,
he was asking the spies, who understood the inner meaning of his
question, whether Job was there. What difference did it make to
Moses whether Job was there or not? Why was that so important
to Moses?

Nonetheless, we now have a new definition of the word *etz*, which
does not mean "tree." Moses and the Israelites already knew that
there were various trees in the Promised Land, so what does this
question regarding *etz* indicate? The Zohar continues:

> Rav Shimon said: "He gave them a wise allusion regarding
> to what they asked before, as is written: 'Is God among us or
> not (*ayin*)' (Shemot 17:7) BEING THE QUESTION OF
> WHETHER ZEIR ANPIN, REFERRED TO BY *YUD*,
> *HEI, VAV, HEI*, IS STAYING WITH THEM OR ARICH
> ANPIN IS AMONG THEM, REFERRED TO BY *AYIN*
> (LIT. NOT) He said: There IN THE LAND, you will
> recognize if it is worthy of this, OF ZEIR ANPIN WHO IS
> REFERRED TO AS TREE, or of this, OF ARICH ANPIN
> WHO IS REFERRED TO BY *AYIN*. He further told them,
> if you notice that the fruits of the land are similar to those
> in the other countries in the world, then "there is a tree in
> it," which is the Tree of Life, MEANING ZEIR ANPIN,
> but not from a higher place. However, if you notice that the
> fruits of the land are decidedly different from other fruits
> in other countries of the world, you will know that from
> Atika Kadisha flows and emerges the Supernal difference it
> contains more than all the places in the world. Through this,
> you will be able to recognize if there is a tree in it THAT IS,

ZEIR ANPIN or not (*Ayin*), ATIKA KADISHA, THAT IS
ARICH ANPIN. That is what you set out to discern in the
beginning, as is written: "Is God among us" and "among us"
is specific SINCE THEY INQUIRED IF ZEIR ANPIN
RESTS AMONG THEM, or not (*Ayin*) REFERRING
TO ARICH ANPIN. Therefore, "And be of good courage,
and bring of the fruit of the land," (Bamidbar 13:20), to
know the difference in them, MEANING TO BE AWARE
IF THERE IS A DIFFERENCE IN THEM OR NOT.
—Zohar, Shlach Lecha 6:36

Here the Zohar hints at the concept of wisdom, which, in fact, has
nothing to do with whether Job was present—as if they would
go into the Promised Land only if he lived there. What is being
implied is that if there were no trees in Israel then the Israelites
would not enter, and if there were trees they would. This, according
to the Zohar, is incorrect. The word "Job" is a code for "wisdom."

The inquiry is related to whether Zeir Anpin—the
Tetragrammaton—was in Israel. It refers to what state of
consciousness existed in the land before they entered. The Zohar
says that different lands have different levels of consciousness and
this was the true nature of Moses' question. According to Rav
Shimon, the question was, what do you experience there, what
do you feel there? To what are you connecting when you enter
the land of Israel? The question was not about the trees, it was
referring to whether God was with them or not, and the Israelites
were uncertain.

Certainty and Ayin

Today, nothing is certain. We can observe that fortunes are lost overnight, lives are cut short. Certainly, there is no certainty. From one point of view, it is hard to see how certainty could be lost. But from another point of view, it is clearly lost. Although life does not usually appear to be uncertain, we cannot be confident about anything and surely we are not assured about what tomorrow will bring, when sometimes we even forget about yesterday.

Here we learn that the Israelites were asking if God was among them or not because they were uncertain. Therefore, the word *ayin* indicates that they wanted to know which level of consciousness they had achieved, whether they were at the level of Zeir Anpin or were they at the level of consciousness of Ayin—meaning Arich Anpin, where there is no more questioning, only certainty. This is a level that most people do not as yet recognize. Nothing is certain, not health, wealth, nor our relationships. We are always in doubt about how long a relationship will last or when a new relationship will begin, and such uncertainties are part of our daily lives. The uncertainty expressed in our generation has existed since the dawn of human existence. Therefore, what Rav Shimon tells us, is that they were asking if there was a level uncertainty-consciousness that prevails throughout the land.

Then there is Job, who is described as having lived yesterday and lives tomorrow; this is what the idea of Job concerns. All of the folklore around Job asks how long he lived; some say he lived thousands of years, while others declare that he never existed. For us, the mystery surrounding Job is only symbolic, he represents uncertainty. What Moses was essentially asking is the same question we can ask ourselves today: are we certain or not?

The Zohar says Moses' question had nothing to do with the physical trees of Israel. In fact, this portion is merely teaching us that we can either achieve certainty or we can go through life without it. This whole portion very clearly shows us, thanks to the Zohar, that we do not have to be confined to the limitations of uncertainty, which, unfortunately, most of the world is in. Without the Zohar, we could erroneously think that this seemingly insignificant story brought future destruction to the children of Israel.

The Zohar explains that the word *ayin*, which means "nothing" or "not," is indicative of the Arich Anpin level of consciousness, and that the *etz*, which means "tree," is a code word for Zeir Anpin. Rav Shimon in the aforementioned section from the Zohar explains that if these are the same trees that appear all over the world, then the consciousness that reigns in that land will be that of Etz haChaim (Tree of Life), and not from a higher plane. However, if they saw fruits in the land that they did not find elsewhere, then they should know that there is another consciousness in the land, which is not extant elsewhere, a Supernal consciousness that flows out of Atika Kadisha, a code word of the Holy Agent, which although it has no meaning in any direct translation, Rav Shimon tell us that its essence has another meaning.

Rav Shimon says that the Israelites wanted to know this from the very beginning because it is written: "Is God amongst us or not?" In other words, if the Israelites waged war on the nation of Amalek, would God be with them? When the Zohar says "God" in this context, the word used is the Tetragrammaton, which has one significance. There are 24 different Names of God, and each Name represents another dimension of consciousness. Rav Shimon says that the question was whether the Tetragrammaton was within them or *ayin*, meaning was the energy of God—the dimension of God at the level of Tetragrammaton—in fact, present or was it at the level of Ayin, the level where Ayin is Arich Anpin or "nothingness"? In other words, bring back samples of the trees so that all the Israelites would be able to observe them and see that they are essentially different from all other trees that they had seen up to this point.

What is the difference between Atika Kadisha, the level of consciousness called "nothing" and Zeir Anpin, which is called Etz haChaim (Tree of Life)? Essentially there are two levels of consciousness in this world. In Beresheet it says that God planted the Tree of Life within this world as we know it and also the Tree of Knowledge. And Adam was prohibited from eating of the Tree of Knowledge and was only permitted to eat of the Tree of Life. Now here, we have another dimension: Atika Kadisha, which is referred to as "nothingness."

What is this dimension? Why would it depend on the Israelites? Why did Moses not tell them? He knew what dimension existed, he knew what Israel was and why they were going to inhabit that land. Is it because God promised Abraham that this is the land for the Israelites? To this day, Jews are still trying to maintain and sustain this land for themselves, and this brings one war running into each other like one continuous war? Whether you have anxiety concerning war or you actually suffer it makes little difference. Both realities bring one to a consciousness that there is always war, whether you live in Israel or not. One needs only to glance at a newspaper. Heretofore, we have failed to raise the question: what is so special about Israel that makes everyone talk about it? This is exactly what Moses was asking of the spies when he instructed them to return with samples of the trees so they would know if these trees were different in this land.

What does Ayin mean and what is Etz haChaim? Etz haChaim is the Realm of Certainty. If Adam haRishon (First Man) lived within this consciousness of certainty, then why did he sin? Why would

Adam want to eat of the Tree of Knowledge and descend into the world that we are in now when he already possessed the level of certainty? Unfortunately, our world of uncertainty exists because of Adam's sin, which brought us into this level of consciousness and, therefore we have uncertainty. We could have remained in the Realm of Certainty—the Tree of Life Reality.

Although Zeir Anpin is the Tree of Life, while in this world, we have the alternative of going up or down. The question we face is, could there be a way to maintain, within our own consciousness, the idea that we never have to fall, as Adam once did? Rav Shimon says that there is a way, if the consciousness of Ayin exists either in the people or in the fruits we never have to undergo a change from one state to another. If we experience a true feeling of contentment that lasts for a long time and almost never disappears, then we are in the consciousness of Ayin. However, if we are in the consciousness of the Tree of Life we also experience contentment, yet at this level we can fall to the Tree of Knowledge level where things are possessed of both good and evil, where one day is good and one day is bad, which is the norm for most people.

The Zohar continues:

> "And they ascended into the Negev, and (he) came to Hebron" (Bamidbar 13:22). HE INQUIRES: "It should have said, 'And they came' in plural." HE ANSWERS: "However, Rav Yosi said it refers to Caleb, who came to pray upon the graves of the patriarchs IN HEBRON. Caleb thought to himself: Joshua, indeed. Moses blessed him with the highest, Holy help and he could extricate himself and save himself from them; what shall I do? He took counsel to pray a prayer by the graves of the patriarchs, to be rescued from the misguided decisions of the rest of the spies."
> —Zohar, Shlach Lecha 6:38

It was predetermined that the spies would come back from Israel with a bad report. Caleb knew in advance that they would return with a negative report and that he would be a part of it, thus he went to Hebron to pray to the righteous souls buried there that he not fall into the uncertainty of the other ten spies. Caleb knew that Joshua would not lose certainty because of the blessing of Moses but that he himself might fall and return with the same answer as the others. The Zohar says the reason Caleb was protected from giving the same report as the other ten was because he went to pray by the graves of the patriarchs in Hebron. He needed the assistance of Abraham, Isaac, and Jacob so that he would not fall into the consciousness of the others. He reflected so as not to fall into the same error.

Why would the ten spies give a negative report? Were they not going into the land with an open mind to find out what kind of consciousness was there? The Zohar says they were all chieftains of the tribes. They estimated that if the Israelites entered Israel, there may not be a necessity for chieftains—they might be out of a job. This is why no one creates durable automobiles or lightbulbs because if they did, there would be no use for their work tomorrow, people would be unemployed.

It says in Jeremiah 31:34, "And they shall teach no more every man his neighbor, and every man his brother, saying, 'Know the Lord: for they shall all know Me, from the least of them unto the greatest of them.'" Was this the same idea? The spies had already established a consciousness of the land because they were afraid that they would lose their post as leaders of tribes. However, they did bring back a tree that was unusual, a grapefruit tree. What did Caleb not see? What was the difference between their level of consciousness, and what was Caleb afraid of?

This is a very difficult and lengthy discussion, but I shall endeavor to present the gist of what the Zohar is saying here and how this applies to us today. As the Zohar said, this was no mere historic record of people who spied and came back with a report. The Zohar says that the actions of humankind determine everything that happens. If there are wars, humankind causes them. If there are recessions they are caused by human consciousness, by human behavior. Where the mind is determines the way things ultimately make their appearance.

When the spies, the tribal leaders, came into Israel, Moses did not ask them if there were trees there, but if there were *different* trees, so they brought back a different tree, which was the reason they knew that this country had unique energy connected to it. However, this was not the only question raised by Moses. Even the best-laid plans can go awry. They still had to look at the quality of the trees, if they bore fruit or not, if they had any defects. Seemingly nothing could go wrong. Why then, if the plan was so perfect, did the anticipated result not come? It was about whether they experienced Ayin or Etz haChaim, which are both good, but at the Level of Ayin we cannot fall into traps.

As we have learned in the classes, even if we are in Etz haChaim, we have only one free choice. Everything is predestined. While we would like to believe that we are in control, according to the Zohar, in this world, we are not in control of any aspect of our lives, certainly not our relationships, finances or health. We have no control over these factors, the only free will that has been allocated to humankind is what level of consciousness one assumes. If we choose the level of consciousness of the Tree of Knowledge then we are stuck in that predetermined plan and have no further control. Whatever that fate has in store for us is how events will transpire. This is a difficult concept because Satan whispers doubts in our ears that such a life is simply that of an automaton. This is a new concept, that we are only living on automatic. We do not feel that we are robotic but we are. Science has not yet declared that human beings are far inferior to the computer, no human being can perform actions at the speed a computer can. Is a computer anything more than a robot? It is certainly not a human being.

We humans think that we have some sort of control, that we are something special in this world. Yet the existence of computers implies that we are inferior in some ways. We cannot even perform at the same level as something that is completely devoid of a mind of its own. The only way the computer furnishes us with information is dependent on what program has been installed; by and within itself it does not do anything. If our capabilities are lower than that of a computer where is our control?

According to the Zohar, we can choose to be within the Tree of Life Reality or the Tree of Knowledge Reality. Do not forget that we can fluctuate between these two realities. There may be times where we can stay in the Tree of Life Reality, which is rare but it can happen, until the point where we cannot maintain that level of consciousness and descend to the uncertainty level, but this depends on us. Then there is a third level: the Level of Ayin, the Level of Nothingness. When Moses asked whether there was *etz* or Ayin it was because he knew that as long as there was *etz*, a Tree of Life consciousness, in Israel that they could sustain it and constantly remain there, it would be a perfect civilization of certainty. We always have the free will to decide whether or not we fall to a lower level. If Ayin was present—there was no longer even free will— there was no longer the possibility that they could decide.

The Israelites learned that everything, from the atmosphere to the environment, is dependent on where they place their consciousness. The consciousness of the other chieftains was one of uncertainty in their positions, and Caleb knew that this would influence the entire environment, and therefore he too would be influenced. Thus for Caleb to try to achieve the Level of Ayin, he had to go to Hebron. What did Caleb do in Hebron? He prayed. What does this mean; did he open up a prayer book? Caleb knew that there was system by which we can connect to the Level of Ayin, where we literally leave the dimension of free will. Who wants to leave the dimension of free will?

If we are looking for misery, God gives us the free will to choose it, and most of us do. For example, people justify why they need a certain procedure or surgery, saying, "I have gone back and forth with it and now I want to get it over with." What kind of a justification is "Let me get it over with"? Do you know the consequences of getting it over with? Do you know what can develop? No. Who says getting something done means you are finished with it? You are only finished with one stage of the process. Now that you have removed this one, you have brought another into focus jumping from one life movie to another. Why do we choose one thing over another? Because we erroneously believe that perhaps a new course of action will finish the job.

Ultimately, in the big picture, there is no free will. Life runs along the pattern chosen. According to the Zohar, if we choose the pattern of the Tree of Life, then this is where we are, this is where our environment is. This will be the affect the whole world will have over us unless we can do something exceptional, unless we do what Caleb did, unless we know how to make the connections, as we do at the Kabbalah Centres. We follow the connections, and when we pray on Shabbat or any other day, we place our consciousness not where we are geographically, but rather at the Holy Temple or with Rav Isaac Luria (the Ari) in Safed. Our consciousness is not of such a high dimension that we can easily connect to the patriarchs Abraham, Isaac, and Jacob, as Caleb could. Instead, we connect to Rav Shimon, knowing that he is certainly in the Reality of Ayin.

With him there is no falling from one level to another. Remember that the snake—meaning Satan—pleaded with God, saying if God did not remove Rav Shimon from this world then he would have no chance of influencing anyone to choose the path of uncertainty. Rav Shimon influences the entire environment, the entire quantum universe that we exist in. He is still influencing it to such an extent that one cannot influence anyone to choose misery as opposed to contentment. And we choose misery, make no mistake.

If we made a list of all of our decisions, we would notice that not only in five out of ten, but in all decisions we have made, we chose the path of misery. And had we asked one more question, we probably would not have taken that route. What the Zohar does is try to expand our awareness. When we make a decision, we must look for questions to raise because the fact that we are satisfied does not mean that we have reached the goal. Whether it is correct or not, this is the life cassette that is now playing. If we have made an inconclusive decision because we have not raised enough questions, then we are in the cassette of uncertainty, whether it is for one year or three years, and this Age of Aquarius is going to move things along much more quickly. This is the difficulty of choosing a path. Regardless of which path we choose, we will see the consequences.

We learn here that Moses told the spies to go and explore the Promised Land and see the consequences. *Is your thought energy-intelligence going to be, if you lose your job, you will therefore change your report to give the idea that this land does not have a consciousness of Ayin?* The consciousness in the land of Israel is Ayin, it will never change. Israel is the only place that has the consciousness of Ayin. Does this mean we physically have to be there to connect to this consciousness? No, but it is stronger if we are there. Our problem is the physical body, which is connected to the Realm of Limitation. The body is what prevents us from travelling the world in a moment. The mind can travel anywhere at will within a matter of seconds.

We can cover any and every area in seconds with the mind. It is the body that prevents us from achieving this because the body functions in a state of limitation and separation, separating one area from another.

In this section of the Bible and the Zohar we are being taught to investigate everything, not only the land of Israel. If we have a decision to make, are we going to enter into such a decision with preconceived ideas like the spies did? Will we arrive at any conclusion? No, because we have already made a decision before a discussion began. When we have preconceived notions of what we can expect at the end, why would we bother to ask questions?

In essence, Moses said that once the spies went in with a preconceived notion, they had no choice but to come back with the information they did. It is the same with each of us every day, if we are employing preconceived notions, we have not taken all aspects into account. Why ask questions? After all what else could we possibly learn when we are under the influence of preconceived notions?

Many misfortunes befall those who enter a situation with preconceived notions. How do we escape this mental trap? We are deeply influenced by our surroundings and friends, most of us will operate according to current norms. For instance, if we are wealthy, it is most likely that we would gravitate towards an area where other wealthy people live. Did we make the decision to live there? Of course not. In other words, we do not truly make independent choices in our lives.

If we do not raise our awareness, then we come in to every situation with preconceived notions, just as the Torah shows us here. Before we even begin to tackle the questions, before we think what is good for us or what will improve our situation, we have been influenced by our environment. We must think of where our decisions will lead us. We must contemplate whether our notions are preconceived or if we are now beginning to raise genuine questions so that a greater awareness can be achieved.

The beginning of this portion has nothing to do with exploring the land of Israel. It has to do with our daily decision-making. What do you want? This was the question Moses raised to the Israelites, do you want Ayin? Moses knew that what they wanted was exactly what they would find in Israel. If you want Ayin, if you want total certainty, that is what you will find. But if you are concerned with everyday mundane issues then your mind is immersed in uncertainty. This is where such a path leads, and from it no improvement is possible. How many of us have experienced something truly different from what we had experienced yesterday or last year? How many can truthfully say we have undergone a transformation? Is this such a difficult a question to raise? Are we just doing the same things we did yesterday?

Satan is so strong, which is what Caleb was afraid of. He knew there is something in the atmosphere that prevents us from raising our consciousness. The spies were supposed to explore but in reality they were not doing that, they were not intending to find anything different than what they had already decided in advance. The entanglements of daily life are such that we often feel we can never escape them. This is what the Bible is here for. The Bible is not a history lesson, it is here to teach us how to immediately escape the maze in which we find ourselves, to find our way out of the narrow corridors few of us can ever leave.

The Bible says at this point that Caleb went to Abraham. If one cannot escape troubles, then what alternative is there? Is prayer the solution? Prayer has never achieved anything for anyone; no matter the religion, nothing has changed. Rav Shimon, like Joshua, was born already blessed by Moses, it was destiny. Joshua would be in the Ayin. Complete, he did not have to travel anywhere, whether he went to Israel or not, he would not be going there in search of anything, since he knew already what existed there. How could he know that he would find the *Ayin*? Moses had already told him that he would find trees because Israel is the land of milk and honey. What is the meaning of the land of milk and honey? This is the land that has the ability to instill an ability of Ayin in the environment if the people are of that kind of consciousness. Unfortunately, this is not the case, and Israel remains a land riven by strife.

We are told in the beginning of this portion that if we want to search out Ayin it is because the idea of it nags at our minds. Where is the fountain of youth that legends have spoken about? Everybody wants to be young again; someone who has lost a limb wants the limb restored, someone who was once wealthy wants to restore the wealth they once had. Where do we find the things that were lost? Moses tells us that we can only find them in the land of Israel. If you want to maintain your wealth, there is only one place you can do that, in Israel. After the fall of Adam, most of us are destined to live outside of Israel, there is no choice. In this lifetime or another even those who were born in Israel will have to take that trip outside the country. However, there is a purpose to being outside of Israel. It is the process of bringing back the sparks that are distributed all over the world; each individual brings back a spark.

However, Moses told the Israelites—who were not going into Israel because they made the golden calf—why was he sending them. He did this for the parents to know what kind of land they were sending their children into.

We have got to be in Israel. Our War Rooms in the Kabbalah Centres have huge pictures of gravesites of righteous souls and a picture of the Holy Temple in Jerusalem, so we can place our consciousness in Israel even while our body is here, wherever here is. Moses also wanted to know if the consciousness of the spies was in the Level of Ayin, because then he could enter Israel as his place is in the Level of Ayin and the spies would influence the country, as we do today in Israel. If their consciousness was not in Ayin, he could not go into Israel.

We cause the uncertainty of war. It is we who bring about such a condition. We have no one to blame but ourselves. The Light demands that we be totally connected to It. We must follow the demands of the universe, this is the natural law of the universe. This is why Caleb went to Hebron and also why we connect with the patriarchs in Israel. They are all on the same level of consciousness; in fact, the Zohar says that from the time that Rav Shimon left this world, we shall never achieve the level of consciousness of his time or the time of the Israelites in the wilderness, which is the known as the *Dor De'a* (Generation of Knowledge), until our current era, meaning today. According to Rav Avraham Azulai and Rav Isaac Luria (the Ari), we are the *Dor De'a*, and we have such an infinite capacity of consciousness yet no one is making us aware of it.

We all think the same way, we all follow the fashion. We have the capacity to look around, question and explore ourselves—*lecha*, which is the second word in the name of the portion. Explore yourself, see where you really are, otherwise you are not going to make any difference. You might see for a moment that things are improving but almost as soon as life starts to get better, there will be a leveling off. There is no such thing as a straight line of action. The only time we find one is when the physical body is about to die. The consciousness stays alive after death but the body is no longer be able to hold on to it. We have the problem of ups and downs because we have a physical body. The problem is not our consciousness.

Death, Resurrection and Cleansing

The Zohar says, Rav Ilai—one of the five students of Rabbi Akiva who remained alive during the plague that killed 24,000 of his fellow students—said that a spirit came to him and told him about a certain garden where they saw many other things, and they went to a place that we refer to as a cemetery. There, when someone died and was buried they immediately sprung up alive, only to die again and descend by themselves into the ground emerging up again. This death and rising kept repeating again and again—a truly remarkable event. The Zohar says that these people who died and rose again were the ones who died in the wilderness, the *Dor De'a* who are being discussed in this portion. Yet, we are really talking about ourselves today. As the holy Ari says, the generation of the *Dor De'a*—the Generation of the Wilderness—is the same generation that returned at the time of Rav Shimon and they are the same people who are returning in our time.

Rav Ilai was speaking with another student and they asked the spirit, "What do they do here?" And the spirit answers: "They do this every day." When they died, the body decomposed immediately but the minute they went back into the ground, they immediately disappeared, the body completely decayed to the point where nothing was left. And each time, part of the evil that they had acquired through their actions was thus cleansed; each time they underwent a burial, they experienced a cleansing. And then there was suddenly a resurrection. So what happened? These people were special and we are special today. As Rav Shimon said, in the past two thousand years, there will not be these kinds of people, there will be other souls, but not those who physically experienced this burial and resurrection because although all the souls were there on Mount Sinai, not all the bodies were there. Yet, since we were all there, all the souls were elevated to that point. However, only this generation who wandered in the wilderness was the one who stood there physically at Mount Sinai, and because of all their evil actions, they underwent this continuous process of death and resurrection. One day, there was complete decomposition of the body, the next day it rose up whole again. What exactly is the message within this strange section of the Zohar?

The reason for burial is that the earth has the power of cleansing the physical body, which contains the aspect of Satan. The Zohar tells us that we have two bodies, we have a body that is part of our soul, which never disappears and always remains with us, and then there is another body that is part of Satan—it is the Satan within all of us. These people were buried one day and resurrected the next. However, what does the Zohar say about this portion of the Bible? When this generation stood on Mount Sinai, they were there in a body without dross but after the golden calf, they drew down the consciousness of the Tree of Knowledge, they went down into this dimension of good and evil, which is the same as we experience in our lives.

The Zohar says that when the Israelites sinned at the time the golden calf, they lost ornaments. Only here do we find the explanation. These ornaments represented the level of consciousness they had achieved on Mount Sinai. This consciousness was not however lost forever, it subsequently came and went.

What this portion is telling us is that today more souls are being born than has happened from the time when the Age of Aquarius began or from the time of the Ari. We now have souls on the planet who were not present at the golden calf incident and, therefore, do not undergo the same problem of a rapid disintegration that we experience today, such as the market going up, then suddenly going down and no one knows why. These rapid changes are indicated by the Zohar, and this is its clue to us. When the Zohar says the people of the *Dor De'a* are born one day and the next they die, it is much the same for many today, who one day are on the top yet the next day are on the bottom. This is the *Dor De'a*, there are no guarantees.

If you want the clues as to the nature of your consciousness, explore your environment. This is what Moses told the Israelites. Moses knew these people's consciousness and that they would influence the consciousness of the land of Israel. It is not simply that the Bible was forecasting for us what we can expect to find in the future. We are living in such a period of daily peaks and lows now. Our body as well as our consciousness changes from day to day. One day an individual may go to the doctor and be given a dreadful prognosis. What ailment did he or she have yesterday? Nothing, everything was wonderful. Suddenly, a husband comes home to his wife and says he is leaving her. Everything seemed to be fine the previous day. One day, there is wealth, the next there is not. For a time, we have it all, the next day we have nothing.

In the portion of Shlach Lecha, the Zohar is teaching us what we can and cannot expect in this Age of Aquarius and it also gives us the antidote for its woes. The antidote is what Caleb and Joshua came back with. The day they came back and everyone wept was the day of Tisha B'Av. I know a lot a people who have Tisha B'Av all year round, not just one day a year. Who among us would not prefer to settle for one day of disappointment a year, rather than having disappointment the whole year round? There are some who welcome even one day a year of contentment. That would satisfy them, let alone 364 days of contentment and only one day a year of Tisha B'Av.

This is what the Zohar tells us the spirit was showing to Rabbi Ilai; the people were experiencing the ups and downs of existence; the body disintegrates, then the next day it is whole. The same is true for us today, the doctor does not know why we may have recovered but we do. What does this tell us? Are we suddenly healed? No.

And the same woe can befall us again tomorrow because as the Zohar says, the next day the same bodies went back into the grave. As we know, a grave is not only where dead people are put to rest; there are many people living in homes that are like cemeteries. This is the consciousness we have to take ourselves out of, it is Satan's consciousness.

When we connect to this reading, we want to escape the rollercoaster of fluctuations. As long as the body is here it is up and down, in and out of the grave, and in daily life we experience highs and lows. Is it possible for this madness to ever end? Just a little story like Caleb's gives us the complete clue. We have no other choice, if we do not pray the way we do at the Centre, we have no choice but to succumb to the ups and downs of life. We learn that to free himself, Caleb had to go to Hebron. The Zohar explains that Hebron is a connection to the dimensions of Abraham, Isaac, and Jacob, and that now, through them, we can reach that level of consciousness.

5 Then Moses and Aaron fell on their faces before all the assembly of the congregation of the children of Israel. 6 And Joshua, the son of Nun, and Caleb, the son of Jephunneh, who among those that spied out the land, rent their clothes. 7 And they spoke to all the congregation of the children of Israel, saying: "The land which we passed through to spy out is an exceedingly good land. 8 If the Lord delights in us, then He will bring us into this land, and give it to us—a land which flows with milk and honey. 9 Only do not rebel against the Lord, or fear the people of the land; for they are bread for us; their protection is removed from them, and the Lord is with us; fear them not." 10 But all the congregation said stone them with stones, when the glory of the Lord appeared in the Tent of Meeting to all the children of Israel. 11 And the Lord said to Moses: "How long will this people despise Me? And how long will they not believe in Me, with all the signs which I have wrought among them? 12 I will smite them with the pestilence, and destroy them, and will make of you a nation greater and mightier than them."

The Doubt of the Chieftains

When Moses sent one chieftain from each tribe, this individual was not simply elected, he was divinely appointed. Rashi and the other commentators struggle to express what this portion is about. When these twelve men returned, only two, Caleb and Joshua, brought back a good report about the land they had investigated. The others said that the land was not good and that there were insurmountable obstacles. Then the Bible says that the whole congregation of the children of Israel rose up against Moses and Aaron and asked again why they had been brought out of the land of Egypt to die in this wilderness. The congregation said, it would be better to die in Egypt than to have to enter the Promised Land and fight with these enemies. Once again this confirms that the story of Passover is not about the celebration of freedom from bondage of Egypt. If Passover was, in fact, about freedom from bondage, then why would the Israelites want to return to Egypt at as soon as any small difficulty arose? Moreover, what did the congregation of the children of Israel say when they heard the good accounts of Caleb and Joshua? They wanted to kill the two men who dared to disagree with the other ten spies. Caleb and Joshua were entitled to their opinion, yet the people were prepared to kill them.

In Bamidbar 14:11, we come to the word *yena'atzuni*, meaning "they will despise me," and within *yena'atzuni*, is the word *nazi*, which appears in the Bible for the first time. It is used when God expresses his disapproval of the Israelites and their behavior toward one another. Some historians say that this hatred started one thousand years ago, and others say that it began in 1933. I do not know why they do not say it originated in the Bible. There has been much research into this one word. The Zohar says in every generation, a few Jews—the *erev rav*—return to engender hatred, not only among the Jewish people but all of humankind. This portion exists to teach us not about the story described, but about the *lesson* contained within it. This point where we see the word *nazi* for the first time is when the hatred, suffering and pain of humankind came into being.

The Zohar says that the spies returned from Israel on Tisha B'Av, the day on which both Holy Temples were destroyed, and that this is the one day of the year ruled by Satan. History teaches us that all the empires of the world wanted to rule the land of Israel. Why? The Babylonians and the Romans wanted to rule the land. However, according to the Talmud, the reason the Temples were destroyed was because of the hatred of one Jew for another. The only reason that the Temples were destroyed was because of the lack of human dignity between Jews, and this lack has continued in every generation since.

Did God decree that these people, these complaining Israelites, would die in the wilderness with the exception of Caleb and Joshua? Why was the decree so severe? If this is a God Who is supposed to be compassionate and full of mercy, why could He not forgive these complaining Israelites? Why did He punish them with death in the wilderness? To teach us the lesson behind the story. No matter the "good" reasons we think we have, there is no justification for treating another human being with anything less than human dignity. We bring negativity with us into this world—from this lifetime and from previous lifetimes—and our work while in this world is to clear the slate. This is why we came into this world. No matter the justification, no matter what our good reasons may be, we must understand that we cannot do our job if we create negativity in this world. We bring our own chaos, pain, and suffering into this life. It does not come from outside of ourselves, it is not given to us by God; it is created by our negative actions.

Moses experienced then what The Kabbalah Centre is experiencing today. There is nothing new here. We are going to remove pain and suffering and there is opposition preventing us from making this happen. No authoritative body wants to remove pain and suffering since it threatens their institution. We are called evil in spite of what we teach—which is human dignity between human beings.

The portion of Shlach Lecha is about the twelve spies going into Israel to investigate the Promised Land. Why did they have to go into Israel after they had witnessed so many miracles, such as the plagues in Egypt and the splitting of the Red Sea and so on? Could they not just believe that God would lead them into Israel? Why did they feel that they personally had to verify whether or not God was telling the truth? The Zohar explains that these twelve chieftains were *tzadikim*—righteous, elevated souls—yet they questioned the voice of God, questioned whether Israel was an appropriate place to enter. When the spies returned, ten of them agreed that this was the land of milk and honey but that the people living there were stronger and more powerful than they were. They said that it was impossible to go into the land. How could they question God's omnipotence, how could they not think that God would facilitate His own people's entry into the Promised Land? Only Joshua and Caleb disagreed and said that the land was good.

Then and now the authorities manipulate the ignorant by telling half-truths; those who find half of what they hear to be true and assume that the rest is true as well. The entire congregation listened to the ten and consequently began to whine and complain. And the complaints were the same as before, "Why did you take us out of Egypt, so we could die in the desert?" This was after the advent of the Giving of the Torah. More so, they asked for a new leader to bring them back to Egypt.

Joshua pleaded with the people not to rebel against the Lightforce of God saying, "If God is with us, what do we have to fear?" The authorities, however, the other ten chieftains asked if they could stone Moses, Joshua, and Aaron to get rid of them, just like they want to get rid of The Kabbalah Centre, today. In 3,400 years, nothing has changed. Some of our teachers and students have been so badly assaulted they had to be treated in a hospital.

The Matter of the letter Yud

In Bamidbar 14:17, the letter *Yud* in the word *yigdal*, which means "to grow" is larger than the other letters. The *Yud* is the least physical in that it is normally the smallest of all the Hebrew letters, which makes it the most powerful because it has less matter. For many years, I was ignorant and did not know there was an enlarged *Yud* in this verse of the Torah Scroll. Meditating on this large *Yud* gives us the opportunity to connect to the consciousness to overcome physicality; not to eliminate the physical but to overpower it.

We tend to forget that the only way to remove pain and suffering is through a change of behavior. The authorities look forward to Tisha B'Av because it signifies pain and suffering. Human beings come and go, but the Lightforce of God remains. In the first verse of Shlach Lecha, it says, "And God says to Moses, send you…." All the commentators are in agreement that this was for Moses' benefit. There is no reference to Moses having made a request of God nor did the request come from the people, rather it was God's idea for Moses to designate the people to explore the land to see if it was the promised land of milk and honey.

The Zohar makes the comment that when we are referring to these twelve chieftains, the tribal leaders, we are dealing with people with a very high level of consciousness, *tzadikim*. This is the Zohar's description of the people who were sent to explore the land. We must also recall that throughout the Bible, certainly from the time of the exodus from Egypt, that it was God who promised this land, not Moses. Is the word of God not sufficient? It was not a question of whether the land was indeed one of milk and honey, which is how it is has been interpreted for 3,400 years, but rather it was for Moses to know whether or not he was the one meant to lead them into the land of Israel.

Moses asks the chieftains to inform him whether there were any trees in the Promised Land and if there were, he requested that they bring back the fruits of the land so the people can verify with their own eyes the type of trees that grow there. Moses's level of consciousness was above time, space, and motion. The Zohar answers that it was not a question of whether there were trees or not, it was about something deeper. The twelve came back and said that the land was plentiful. They even brought back one branch that was so heavily-laden with fruit that it took two men to carry it. The Zohar says that if you inject the truth with a lie it may not be accepted, but if you inject a lie with a bit of truth, that lie could be acceptable. As a righteous person, how was Moses going to ascertain whether or not he was to lead the people into the land of Israel? Unlike Joshua and Caleb, the other ten chieftains began to quibble about what would happen to their leadership positions, and when they tried to lift the fruit-laden branch they could not. Only Joshua and Caleb could easily lift it, and this was due to Moses' influence. Moses inserted a *Yud* into the name Joshua indicating that what is more is less, the more physical in nature something is the less it would be. The *Yud* is the first letter of that most powerful system—the Tetragrammaton. The Zohar indicates that there was a transformation within this tree and the branch became light again.

Once the other ten said that there were giants living within the land and that the cities were well-fortified, despite the objections of Joshua and Caleb, the Israelites felt as if they had been cheated by God. They began to weep and complain. Caleb and Joshua demanded to know why the people were rebelling against the word of God.

The large letter *Yud* in the word *yigdal* raises us to the level of Binah. The *Yud* has the least amount of physicality, it is like a dot, so why is the *Yud* written in a larger size here? It is to indicate that we should reach levels of consciousness where challenges are actually opportunities that can bless us. These ten chieftains became obsessed and self-righteous. What happens when we are under pressure? Do we negate others? Do we only survive at the expense of others? Certainly not, we need to treat others with human dignity at all times and under all conditions. The spies had their own agenda. They twisted everything around. They looked at this beautiful Promised Land and could not see its goodness. They could only think about whether they were going to retain their positions. Although they were speaking about one of the world's greatest energy centers, they saw something else entirely.

We begin to lose that basic principle of self-sacrifice for the greater good. We can be righteous until push comes to shove. This is what happened here in the portion. Rashi says that these events sealed the fate of the two Holy Temples. We are the same souls who were present at the exodus and we were present when the spies came back with their report. We were present before the fate of the Temples was sealed. When we connect with this reading, we can take this tragedy and use it as an opportunity for cleansing. Nothing can strike us down without something within us causing it to happen. When we are confronted with a challenge and we align ourselves with the consciousness of responsibility, we are immediately cleansed and the challenge falls away. The ten chieftains were now destined to die in the wilderness. Only Caleb and Joshua would enter the land of Israel. Taking responsibility is not the road to death. We can only cleanse ourselves and in doing so permit our consciousness to change.

This is not just a story, this portion, this week is filled with the same kind of energy that prevailed during the golden calf incident. What happened next was that the evil people—*erev rav*—blamed Moses. When we abdicate responsibility and lose touch with human dignity, our lives will be filled with chaos. With the Light and lesson of this reading we have the opportunity to turn a tragedy into a blessing.

However, if we deny our responsibility, it can never happen. We have an opportunity to transform the chaos we have inflicted on others by assuming responsibility with the power of the mind and the tools that were given to expand this physical reality into a Flawless Universe.

What makes this section difficult to understand is that two of these spies—Caleb and Joshua—returned with a positive report, and they did enter the land of Israel. Who were these other ten? They were heads of tribes, they were righteous people. Did they not believe—as God had promised—that He would always be present to take care of them, as He had in the past? Why would they have doubts because they met up with the giants? What transpired was that these ten righteous people had an epiphany about what would happen when the nation of Israel entered the land. They saw that they would then be out of a job. The Zohar says that this story is giving us perspective on our own lives; just because we put into practice the principles of Kabbalah there is no guarantee of removal of chaos.

The Zohar explains that this story has nothing to do with spying out the land, it is about our journey through life. The word the Bible uses is *yaturu*, which does not mean "spy" but "to tour." It is very clear that the Bible is indicating the journey we each embark on the moment we take our first breath, a journey filled with a mixture of many good and bad times. The Zohar says this journey, which we begin in a miraculous way, takes into account reincarnation. When we really think about life, how we came into this world, from beginning to end, it is an incredible feat.

The Zohar says that from birth to twelve years old for a girl and birth to thirteen years old for a boy, we are under the jurisdiction of Satan. From the moment we enter this world and through these formative years, we are conditioned and programmed by Satan on one basic principle, and that is doubt. Is this why the subject of immortality has been scorned and even mocked? We are told by everyone around us that immortality cannot be possible. Even though both the science of today and nano-technology tell us that it is indeed possible, we still see aged and infirm people, as well as so many dying. Are we to believe that we can correct this situation? Our minds have been programmed during our formative years to think that our latter years are the beginning of the end, therefore what kind of path is it that God has placed us on? This is what Shlach Lecha is dealing with. These people were righteous, they believed, but in a moment of weakness they doubted. The Zohar says we perpetuate our own chaos. I believe the Zohar. If we cannot embrace the fact that we are the perpetuators and the creators of our own chaos, we cannot make it on this journey because then we become ensnared in the trap of blaming God for our divorce or a plethora of other excuses. The tribal leaders were righteous, yet they also thought about what would happen to their lofty positions.

The physical body is illusory, yet the soul continues after death without interruption. Whether in this lifetime or a past lifetime, correction remains to be dealt with until we come to the understanding that we are responsible, that we are the creators and the perpetrators of our own chaos, and that we alone can remove this chaos. The Zohar tells us that God did not intend for us to believe death is inevitable. This world really is a bed of roses, we just need not get in its way.

13 And Moses said to the Lord: "When the Egyptians shall hear, for You brought up this people in Your might from among them, 14 they will say to the inhabitants of this land, who have heard that You, Lord, are in the midst of this people; inasmuch as You, Lord, are seen face to face, and Your cloud stands over them, and You go before them in a pillar of cloud by day and in a pillar of fire by night; 15 now if You shall kill this people as one man, then the nations which have heard the fame of You will speak, saying: 16 'Because the Lord was not able to bring this people into the land which He swore to them, He has slain them in the wilderness.' 17 And now, I pray You, let the power of the Lord be great, according as You have spoken, saying: 18 The Lord is slow to anger, and abundant in loving-kindness, forgiving iniquity and transgression, and that will by no means clear the guilty; visiting the iniquity of the fathers upon the children, upon the third and upon the fourth generation. 19 Pardon, I pray You, the iniquity of this people according unto the greatness of Your loving-kindness, and according as You have forgiven this people, from Egypt even until now." 20 And the Lord said: "I have pardoned according to your word. 21 But truly, as I live and all the earth shall be filled with the glory of the Lord— 22 because these men that have seen My Glory and My Signs, which I wrought in Egypt and in the wilderness, yet have put Me

to the test these ten times, and have not hearkened to My voice; 23 surely they shall not see the land which I swore to their fathers, neither shall any of them that despised Me, see it. 24 But My servant Caleb, because he had another spirit with him, and has followed Me fully, he, I will bring into the land where he went; and his seed shall possess it. 25 Now the Amalekite and the Canaanite dwell in the Vale; tomorrow turn and go into the wilderness by the way of the Red Sea." 26 And the Lord spoke to Moses and to Aaron, saying: 27 "How long shall I bear with this evil congregation, that keep complaining against Me? I have heard the complaining of the children of Israel, which they keep complaining against Me. 28 Say to them: 'As I live, said the Lord, just as you have spoken in My Ears, so will I do to you: 29 your carcasses shall fall in this wilderness, and all that were numbered of you, according to your whole number, from twenty years old and upward, you that have complained against Me; 30 surely you shall not come into the land, which I lifted up My hand that I would make you dwell in, except Caleb, the son of Jephunneh, and Joshua, the son of Nun. 31 But your little ones, that you said would be a prey, I will bring them in, and they shall know the land which you have rejected. 32 But as for you, your carcasses shall fall in this wilderness. 33 And your children shall be wanderers in the wilderness forty years and shall bear the brunt your infidelities, until your carcasses

be consumed in the wilderness. 34 According to the number of the days you spied out the land, forty days, for each day you shall bear your iniquities for one year, forty years, and you shall know My displeasure. 35 I, the Lord, have spoken, I will surely do so to all this evil congregation, that are gathered together against Me; in this wilderness they shall be consumed, and there they shall die.'" 36 And the men, whom Moses sent to spy out the land, and who, when they returned, made all the congregation to complain against him, by bringing up an evil report against the land, 37 those men that did bring up an evil report of the land, died by the plague before the Lord. 38 But Joshua, the son of Nun, and Caleb, the son of Jephunneh, remained alive from among those men that went to spy out the land. 39 And Moses told these words to all the children of Israel; and the people mourned greatly.

The Destruction of the People by God

Moses was again told by God, "I will make you into a great nation," and Moses said, which I think is totally incomprehensible, that the Egyptians would witness what God did to the Israelites. Why would Moses be concerned if the Egyptians saw what God did to the Israelites? God was ready to destroy them at that moment and start all over with Moses, and only because Moses intervened did God retract His threat. This story is hard to imagine.

Do you understand why the Zohar says if anyone just reads the Bible for the sake of the story, there is no message received? They would get the wrong signal. Why should so many perish? On the other hand, how could the Israelites conduct themselves in such a manner? Again, we are reminded that Rav Shimon said that the whole Bible is a code, that we should not pay attention to the translation. Now that we have translations in English, French, and Spanish, do we grasp the Bible better? Thinking that we do is a trap because now people believe that they comprehend simply because they understand the language. There are concealed messages in the Hebrew text, and we have already explained why it was presented in a story form.

What we are receiving here, what God is teaching us, is the consequences of our actions. In this universe of ours the law of cause and effect reigns. Whatever we do will bring a direct response or consequence. If we are going to be evil, we should expect an effect that will somehow create chaos in our lives. But nonetheless, we still perform evil deeds all the time.

Thirteen Attributes

Bamidbar14:17 contains a large letter *Yud* in the word *yigdal* (will grow), as well as the prayer known as the Thirteen Attributes, which Moses brought through when God wanted to destroy the children of Israel. The Thirteen Attributes is a powerful prayer, a powerful configuration of letters, words, and verses that can reverse the negativity we have brought into this world. This is why we incarnate; we want to create a clean slate for ourselves. As long as we have negative activity in our life cassette program, consequences will be present. There is no way to change this law, which is, in fact, the only law of physics. All the rest of the laws of physics are slowly but surely disappearing, except for this law of cause and effect.

We have a great opportunity with this prayer that is not really a prayer. Through it the Lightforce of God causes the darkness to disappear. We do not know how or why but we know that when the Light appears, darkness cannot coexist with It. We have this opportunity because the cause of all misery, pain, and suffering is human negative activity. We all possess the frailties of human nature. If we did not have this opportunity there would never be a way to be rid of chaos. So many lifetimes are behind us, and now we must erase the negativity of those lifetimes. We have this chance with this reading. More than likely we are all going to become better people because we have this opportunity to draw the Light into our lives and remove the darkness. It is then up to us not to repeat the same offenses toward our fellow man.

Also in the section, God called these Israelites the chosen people and then asked when this evil congregation would stop complaining. Three times in one verse God said that they complain too much, stressing the idea that we are a complaining people. Why could God not say it just once? Did He not think that the message was coming across? This is one of the most difficult sections; there is nothing more annoying than complainers but we have to believe this story. Perhaps this is why we are better off sometimes not knowing why the section exists. Remember that we were all present there at the time of this story. God said that Israelites aged twenty and over would die. We need to remove from our hearts the idea that others in past lifetimes or in this one have done us wrong. We tend to remember that which has been done to us and harbor it as a grudge. Yet, we are told, here once again that just because someone has treated us with a lack of human dignity does not permit us to retaliate in kind.

Does the Bible not say love your neighbor as yourself? What Shlach Lecha is saying is that we do not have to love everyone, which seems contrary to *ve'ahavta lere'acha kamocha* (love your neighbor as yourself). What, then, is the answer? I have asked many people over the years how they would interpret this and how they explain it, as well as how they understand what love means. The answer is so simple, the Zohar says "Love your God." But how could we possibly love something or someone we have never seen, never been in touch with? Certainly God is not in that category of love. The answer is, we learn to love God through our relationship between ourselves and God. The Zohar explains that it is not a question of loving God but rather one of connecting to God, and this is the lesson. God is compassionate, therefore we must be compassionate. If God extends mercy, we must extend mercy. This is what love is about, connecting to attributes of the Lightforce of God.

By the same token, when another individual extends compassion, we have no choice but to return it. What happens if someone hates us? We are told that to understand their negativity, we have to feel the lack of compassion of that individual and see in them the consequences of their behavior, and most importantly, we have to understand that we, too, could fall into this trap.

Therefore, we hope to make the connection to the large letter *Yud*, the antidote to our offense. This is the answer to all human suffering—whether it is individual, collective, national or international. We must treat everyone with human dignity, irrespective of who the person is. We can never forget our responsibility of extending human dignity.

The Israelites and Doubt

Moses replied to the wrath of God by begging Him to please spare the people. God says: "How long will they despise Me?" In this portion, God wants to get rid of these complainers, telling Moses that only he would remain. Moses pleaded with God. He worried what the other nations would say if they saw that the Israelites could not compose themselves. If they saw that their God was willing to kill them, those nations certainly would not think that the Israelites were fit to be the Chosen Nation. God heard Moses and refrained from killing the Israelites that day but that complaining generation all perished during the next 39 years in the wilderness and none of them reached Israel.

Moses asked, what will the other nations say? How will pain and suffering be removed if not by the Israelite? Moses knew that the whole world, not just the Israelites, had to participate in the removal of chaos. But if the Israelite was not to lead the pack, the rest would not follow. Only if the entire Lightforce of God is revealed will the darkness disappear and not return. The purpose of The Kabbalah Centre is, as Rav Ashlag said, to disseminate information, nothing new is being said here, no great ideas are being expounded. All the people were present at Mount Sinai and the Ten Utterances were given in all seventy languages of the world. The reason the Israelites were chosen is because it is their purpose and obligation to provide humanity the instruments, such as the Hebrew language, to remove chaos and darkness. The Zohar states that it alone is the instrument for connecting to the Tree of Life.

40 And they rose up early in the morning, and got them up to the top of the mountain, saying: "Behold, we are here and will go up to the place which the Lord has promised; for we have sinned." 41 And Moses said: "Now why do you transgress the commandment of the Lord, seeing it shall not prosper? 42 Go not up, for the Lord is not among you; that you be not smitten down before your enemies. 43 For there the Amalekite and the Canaanite are before you, and you shall fall by the sword; because you have turned away from following the Lord, the Lord will not be with you." 44 But they presumed to go up to the top of the mountain; nevertheless, the Ark of the Covenant of the Lord and Moses, did not depart from the camp. 45 Then the Amalekite and the Canaanite, who dwelt in that hill-country, came down, and smote them and beat them down, to Hormah.

Bamidbar 15:1 And the Lord spoke to Moses, saying: 2 "Speak to the children of Israel, and say to them: 'When you come into the land you are to inhabit, which I give to you, 3 and will make an offering by fire to the Lord, a burnt-offering, or a sacrifice to fulfill a vow clearly uttered, or as a freewill-offering, or in your appointed seasons, to make a sweet savor to the Lord, of the herd, or of the flock; 4 then shall he that brings his offering present to the Lord, a grain offering of one-tenth of an ephah of fine flour mingled with one-fourth of a hin of oil; 5 and wine for the drink-offering, one-fourth of a hin, shall you prepare with the burnt-offering or for the sacrifice, for each lamb. 6 Or for a ram, you shall prepare for a grain offering two-tenths of an ephah of fine flour mingled with one-third of a hin of oil; 7 and for the drink-offering you shall present one-third of a hin of wine, of a sweet savor to the Lord. 8 And when you prepare a bullock for a burnt-offering, or for a sacrifice, to fulfill a vow clearly uttered, or for peace-offerings to the Lord; 9 then shall there be presented with the bullock a grain offering of three-tenths of an ephah of fine flour mingled with half a hin of oil. 10 And you shall present for the drink-offering half a hin of wine, for an offering made by fire, of a sweet savor to the Lord. 11 So shall it be done for each bullock, or for each ram, or for each of the he-lambs, or of the kids. 12 According to the number that you may prepare, so shall you do for everyone according to their number. 13 All that are home-born shall do these things after this manner, in presenting an offering made by fire, of a sweet savor to the Lord. 14 And if a stranger dwells with you, or whoever may be among you, throughout your generations, and will offer an offering made by fire, of a sweet savor to the Lord; as you do, so he shall do. 15 As for the congregation, there shall be one statute both for you, and for the stranger that dwells with you, a statute for ever throughout your generations; as you are, so shall the stranger be before the Lord. 16 One law and one ordinance shall be both for you, and for the stranger that dwells with you.'" 17 And the Lord spoke to Moses, saying: 18 "Speak to the children of Israel, and say unto them: 'When you come into the land where I bring you, 19 then it shall be, that, when you eat of the bread of the land, you shall set apart a portion for a gift to the Lord. 20 Of the first of your dough you shall set apart a cake for a gift; as that which is set apart of the threshing-floor, so shall you set it apart. 21 Of the first of your dough you shall give to the Lord a portion for a gift throughout your generations. 22 And when you shall err, and not observe all these commandments, which the Lord has spoken to Moses, 23 even all that the Lord has commanded you by the hand of Moses, from the day that the Lord gave commandment, and onward throughout your generations; 24 then it shall be, if it be done in error by the congregation, it being hid from their eyes, that all the congregation shall offer one young bullock for a burnt-offering, for a sweet savor to the Lord—with the grain offering, and the drink-offering, according to the ordinance; and one he-goat for a sin-offering. 25 And the priest shall make atonement for all the congregation of the children of Israel, and they shall be forgiven; for it was an error, and they have brought their offering, an offering made by fire to the Lord, and their sin-offering before the Lord, for their error. 26 And all the congregation of the children of Israel shall be forgiven, and the stranger that dwells among them; for in respect of all the people it was done in error. 27 And if one person sin through error, then he shall offer a she-goat of the first year for a sin-offering. 28 And the priest shall make atonement for the soul that erred, when he sinned through error, before the Lord, to make atonement for him; and he shall be forgiven, 29 both he that is home-born among the children of Israel, and the stranger that dwells among them: you shall have one law for him who errs unintentionally. 30 But the soul that does anything with a high hand, whether he is home-born or a stranger, the one brings reproach on the Lord; and that soul shall be cut off from among his people. 31 Because he has despised the word of the Lord, and has broken His commandment; that soul shall utterly be cut off, his iniquity shall be upon him. 32 And while the children of Israel were in the wilderness, they found a man gathering sticks upon the Sabbath day. 33 And they that found him gathering sticks brought him to Moses and Aaron, and unto all the congregation. 34 And they put him under guard, because it had not been declared what should be done to him. 35 And the Lord said to Moses: "The man shall surely be put to death; all the congregation shall stone him with stones outside the camp." 36 And all the congregation brought him outside the camp, and stoned him with stones, and he died, as the Lord commanded Moses. 37 And the Lord spoke unto Moses, saying: 38 "Speak to

**the children of Israel, and bid them that they
make them throughout their generations
fringes in the corners of their garments, and
that they put with the fringe of each corner
a thread of blue. 39 And it shall be to you
for a fringe, that you may look upon it, and
remember all the commandments of the
Lord, and do them; and that you go not about
after your own heart and your own eyes, after
which you use to go astray; 40 that you may
remember and do all My Commandments,
and be holy to your God. 41 I am the Lord,
your God, who brought you out of the land
of Egypt, to be your God: I am the Lord,
your God."**

Airborne Disease and the Destruction of the Temple

In the Bible, the reference to the wilderness or the desert is the place
of Satan. As we learn from the Zohar, not only are we familiar in
Kabbalah with the idea of airborne diseases, we are going to find
who the carriers of these diseases are. The portion of Shlach Lecha
indicates to us that there is another tool, and we are fortunate to
be studying it here, for without interpretation, this portion makes
no sense. This story becomes illogical from the moment when God
told the Israelites that this was their land, yet they do not trust God,
so they send spies. The Zohar clarifies for us that that these spies
were the chieftains of their tribes, righteous people who looked at
the land and saw that it was everything God had said. Only in the
Zohar do we find that these chieftains question whether they will
still be heads of the tribes once in the Promised Land.

The Book of Bamidbar is probably one of the most interesting books of the Seven Books of Moses. This story about how the spies came back and said ugly things about the land of Israel and how the entire congregation wept upon hearing the report shows us something about our own consciousness. Consciousness is all that we possess and yet it is so weak, and we are so reactive. If today is bad, our whole life looks bad, this is human nature. The Zohar says this day was Tisha B'Av, the day that belongs to Satan. The result of his control of that day brought about what we read of in this section. Because the Israelites spoke evil, the Temple was destroyed 1,400 years later, and this was also the seed level of the Holocaust. God here refers to the Israelites as *nazi*.

Furthermore, this moment is where the idea of disease spreading from evil speech emerges from. Those who perpetuate evil speech bring airborne diseases into the hospital and into our homes. We need to quarantine all those who speak evil. Its effects can span centuries, they can emerge 1,400 years later. We most certainly have something here that is applicable contemporaneously, as the environment is becoming more and more hostile each and every day. Attending the Kabbalah Centre War Rooms is the only protection I know from the toxicity of our environment. Just two of the chieftains, a small voice to be sure, said that the land is good. These days, newspapers only print bad news, good news does not make the headlines.

One could go through this portion every year for a lifetime and not discover that the word *nazi* appears in this portion. This is the definition, given by God, of the *erev rav* who were those people who uttered evil speech. God wanted to get rid of all of them and start again with Moses. Moses received from God a cure for all airborne disease. Today, we receive the prayer that is the most powerful connection against all forms of negativity, the Thirteen Attributes of God, which is sung three times a year. This prayer eliminates all of the diseases created by evil tongues. It concentrates the power of the immune system and that is the way it eliminates disease. Unfortunately, most of us do not see the connection to evil speech. If the effect is felt the same day, we would see how lethal it is but it is only after many years, perhaps, that we are afflicted. Such afflictions are the result of evil speech we may have practiced years earlier. The universe is not random, for every action there is an equal and opposite reaction.

With this reading, we can banish all airborne diseases and afflictions. It gives the body a chance to regenerate, and we can convert our negative activity into something positive. This entire section revolves around what the chieftains reported. Did their negative report help anyone? It did not help the perpetrators. Because of their evil tongue, they perished in a plague. This is the crux of the section.

There is much more in the Bible that tells us about human nature. We are born with the DNA of a negative inclination, as it says in Beresheet 8:21: "…the heart of man is evil from youth." This is intended to cleanse us, it is all part of our purification because too often our consciousness degenerates, yet we can also use our consciousness to regenerate. Doctors want to suppress the immune system when what we need to do is strengthen it.

The Source of Human Suffering

Shlach Lecha is the portion we do not like to talk about. This section contains the beginning of the destruction and downfall of the Israelites then and all of humanity to this day. It is the source of all human suffering throughout the ages. The Israelites were only three days away from perfect peace, from entering into the land of Israel and eradicating chaos once and for all. Moses had to know what the consciousness of the Israelites was, whether they were ready to enter the Promised Land or not. God said sending the chieftains to find if there were trees was intended as a way for Moses to discover what their consciousness was when they arrived in Israel. The real question was whether or not the Tree of Life was there. Caleb and Joshua were the only ones to return with good comments, as they were coming from the level of consciousness of the Tree of Life. The other ten came back with a consciousness of the Tree of the Knowledge of Good and Evil, they said that the land was good but that there were giants.

This caused the decree that the Israelites were not going to enter Israel, since they were in the consciousness of the Tree of Knowledge and did not want to give up their materialism. This is why people become stuck in the Tree of Knowledge Reality. The universe is filled with so much chaos that even the good people among the Israelites joined in with the worries of those ten people. Why did they look for chaos, something that was evil, why did they agree with the ten and not the other two? Why did the Israelites become caught up with the evil people? Rav Shimon said that if you are raised in an evil community or family, you get caught up in it. Once the Angel of Death is given permission to strike, he does not know how to make a distinction.

Next, the Israelites looked for who to blame for not being able to enter Israel. They blamed Joshua and Caleb saying that had they not had this good report the whole thing would not have started, when all they did was tell the truth about the Tree of Life. And as we know, when we are connected to the Tree of Life we can remove chaos.

This is the most terrible portion of the year in terms of the ugliness of the evil *erev rav*. We have the big *Yud*, the smallest aspect of materialism, and because it is so powerful it has been expanded to give us an extra boost of energy so that we will not always try to find whose fault it is but take responsibility for our own actions. This is the true Israelite, someone who is accountable. The Zohar says a goy is someone who worships materialism and not someone who is not Jewish. The *Yud* will take us out of the mindset that blames instead of taking responsibility.

Conclusion

Why do we do the *Petachat Eliyahu* connection every day? It is to open ourselves to others. An opening in our heart means that when we see in someone else something that we do not have, something that we desire, our open heart can help us to receive that which we need. In the prayer *Yehi ratzon* it says "save me from *chaver ra* (an evil friend)." The concept of an evil friend seems contradictory. How can someone be a friend and also be evil? Think of the twelve spies, were they evil people? No, they were spiritually elevated, righteous people. What happened? The Zohar explains that they became closed to others when they began thinking about their own positions and not the greater good. From this we learn the importance of being open-hearted even when a crisis is reached. There will always be someone who has something we do not have, and encountering this is our opportunity to open ourselves to others and not become envious, not become a *chaver ra*. We cannot be a friend only on the surface. Open-heartedness allows us to empathize with others, as well as to be content with what we have and be happy for what others have.

In the portion of Shlach Lecha, why does God tell Moses to send spies to the land of Israel, why put a stumbling block in front of a blind person? The Zohar explains that in this way, Moses would know if that person would be the right leader. He had to test the consciousness of the spies, who were the leaders of the twelve tribes.

Moses needed to see if they would come back with a report of the Tree of Life, if they would be open-hearted to those who have something they did not. This is what puts us to the test and is really what constitutes a true friend.

The Zohar explains that although the spies were *tzadikim* (righteous souls) and friends, they still feared that if they entered the land of Israel they would lose their position as leaders, they did not think further than that. They did not think that entering the land of Israel would mean *Mashiach* (Messiah) and they would not need a job in such a case. When the spies returned, ten of the leaders said that the land was good *but* they could not fight the indigenous people because they were giants. Two of the chieftains, Caleb and Joshua, disagreed and emphasized that God was with them and thus they could do anything, and for this the Israelites wanted to kill them. If someone has a different opinion should they die? Why did the community side with the ten negative spies? Why did they not connect to the miracles that they had already experienced?

We need to open our hearts and not be an evil friend. The Zohar explains that only with an open heart can we really love someone. We need to work on this idea because we are deep asleep and we do not have open hearts. The problem of the ten spies and the children of Israel was that they did not have open hearts, which is why God said to Moses, "Let us get rid of them." If we have an open heart we can get rid of any form of chaos, we can even eliminate Satan.

BOOK OF BAMIDBAR:

Portion of Korach

PORTION OF KORACH

Bamidbar 16:1 Now Korach, the son of Izhar, the son of Kohath, the son of Levi, with Dathan and Abiram, the sons of Eliab, and On, the son of Peleth, sons of Reuben, took men;

The Nature of Korach

The Revelation of the Bible on Mount Sinai took place before the Korach incident. That being said, what choice did Korach have? Was this event predestined? If the Torah Scroll was presented in its entirety on Mount Sinai in the form of revelation, was he then merely acting out his role to rebel and to create a dispute?

The Zohar questions the actions of Moses himself. The Bible says Moses wrote about his own death, which is the death of the illusory level. Nevertheless, the Bible is not religion because if it were, then all has been predestined and we are merely participating as automatically as robots do, nothing more. Korach was merely following his own destiny. The fact that he was so consumed by the Desire to Receive for Oneself Alone was already predestined. Thus, we see that here we have the old conflict of faith versus free will.

The Zohar says that it was Moses who wrote the entire Torah and brought it to the nations of the world. The Ten Utterances included everything. The Torah Scroll is just a more elaborate form, but all of it is included within the Ten Utterances. How could Moses possibly write about his own death before it happened?

As we learn about in the Study of the Ten Luminous Emanations, when one plans to travel from New York to Los Angeles in a week's time, thinking about taking a stroll on the beach (and there is nothing that prevents that trip from taking place), the footprints on the beach that one thinks about today are already established. This is according to modern physics. The event is already a foregone conclusion. The footprints are there, made by the person who thought about it and who will physically walk over that footprint a week later.

The Zohar, explaining the first verse, says:

> "And Korach...took" (Bamidbar 16:1). HE ASKS: "What is the meaning of 'took'?" HE RESPONDS: "He took faulty counsel for himself. If one chases after something that does not belong to him, it escapes from him and he even loses what he has. Korach chased after something that was not his. Therefore, he lost what was his and no one else gained. Korach turned to disagreement. What is the meaning of disagreement? Distancing and repulsion; the distancing and repulsion of what is Above and Below; and whoever wishes to postpone the restoration of the universe will become lost from all the worlds. Conflict is a distancing of peace, and whoever is in conflict about peace is in disagreement with His Holy Name because His Holy Name is called 'Peace.' Come and behold: the world does not exist except through peace. When the Holy One, blessed be He, created the world, it could not endure until He came and made peace dwell upon them. What is it? It is the Shabbat, which is the peace of the Upper and the Lower grades. And then the world endured. THEREFORE, whoever creates dissension about this PEACE will be lost from the world."
> —Zohar, Korach 1:3-6

This portion begins with, "And Korach ... took men," which is a corrupt translation. In Bamidbar 16:1, in the Hebrew scripture, there is no use of the word "men." The Bible says: *Vaykach Korach ben Yetzar, ben Kahad, ben Levi,* which means "And Korach took, Korach son of Yetzar, son of Kahad, son of Levi." There is no more to the verse. Therefore, whom did he take? Translators say that he must have taken men because he took men later. But this is not what the biblical verse says. Because of this translation, which does not include the word "men," the Zohar raises the question, "What does it mean, 'Korach took…'? What did he take?" The Zohar answers that he took evil advice. Anyone who is chasing after that which is not his finds that what he hunts flees from him—even that which he is entitled to. There is an old saying of the Talmud and the Zohar: "If you run after honor, honor runs away from you, and if you run away from honor, then honor runs after you."

Korach ran after that which was not destined to be his. What was the evil advice he took? From the literal description in the Bible, he was raising a rightful objection, one that we have raised before. Why were all these particular honors given to one family? Yet the Zohar says that this is not what Korach took for himself because his internal inclination was to seek out dispute. He took what he sought. He was a man destined to thrive on dispute. That which could benefit humankind was something he, like the Egyptians, sought to remove from this world. What, exactly was he seeking to remove? Korach did not want the one unified whole, called *Shalom* (peace), whereby two completely different people can peacefully coexist despite the fact they may not necessarily share the same preferences or values. How is it possible for two opposites to be part of the same whole? Take the analogy of a lightbulb, which contains two opposite elements that somehow manage to create light. The fact that a lightbulb consists of opposites is in no way a reflection of separation or *machloket*, which means "dispute" and comes from the root word *lachlok* (to separate).

Rav Shimon says there are those who dispute peace and create separation on His Holy Name, because His Holy Name is called Peace (*Shalom*). From a kabbalistic point of view, God has many Names and each Name represents another form and channel of His energy. In other words, there are higher and lower intensities of energy. For instance, the Tetragrammaton—*Yud, Hei, Vav,* and *Hei*—represents a channel for dispensing higher forms of energy. The Name *Alef, Daled, Nun,* and *Yud* is a lower form, *Elohim* is another form and *El* is another. There are many Names that represent different levels of energy-intelligence but they all embody *Shalom*, all are unified.

The fact that we are not completely alike, that we do not necessarily agree with everyone else, and do not have the same level of intelligence, should not be a reason for disagreement, according to the Zohar. Cain brought the sacrificial flax because his internal characteristic was one of negativity—he was Left Column. When Abel brought the sacrifice of sheep, we know it is a channel of positivity since wool warms; it is Right Column energy. These two sacrifices are not in conflict.

The Zohar raises a question about Bet Shammai (House of Shammai) and Bet Hillel (House of Hillel), two scholars who represented two different schools of thought during the period of the Tannaim. These two schools had vigorous debates on matters of ritual practice, ethics, and theology. One school of thought said "yes," one said "no;" one said "forbidden," the other said "permitted," and both are correct. How could both be correct? The answer according to the Zohar is that each was coming from his own level of consciousness.

Bet Shammai stemmed from the aspect of Cain, from a negative aspect and therefore everything was prohibited, everything was negative as with the Left Column. This does not make it bad; it is simply the aspect with which he was connected. Bet Hillel was more compassionate, more permissive because, according to the Zohar, he came from the aspect of positivity, Right Column. Each was sourced in a different aspect.

Korach sought division. He wanted an operating system where plus and minus did not work together. He wanted only one pole, only one understanding, to exist. He wanted a spiritual structure where two cannot both be right. This is *machloket* (conflict; division). And Satan enters where there is *machloket*, where there is not a condition of one unified whole; where two people with opposite opinions cannot live alongside each other. Why is this a problem? Because they are not presenting the unified whole, which is this cosmos. The atom operates on the basis of a unified whole.

Thus Korach did not take people, he took himself. And anyone that agreed with him was right. Whoever disagreed with him was wrong. The Zohar says it was not a dispute for the purpose of creating harmony. He could have rightfully raised the same question but his intent was dispute, not to create a unified whole. He was saying "one side" as if to say there is only one opinion. Many people today consider what they believe to be the correct opinion and that there is no other opinion. God has different Names because there are different aspects to the same unified whole. Therefore the Zohar concludes that the world exists only on a foundation of peace.

This is important to repeat: If two people are in a disagreement because both want to be right, then they are both wrong. If they initiated a dispute of differences, it draws them apart and has not brought in the Name of God but instead has brought in the force of Satan. Satan's internal energy-intelligence is one that does not reflect the vision of peace—it is opposed to a unified whole and creates division.

This is what Korach wanted. He wanted division. He wanted the energy force in this universe to not operate with plus and minus together, as it does in the lightbulb. He wanted there to be only one pole because, in his view, there should only be one understanding, only one person who is right. When two people with opposing views want to be right, this is what creates conflict. We immediately shut out each other's essence. Opposites have to be a part of one unified whole, and Korach did not want to recognize that. He wanted only one point of view to rule, which is the essence of Satan. Therefore, the Zohar says that as long as there is disharmony, there can never be perpetual peace in this world. Irrespective of what position anyone takes, if you take a position that yours is the correct position and someone else's position is incorrect, the world cannot exist in accord.

The divisions that we see in the form of war or holocaust are only the result of humankind's negative and inhumane actions. "If someone's mind is not focused on peace," says the Zohar, "then what follows is the Satan." However, the Satan is not the enemy, the Satan is the *result* of a short circuit. It is the same as the lightbulb. Where is the Satan in the lightbulb? When we see there is a short circuit in the bulb, what appears? A black spot. Black is indicative that there is no flow of energy, and that little black spot indicates that the lightbulb has burnt out—and this is Satan. He is the result of a short circuit in energy.

If the revelation of the Bible at Mount Sinai already had within it that Korach would behave this way, how do we reconcile predestination and free will? Did Korach have a choice? It says in the Bible that Adam sinned when he ate from the Tree of Knowledge. Was this predestined or did Adam have free will? According to the Zohar, the golden calf and all that is described in the Bible was established 2,000 years before the creation of the world. The Bible is the cosmic blueprint not only for Creation but also for the development of all entities, of all the manifestations we experience on a physical level. Everything was predestined. If this is the case, then are we are merely following the dictates of that which was established? Again, I ask, where is the free will?

Two Levels of Reality

There are two levels to reality, as we discussed earlier concerning the footprints. For those who have read the Star Connection, I discussed there the grandfather paradox. There is a problem with travelling back in time. If I go back in time and prevent the marriage of my grandfather to my grandmother, then of course my parents may not be born, and I would not be born. And if I am not born, then I cannot go back in time and prevent the marriage. The Zohar provides an answer to this perplexity.

The Zohar says that Moses was born with the same level of consciousness that he was connected to before birth as after birth. Moses was an unusual man. This means that in the case of Moses there were not two aspects of reality. There was one real reality: the reality of seeing everything as it is, as well as the illusionary reality. Here is an example to illustrate this: If I imagine putting up an 84-storey building. Is the building built already or not? It is built already. Everything that will ever enter that building has been predestined before. Therefore, what is happening on a physical level is what has already been concluded in my mind.

No one believes that the building goes up of its own accord. It has been predesigned and predestined. However, the building and my thoughts about that building are not the same. Now, we do not consider humans to be made up of only a physical nature— we are intelligent thinking beings. Meaning that for the most part, whatever we do is done with forethought before it becomes manifested, before it becomes physical reality. Therefore, there are two levels of consciousness: there is the physical reality, which has no free will; once the blueprint is established, once the architect has drawn up the plans, that is what the building is going to be with no changes unless we go back to the drawing board again and alter the plans. Yet the changes do not take place in a physical reality.

Therefore, what the Bible is telling us here concerning the nature of physical reality is that Moses never left the realm of the True Reality, he was never involved in the physical illusions as were Korach and all other people. Moses saw from the beginning to the end. For most people the beginning and the end are not always the same. We begin with a certain plan and then we go off on a tangent— which has little resemblance to the original idea. For example, an individual begins a particular type of business. By the time they get through the manifestation, the business has almost no connection with the original thought. Therefore, when discussing someone who is connected to the state of consciousness that Moses was born with, this was something he did not have to develop.

The Zohar says we have the potential to revert back and connect with the consciousness of Moses. Go right back and connect with that consciousness, which is above the physical reality. At this point there is no connection between the physical reality and the metaphysical reality, they are two separate and distinctive entities that have no relationship with each other. It is almost no different than thinking about putting up a physical building. Am I connected with the physical building as I visualize the building? Yet, is not the entire building there before I even put it up? In fact, it might even be a building more closely to my liking because after the building is put up, then I may think I should have done it this way or that way, at which point the physical reality does not even resemble what I really had in mind. This happens to all of us.

Thus when the Bible reveals for us the physical aspect, it is revealing the physical perspective that we all become ensnared by on the material reality level. However this does not mean we have to get caught up in the physical reality, we can live and exist on a level of consciousness where the mundane physical reality has no effect upon us. Mind over matter exists, we can shape the world to our wishes.

The Zohar raises the question, "How could Moses write about his death?" and then answers that it was because Moses put together all the potentialities—all the letters were there. It is as if all components for a building are present in advance—the cement, the plumbing, the electrical wiring. How it manifests is dependent on us, however. We could put cement or steel reinforcements in the wrong place or in the right place.

We get consumed by the physical reality, as did Korach, when he fell into the trap of the Satan. He fell into the trap of honor and lost sight of the big picture. Most of us somehow think the whole world could not exist without us, that our business cannot function without us, and yet we never stop to think that, after 120 years or so, none of us will be here. Does this mean the world comes to an end? No, of course not.

For the most part, everyone thinks without them everything will become chaos. But the world continues. The very fact that we believe the physical reality is totally dependent upon our existence is part of its illusory nature. This is what Korach was attempting to do, to push away the aspect of *Shalom*, where two opposite opinions are not in dispute and create one unified whole. Such are the illusory ways of the physical reality.

Therefore, when the Bible says, *Vayikach Korach*… "Korach took…" at that moment, Korach took the course of the physical Illusionary

Reality. He fell into the trap of the Satan—before this moment, the choice was his. This was not a question of the honorary position with which Aaron was bestowed but rather something that Aaron worked hard to achieve and make the connection to through the aspect of "chasing peace" (*rodef shalom*). Aaron desired to make peace among all the Israelites. This was his life's endeavor. He was not seeking the priesthood position, he was seeking to become connected to the attribute of Sharing (*Chesed*), which is the Lightforce of God. Therefore, he achieved this state of consciousness and was given the priesthood, and Korach said, "Who says the priesthood should go to Aaron? It should be mine." And this was Korach's mistake.

The Bible does not mean that Korach took all these people with him. The vocabulary, structure and the grammar do not support this idea that he decided to take people. Korach was a man who always sought out *machloket*, meaning "quarrel," "division" or "separation"—which is closer to the true meaning of the word. The Zohar says Korach attempted to expound the idea that this universe is fragmented.

If there is total and complete unity in the universe, this should apply to the individual as well because we are not separated from the universe, nor is the universe separate from us. But in our reality, the eye is fragmented because the eye cannot hear. The fact that we cannot see voices today or hear images is *not* because each part of the brain functions individually nor is it because the five senses do not have the ability to grasp different concepts. Every one of our senses is contained within the other—there is total unity.

Korach made every attempt to prevent the idea of unity from seeping into the world because he did not believe in a unified universe. The Zohar says, therefore, those who make an attempt to be *docher Tikkun ha'Olam* "to remove or push away the correction of this world" will be lost from the world. This is because the purpose of *Tikkun ha'Olam* is to correct this world that appears to be in a fragmented state.

Korach attempted to maintain the division—division of thought, division of consciousness, division of sections of the universe, division of people. After all, if Americans speak English, and the French speak French, and neither one has knowledge of the other's language, there must be division. But little do we know that the reality is when we hear someone speak a language we do not understand, it does not mean we cannot achieve an awareness of what that person is communicating. At one time, everyone knew what everyone else was saying; there was only one language— Hebrew. Why is the Zohar compelled to state that there was one language, and that this language was Hebrew? The Bible, in Beresheet 11:1, says that there was "one language" *safa echad* and things were "unified," in *achdut*. What comes first? The fact that there was a language and thus there was unification or were these two separate incidents? There was one language and there also happened to be a unification of all people on the Earth because there was only one language.

On what do we base this Grand Unified Theory when around the world, all we see is fragmentation? We see different nations, all separated. We see fragmentation within communities, within families, within the individual. Have you heard the expression: He is torn—meaning fragmented; there are two parts within him that do not seem to merge with each other. This is how the world appears. And then Einstein comes along and the world begins to seek out the idea of a Grand Unified Theory. Billions of dollars per year are spent on finding this element that creates unity.

The Zohar says the answer is simple, in Beresheet there was one language. However, the peace that existed then was not because there was one language; it was because that language was Hebrew. The Hebrew letters are not merely symbols that provide those living in Israel with a language, it is a language that unifies. One might ask, "But take a look at Israel today, why does the language not merge all of these disparate people into one?"

The Zohar says Korach spoke Hebrew, like the Israelites—but they did not believe the Hebrew language was a unifying force; they did not believe that humanity could bring the world together; they did not believe that fragmentation could be terminated. What they did believe was that fragmentation, which is limitation, must exist in the universe. Korach made an attempt to remove or push away the *Tikkun ha'Olam*, the Correction of the World. He did not want to permit the idea of unity to exist, the idea that we are all one, and at the same time separate individuals. There is no contradiction. We can all be different and yet be unified—each one serving a purpose. Like the body, all the parts are of one unified whole, yet each part, organ, limb is unique, serving a different purpose. It is the same as with the simple lightbulb. When a plus and a minus become a circuit of energy, each one complements the other. This world must have different aspects to achieve correction. Before light can appear in a room, one must flip a switch, which ignites a circuit in the lightbulb, unifying both the plus and the minus poles as one unified whole.

There is no room for discussion about whether or not the world is one unified whole. Quantum has confirmed that the world is one. This is the conclusion of science. Scientists implicitly believe in a quantum universe, that all is entwined, all is interconnected, all is interrelated. However, there is the question, if the world is one, what makes it one? We observe the world to be divided, full of fragmentation and limitation. If it were one, people should be able to hear the whole world at the same time, they should be able to see the entire world at the same time. And yet we can only see or hear as far as our immediate surroundings. This is a contradiction. To achieve mastery over our situation, we must have control over the physical world. But we cannot control physicality until we decide not to be like Korach, not to be a person who is determined that the metaphysical and the physical should not be one unified whole.

The existence of unseen forces has been validated by science and is no longer a point of discussion. The scientific understanding is that everyone and everything is connected. It only appears that we are not all one; that the table is not one with the chair, that they are interrelated. Although the table is here and the chair is over there, science deduces that there is no space, time or motion between them—space is an illusion. Without this comprehension, we cannot approach the idea of control. Everything of a physical nature is illusion.

In the image of a goblet below,

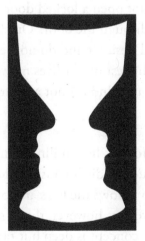

what do you see? Do you see a goblet or an image of two facing profiles? We can see both images but not at the same time. We toggle back and forth. Both exist and yet are not seen at the same time. Both are here, and yet are not here. An illusion is something that has no eternal stability. People are illusions because they come and go. Health is an illusion because it comes and goes. Something that is not illusory remains permanently, eternally.

In this world, things that comprise a physical reality are an illusion. There is nothing that is real except consciousness. Because we do not understand something, it does not necessarily mean we should reject it. The Zohar says the reality of existence is only what we think, what we believe or what we desire.

If someone desires a billion dollars to be put in front of them, would it happen? Yes, but they might not see it. The fact that we do not see it does not mean that it does not exist. Where is it? Firstly, we cannot receive something if we do not believe it can exist for us. We may say that we want a billion dollars to be placed on the table in front of us, and we will believe that part but do we have the consciousness of certainty required?

Do we believe we cannot open a locked door without the key? Do we believe we can go through the door? Our belief is temporary. It is not a question of I desire it and do not see it. We believe in it for this moment but the rest of our lives may be taken up with the illusory thought that our mind cannot accomplish what we would like it to.

If an individual, God forbid, has an illness, his mind, according to science should eliminate the disease just by declaring: "You (illness) do not exist." This also follows the laws and principles of the Zohar. The mind is our only reality, however, this is something difficult to grasp. Not because the concept is deep but rather because, when we look around us and see this physical reality as it is, how can we say it does not exist? Whether we comprehend or not, there are still many things we do not understand, yet we still continue on with them.

When one entrusts a physician with their life, and asks the question, "Are you sure that this procedure you recommend will cure me?" The common reply is, "No, I cannot guarantee it." Why is the doctor unsure? How can we entrust our lives to someone who is not sure? What do doctors mean when they say they are not one hundred percent sure? Is it because the statistic of the particular procedure is that one out of a million do not survive? Someone has to be the one out of a million. The consciousness that establishes this story as the only reality reveals the way our minds have decayed and until we come to this understanding, we have no control over the world.

According to science, humanity should have control over the physical world and the Zohar tell us that humankind's activity, humankind's actions, causes the disunity between two tectonic plates. Korach did not have the consciousness of unity of Upper and Lower, the metaphysical and the physical. Metaphysical is not a term that is distant from us. Thought-consciousness is metaphysical. Can you put your finger on it? No. Anything relating to that which we cannot package or encapsulate is metaphysical. The word metaphysical means it is above the physical reality. Korach did not believe we can unify. He did not believe that this physical reality and our minds are interrelated. He did not believe we can make anything physical react according to our consciousness.

The Zohar says the story of Korach is not about a man who rebelled, and then, subsequently, an earthquake manifested. Does the Bible merely want to reveal to us some old history that occurred in the wilderness? Of course not. The Zohar makes it clear that every word, every letter, is a force we should take advantage of. But we must first have certainty, we must believe in it because if our consciousness is not there, we are not there, and we cannot have control. We see the absence of control all around us, whether it involves wealth, health or happiness.

Says the Zohar, because Korach did not believe this world is unified and did not believe we can master physicality by virtue of the metaphysical, by virtue of the conscious mind, his consciousness was opposed to Peace (*Shalom*). Peace has eluded humankind since Cain and Abel; from that moment on, there was no more *Shalom*. They created a separation. They divided themselves. Rather than being one, a unified whole, two aspects of the same whole, they created a condition that was the opposite of *Shalom*. This was Korach's idea. *Shalom* does not mean an expression of peace, meaning no more wars, no more bloodshed. This is not true. No more war or no more bloodshed does not mean that there is peace. A person can have internal conflict without bloodshed, without the use of armed force. The notion of *Shalom* means that we come to a realization, and we create *Shalom*, not only within our own family, not only within our own environment, but we create *Shalom* also throughout the world. The power of unification, of unity, is when the unseen as well as the seen—both realities can be joined.

The Zohar says Korach divides (*cholek*) Peace. Peace is a phenomenon, it is an actual entity that is all around us. All we have to do is have a consciousness that it is present, then we will be amazed by how control suddenly appears in our very hands. However, humankind does not believe there is peace in the world. We do not believe there is peace within ourselves. The Zohar says the one who is *cholek* brings fragmentation and separation into *Shalom*, which means His Holy Name.

The Power of the Hebrew Language

Abraham the patriarch considered the letters of the Hebrew Alef-Bet to be so powerful because every letter of this alphabet created the universe. The world was created with the letter *Bet*, and every constellation, every planet, as well as the elements of fire, water, and air were all created by Hebrew letters. Now, if a letter can control so vast a universe, so vast a star as the sun, then these letters in our hands should be able to produce, if not the creation of universes—which is possible, according to the Zohar—then at least, the injection of a positive force into this universe of ours.

When I first entered the world of Kabbalah, I realized that when we recited the prayers in other languages instead of Hebrew, we were not able to achieve the intended connections. These translations took away the one advantage we all have—the Hebrew language. There is no other power at our disposal that can bring control to our lives the way these letters can. Therefore we have an Ana Beko'ach, which is also structured very specifically, and the *Shem HaKadosh*, which does not mean the Holy Name of God. As we have learned, the word *Kadosh* does not mean HOLY, it means WHOLY. These letters constitute unification, a wholeness. This is the secret of the Grand Unified Theory—*Shem HaKadosh*.

These letters are structured in such a way to indicate to us, a weapon, a tool, a force by which we can create unity. What does this do for us? In simple terms, we bring unity to the entire universe. Does this mean we can create unification between nations? And thus there is no necessity for bloodshed? Or does it also indicate that the ears can see, that every part of our body takes in everything that exists in the universe. This is the singular purpose of the reading of the Torah, and the reading of everything that is contained in this portion of Korach.

This portion is for the express purpose bestowed by God and the sages to give us tools by which we can prevent all of the disasters that are always occuring in our lives, like earthquakes. Maybe, God forbid, this week there was meant to be an earthquake. Certainly, with this reading, this week there will not be an earthquake. Why not? Because there are at least ten people who have the consciousness that the portion of Korach will stave off an earthquake. Unfortunately, this energy only remains for six days following the Shabbat this portion is read.

However, those who have this unifying consciousness will find their vision is improved, their hearing is improved. Meaning they will hear and see things that they did not hear and see the week prior.

We are not in a game of morality: do not steal; do not kill; do not do this or that. The whole world does not listen to these laws because the world is not ready. Even on Mount Sinai, the world was not ready to listen to the Utterances, commonly known as commandments. In fact, it is human nature that when we are told to do something, we will look for every avenue to do the opposite. Therefore, the Ten Utterances could not have come down to us as an idea of do or do not do. They are ten packets of energy placed in this world to be used by those who know how to remove fragmentation, how to remove the disunity.

If there is total unity among people who wish to steal or murder, they will succeed. The Zohar says the generation of the Tower of Babel were people completely unified in their evil objective and negativity because they had achieved unity through the Hebrew alphabet. Therefore, the only choice left to God was to create many languages, thereby disrupting the unity that existed only as a result of the power of the Hebrew Alef-Bet.

Thank God, there are tens of thousands of people today who although they do not know the Hebrew Alef-Bet, scan the whole prayer. It does not matter if they do not understand a word they are reading, the eye is just as effective as a bar code scanner in the department store. This one act of scanning the barcode of a product has many functions.

2 and they rose up in the face of Moses, with certain of the children of Israel, two hundred and fifty men; they were princes of the congregation, the elect men of the assembly, men of renown; 3 and they assembled themselves together against Moses and against Aaron, and said to them: "You take too much upon you, seeing all the congregation are holy, every one of them, and the Lord is among them; why then do you lift up yourselves above the assembly of the Lord?" 4 And when Moses heard it, he fell upon his face. 5 And he spoke to Korach and to all his company, saying: "In the morning the Lord will show who are His, and who is holy, and will cause him to come near to Him; even him whom He may choose will He cause to come near to Him. 6 This do: take you censors, Korach, and all his company; 7 and put fire therein, and put incense upon them before the Lord tomorrow; and it shall be that the man whom the Lord does choose, he shall be holy; you take too much upon you, you sons of Levi." 8 And Moses said to Korach: "Hear now, you sons of Levi: 9 is it but a small thing to you, that the God of Israel has separated you from the congregation of Israel, to bring you near to Himself, to do the service of the Tabernacle of the Lord, and to stand before the congregation to minister to them; 10 and that He has brought you near, and all your brethren, the sons of Levi with you? And will you seek the priesthood also? 11 Therefore you and all your company that are gathered

together against the Lord; and as to Aaron, what is he that you complain against him?" 12 And Moses sent to call Dathan and Abiram, the sons of Eliab; and they said: "We will not come up; 13 is it a small thing that you have brought us up out of a land flowing with milk and honey, to kill us in the wilderness, that you need to make yourself also a prince over us? 14 Moreover you have not brought us into a land flowing with milk and honey, nor given us inheritance of fields and vineyards; will you put out the eyes of these men? We will not come up." 15 And Moses was very angry, and said to the Lord: "Do not respect their offering; I have not taken one ass from them, neither have I hurt one of them." 16 And Moses said to Korach: "Be you and all your congregation before the Lord, you, and them, and Aaron, tomorrow; 17 and take you every man his fire-pan, and put incense upon them, and bring you before the Lord every man his fire-pan, two hundred and fifty fire-pans; you also, and Aaron, each his fire-pan." 18 And they took every man his fire-pan, and put fire in them, and laid incense thereon, and stood at the door of the Tent of Meeting with Moses and Aaron.

Power of Incense

At this point in the reading, we can concentrate on cleansing the negative forces from our homes, and from the mixed multitude (*erev rav*), and construct a protective energy shield around us against negativity. This is the power of the incense.

19 And Korach assembled all the congregation against them to the door of the
Tent of Meeting; and the glory of the Lord
appeared to all the congregation. 20 And the
Lord spoke to Moses and to Aaron, saying:
21 "Separate yourselves from among this
congregation, that I may consume them
in a moment." 22 And they fell upon their
faces, and said: "God, the God of the spirits
of all flesh, shall one man sin, and will You
be angry with all the congregation?" 23 And
the Lord spoke to Moses, saying: 24 "Speak
to the congregation, saying: 'Get you up from
about the dwelling of Korach, Dathan, and
Abiram.'" 25 And Moses rose up and went to
Dathan and Abiram; and the elders of Israel
followed him. 26 And he spoke to the congregation, saying: "Depart, I pray you, from the
tents of these wicked men, and touch nothing of theirs, lest you be swept away in all
their sins." 27 So they went away from the
dwelling of Korach, Dathan, and Abiram,
on every side; and Dathan and Abiram came
out, and stood at the door of their tents, with
their wives, and their sons, and their little
ones. 28 And Moses said: "Hereby you shall
know that the Lord has sent me to do all
these works, and that I have not done them
of mine own mind. 29 If these men die the
common death of all men, and be visited
after the visitation of all men, then the Lord
has not sent me. 30 But if the Lord make a
new thing, and the ground open her mouth,
and swallow them up, with all that belongs

to them, and they go down alive into the pit, then you shall understand that these men have despised the Lord." 31 And it came to pass, as he finished speaking all these words, that the ground did cleave asunder that was under them. 32 And the earth opened her mouth and swallowed them up, and their households, and all the men that were with Korach, and all their goods. 33 So they and all that belonged to them went down alive into the pit; and the earth closed upon them, and they perished from among the assembly. 34 And all Israel that were about them fled at the cry of them; for they said: "Lest the earth swallow us up." 35 And fire came forth from the Lord and devoured the two hundred and fifty men that offered the incense.

Unification

We have the secret that cannot be denied or concealed any longer. It is the power of the Zohar. By this one act of scanning the Hebrew Letters, we can accomplish unification within our own bodies, within ourselves, within our families, and within the whole world.

The cause of earthquakes is the beating of two tectonic plates against each other, and they do so because they are two fragmented halves. If brought into unity, then they can live side by side—which was the original intent of God when he created these seven plates, continents, in the first place. The reason there are seven is because this distinguishes the *tikkun* (spiritual correction) of people.

It is not easy to come to the consciousness of unity, which is why we need the Zohar for support. For example, when a bank manager calls a patron and says, "Look, you are overdrawn," is it easy to convince that individual to extend and increase the loan? Yes, when there is complete conscious awareness of our individual power, supported by a system then, if you are having difficulties in a business, it becomes a total illusion—like the diagram of the goblet and the two faces: you can see there are two images but you cannot bring them together at the same time. What does an illusion mean? You ought not to believe in it.

A stage magician can make the Statue of Liberty or a Boeing 747 disappear, and we all know it is an illusion but at the same time we did see them disappear. Even though the eye saw the disappearance of the Statue of Liberty, we call it an illusion. Why? Because we know that, somehow, there is no disappearance.

To use the example of a bank manager again. Imagine the bank manager calls and tells his patron, "You have no money in your account, you are overdrawn." Can that be changed by consciousness alone? Yes, there is no question we can do it. From the point of view of the Zohar, which, more importantly, science substantiates: there is nothing in this universe but consciousness. The scientists say: "Do not be governed by the physical reality you see about you because that physical reality is only governed by what you believe it to be." Let us believe them, and let us also believe the Zohar. I do not subscribe to the idea that God created a universe that was destined to remain fragmented. The Zohar says the world stands on *Shalom*. And we now know that *Shalom* not only means peace, it also means unification. To be a good place in which to live, the world must consist of *Shalom*.

Concerning the portion of Naso, the Zohar says Moses told Rav Shimon that in the Age of Aquarius, "Only your book, the book of

Zohar, will bring about the realization of *Mashiach* (Messiah), will bring about the realization of the Tree of Life in this world."

The Zohar says:

> "But the wise shall understand" (Daniel 12:10), since they are from the side of Binah, which is the Tree of Life. For them, it was said, "And they who are wise shall shine like the brightness of the firmament" (Daniel 12:3) with your composition, RAV SHIMON BAR YOCHAI, which is the book of the Zohar, from the Light of the Supernal Ima CALLED repentance. They do not require a test and because Israel in the future will taste from the Tree of Life, which is this book of the Zohar, they will leave the exile with Mercy. It will hold true about them that "And the Lord did alone did guide him, and there was no strange god at his side." (Devarim 32:12)
> —Zohar, Naso 5:90

The Tree of Life is the consciousness of humankind. We do have this consciousness. The Zohar explains we have two bodies, we have consciousness, which is called the Tree of Life, and then we have our physical body, the eyes, which can theoretically only see, and the nose that can only smell. Expand the physical eye and see beneath that which you cannot see. Maybe you can only hear a heartbeat. Can you see a heartbeat inside the human body? Yes, we can see it on the screen but we cannot see the heartbeat itself without the assistance of technology. In the same way we can observe it on a screen, we should be able to see the heartbeat with the naked eye. As we hear the heartbeat with a stethoscope, we should be able to see it. A physician who is fragmented can sometimes come to an incorrect diagnosis because all his faculties do not operate as a unified whole. The mind thinks one thing, the ear hears another, and the eye sees still another—but the world was not originally established this way.

We have a code name for this, and it is a beautiful name, the Tree of Life. What does the Tree of Life mean? It means that this Zohar, the letters, the ideas are absolutely correct. At the same time let us understand the nature of a person like Korach, who did not believe in the essential unification of this universe, who saw everything as fragmented, who saw every human being as separated from the others. This is what the Bible tells us. When you begin to delve into each word it becomes beautiful, it is not merely a chronicle of history.

Korach's consciousness was trained to see this world as a place of fragmentation, a world where we cannot achieve our desire, and a place where one would not even dare ask for miracles. This is completely contrary to the Zoharic interpretation of what a miracle is. Take for example the Splitting of the Red Sea, most Bible readers of all religions understand the Splitting of the Red Sea to be a miracle, a phenomenon created by God—and by God alone. The Zohar says this is a total corruption, and not at all what the Bible says. We, meaning humankind, are the only ones who can create miracles, where does it say otherwise in the Bible?

In the portion of Beshalach, which contains the Splitting of the Red Sea, we find the Israelites with the Red Sea in front of them and the Egyptians behind them. Naturally, they begin yelling to God, and God says to Moses, "Why are they yelling to Me?" Well, who else should we pray to if we have problems? God's response was, "If they want to create the miracle of the Red Sea, they have to jump in." How does one jump into a sea that is probably 300 feet in depth? This is what Moses was told by God.

Everything in this physical universe is possible: from acquiring loans, to feeding oneself and one's family. The king of Morocco stood up to the Nazis, saying, "No, you will not take one Jew from this country." What brought about this miracle in Morocco? The Jewish community in Morocco were creating miracles each and every single day. They were tapping the energy of the Zohar that was there in that region.

This is the structure of the Grand Unified Theory. The Hebrew letters, each of which created the cosmos, provide us with the assistance and support to have control over the cosmos. We must study the Zohar because when we read the letters, the words— the further we delve into them, the stronger the connection, the stronger the channeling. At the very minimum, we have made connections to a Grand Unified Theory, which means there is no fragmentation, there is no limitation, there is no chaos, and there is no disorder. This is what this portion is about, nothing more and nothing less.

Swallowing up

There is another Zohar section that I would like to discuss. It is in the last few verses of the Bible portion of Bamidbar—a section to which very few pay attention. It discusses the tribe of Kohath, one of the three tribes of Levi and each one had a certain chore to fulfill concerning their service in the Tabernacle. In this verse it states what each should do. The Zohar discusses this section in the portion of Korach because Korach was also from the tribe of Levi and the interpretation is the same essential idea.

The Zohar tells us the following:

> Rav Elazar says: "This shall be the service of the sons of
> Kohath in the Tent of Meeting, the Holy of Holies."
> (Bamidbar 4:4) During the period of time when the sons
> of Kohath came to take the Holy of Holies, the priest
> approached and covered everything prior to their approach,
> and they never saw what they carried. Instead, everything
> was covered from them, as it says, "At the breaking of the
> camp, Aaron shall and his sons shall go in, and they shall
> take down the veil of the screen...." (Bamidbar 4:5) Most
> of the casings for the Temple's utensils were colored blue.
> The significance of blue was already explained and taught.
> After everything was covered, the children of Kohath, who
> carried it, came near. They did not get any closer than the
> poles that extended out, as it is written: "...and when Aaron
> and his sons have finished covering the sacred objects...as
> the breaking of the camp, then shall the sons of Kohath
> shall come to bear it...." (Bamidbar 4:15)
> —Zohar, Korach 6:26

Aaron was told they had to disassemble and assemble the Tabernacle
containing the Holy of Holies, the Ark that contained the Scroll,
the broken Tablets that Moses brought down from Mount Sinai—
only the Kohens (Priests) were permitted to touch it. The tribe of
Kohath was not allowed to see the Holy of Holies in its naked state,
when the Holiness would be "swallowed up; *nivla*" because they
could die.

But actually what is being discussed here is the duty of the Priest to
cover up the Ark, so it should not be seen because if the people saw
the physical configuration of the Scroll as it was being swallowed
up, they would die. The Hebrew word for "to cover" is *kisui* but
the word used in the Torah is *nivla*. The reason the Bible uses the

word *nivla* is because when the Priest spread a sheet around the Ark it was as if this sheet swallowed up the Ark. When we put food in our mouth, do we place a covering over the food? No. As soon as we close our mouth what happens? It is swallowed up. The food was not concealed, and therefore we could not see it, because even in concealment we can still imagine it. The idea of swallowing is that the item ceases to exist. When you cover something, it has not been swallowed up, it is actually right there in front of our eyes still but an illusion enters and we do not see it.

This discussion relates to Korach and the 250 men who were swallowed up by the earth. The reason the Zohar introduces the idea of having the right consciousness (and the Priest had the right consciousness) is because he not only could make things disappear, he could make it as though they did not exist.

In the case of cancer, if the cancer is covered up or cut out, does it mean it is no longer there? No. It has to be like *bila hamavet la netzach*, which means "death is swallowed up forever." This is what the Bible says took place on Mount Sinai. The revelation of Light not only removed death but swallowed it up.

Swallowing something means that it has no power to express itself. In the same way that a slave is no longer a free person, able to use their mind and body. Death was swallowed up, means it disintegrated from being a force. When one eats a piece of fruit, chews it and digests, it is no longer a piece of fruit. Death was not merely concealed, it was swallowed up.

It is the same idea with the power of the Priest (Kohen). Korach wanted this power for himself. In essence, he was saying, 'I'm a Levi, and Aaron is also a Levi. If he has the power to make physical matter disappear as though it does not exist, then why not me?' The Zohar says Korach saw things that were not part of him. He did not achieve the degree of consciousness that the Priest had—the consciousness of one who channels blessings or healing.

The Zohar continues:

> Therefore, burnt incense, which is inward, and all that is in secret, is given over to the Priest. Therefore, "Aaron took as Moses commanded, and ran into the midst of the congregation...and he put on incense and made atonement for the people." (Bamidbar 17:12) because it is of the innermost, the secret of the priest WHO IS ALSO WITHIN. "And he stood between the dead and the living..." (Bamidbar 12:13) that is, between the Tree of Life and the Tree of Death. Then the Right causes one to approach the other, MEANING THE TREE OF LIFE, THAT IS RIGHT, COMES CLOSE TO THE PRIEST, WHO IS RIGHT, "...and the plague was stayed." (Ibid.) Praised is the priest's lot, since the priest has power Above and power Below, and he is the cause of peace Above and Below. And at all times, the Left serves the Right, of which it is said: "...that they may be joined to you, and minister to you..." (Bamidbar18:2); and the Right THAT IS INCLUDED in the Left is prevalent in the Temple.
> —Zohar, Korach 6:27

The Priest was a pure channel, he was Wholy (*Kadosh*), he was complete—meaning the two bodies within his being did not interact with each other as separate entities but rather as one body. The Tree of Life completely swallowed up the negativity that existed in the other aspect. Korach wanted this power of swallowing up but he recognized only fragmentation in the universe. He did not believe in the idea of unity. Therefore, says the Zohar, he wanted that which did not belong to him. He wanted the High Priesthood.

As was mentioned previously, Aaron, who was a Levi, became the High Priest because the significant characteristic of Aaron was that he always made attempts to bring peace, whether it was in a family quarrel or between a man and a wife, friends, and so on.

We need the support the Zohar brings so that we can come to the realization that all is one—the world is not separated. If we need money now and it is not in our grasp, we still know if it is in the bank, it is ours, and so we smile. Could this be true? The answer is yes. The only reason we do not believe it is true is because of the consciousness of Satan that is the 1 Percent. This 1 Percent body is destined to inflict all the pain that we suffer. Our suffering is caused by this one entity in us that was not swallowed up; which did not become part of the Tree of Life. The reason seemingly far-fetched things are not within our grasp is because we have already established in our minds there is no hope; that there is no way we can save the situation. It is because we, not God, decided this.

Nanotechnology

This portion is named after Korach, revealing to us that this individual represents something significant. But anyone who knows the story might ask the question: "Why would we want to name a section in commemoration of someone like Korach? Usually we reserve this honor for someone great." Another question we could raise is: "Of what significance is this incident? What meaning does it have for us today?" By answering the second question, we can answer the first one: the revelation of nanotechnology is right here in this section.

For many of us, religion is something very much part of our lives. Few people can truly give up religion. We have an attachment to it, after all, it is something that has been around for 3,400 years. It is not so easy to give up. Even considering that religion and science are converging is difficult to accept.

The first word of this portion gives us one of the most critical components in the success of nanotechnology. We have the application of nanotechnology right here. Science says it will not be ready for fifty years, yet for those of us who do not want to wait, it is our right to choose and accept many of the ideas that have been presented by Rav Ashlag over the past 82 years. Although they may seem outlandish, it seems that everyone who comes to the Kabbalah Centres finds there is something to these futuristic concepts we speak about.

The first word of this portion indicates that we can restore and restructure physicality, which is what nanotechnology is about. Science tells us everything that exists on the physical level will no longer be in the shape that it appears in today. According to science, everything is going to change. Nanotechnology lets us be anything we want, and its advantages bear the stamp of simplicity. In science currently, the more complex, the greater the reason for a Nobel Prize.

The reason kabbalistic nanotechnology is for the layperson is because it does not seek to pursue a scientific endeavor. In today's model of science there is no one who can help you grow a new heart, a new lung or tooth, which presents itself as a choice for the individual to deal with. The individual is the only solution.

Teachers can aid us but nanotechnology demonstrates it is only the individual who can make it effective. Scientists do not even begin to think in these terms, and because they prefer to stay within the narrow constraints of the physical world, they will be totally unsuccessful.

There is one prerequisite: nanotechnology is dependent on the consciousness of the individual. Fifty years from now, with nanotechnology, we will understand there is no reason why we cannot remove a tumor without surgery, which has never so far been an alternative. In the absence of anything else, we use a primitive form of medicine. However deploying the framework of nanotechnology depends upon the consciousness of the individual. This will not be the first time the lessons of Kabbalah have sounded improbable, if not impossible.

The first word of this portion tells us that if we possess any shred of jealousy, if we wish others harm or treat others with anything less that human dignity, nanotechnology will not work for us. This physical aspect of moving atoms from one place to another is like the Star Trek maxim: "Beam me up Scotty!" Captain Kirk may be able to travel a trillion miles away, and we say that is science fiction, which is entertaining but not practical. What about real life? Science tells us that such things are absolutely possible. We can understand this as the body consists of 99 percent atoms, so we can teleport 99 percent of a body to another place, to another part of the universe. Then we have to figure out what to do with the one percent—if the physical body is compressed, it becomes one percent of its original size. Science is beginning to think as kabbalists do. Kabbalists have been talking about eliminating time, space and motion for years.

Everything that comes in the way of chaos is represented by time, space, and motion. What grows in a tumor is space. All of this plays a vital role in whether or not we can restructure our society. It depends upon the degree to which our consciousness has been developed. Without this we cannot reach the ultimate achievement of removing hatred, jealousy, and envy—the idea known to Kabbalah for four thousand years: we are all part of God.

We are told that God is up there, and we believe it. Nevertheless, when disaster strikes, belief evaporates. The way we become God is to say we have it all. What does God lack? He lacks nothing. Knowing this, concepts like jealousy, morality, and ethics disappear. The reason to not steal is not and has never been because it is morally wrong; it is because stealing removes us from our destiny to have control in this physical world. Why should we be jealous, envious or hateful when we have it all? This is what needs to be in our consciousness. Jealousy is an illusion. What we do not see today, we can have tomorrow. These are the ground rules for achieving what we have all been dreaming of, what civilization has been envisaging since the fall of Adam.

The first word, *Vayikach*, which means "And [Korach] took," tells us that Korach wanted what did not belong to him. His consciousness was *vayikach*—he wanted to be a taker. Is God a taker? No, God has no lack, God is totally fulfilled. There is nothing for God to take; God has everything. Energy moves outwards. Energy wants to move, to initiate.

The body needs energy always available, it does not have it within itself. This is Rav Ashlag's great revelation: everything has the atom within it, the neutron, proton, and electron. And within each atom is consciousness. This is why electronics have a problem and why we hear about free radicals. Within free radicals there is a Desire to Receive for the Self Alone, which needs to be converted to a Desire to Receive for the Sake of Sharing. This is the way we can become like God. Without having this consciousness, we cannot achieve all of our aspirations.

This has nothing to do with ethics. The purpose of existence is to gain fulfillment. A void, a vast lack is the chaotic nature of the human being. Thus we have the story of Korach, who wanted something that was not his. It was not an elected office he was

seeking to take away from Moses. Why was Aaron chosen for
the Priesthood? Aaron shared, he was selfless, and in this way the
position was appropriate for him. Korach, on the other hand, was
filled with Receiving for the Self Alone, which is a force in direct
opposition of the nature and function of High Priest.

Another amazing idea presented in Kabbalah long ago, and now
again today, is that we can control earthquakes. Earthquakes and
other natural disasters are often described as acts of God, but the
Zohar says, "No." Korach and the 250 people with him who were
of the same consciousness, were swallowed up by an earthquake
that took place within inches of where Moses and the others stood.
From this we understand the nature of earthquakes.

Nanotechnology helps us to understand what earthquakes are.
Atoms. And this portion tells us how nanotechnology works, which
is for the most part through sharing, not thinking of oneself. You
may ask: *But if I don't think of myself, who is going to think of me?*
There are many who still live by that credo. Yet the way to have the
fulfillment we desire is to think of others before ourselves. What
significance can we draw from this lesson? It is telling us about
the methodology one must have in their consciousness to achieve
the removal of all chaos. There is only one way, and kabbalah
demonstrates it. To remove a cancerous tumor one must go deep
into the very nature of the atom—to the source. We have Abraham
the patriarch, who tells us where we have to go to make things
disappear. Nanotechnology confirms we can make physical things
disappear. It is possible.

However, a tumor will reappear unless it disappears for good. We
know this is true because Korach was like a cancer to the nation
of Israel. He was an example of the Desire to Receive for the Self
Alone. He held everything back from moving ahead. As a result,
he was swallowed up without a trace—as if he had never existed.

The same is true for all forms of chaos. The way to remove cancer or any chaos is to make it permanently disappear. Each of us has to become a Houdini.

The scourge of this country is cancer. How does one overcome the enemy from within? According to Kabbalah, and to this portion, the way cancer can disappear is through nanotechnology. We have to take that first step at the nano level, which requires a high degree of consciousness. We have the nano robots—the Hebrew letters and the 72 Names of God as our tools. For example, in the afternoon prayers we say *Ve ani tefilati et ratson…* which creates for us a nanotechnology of unity. With this prayer we are transforming the essence of every afternoon from a state of judgment to a state of positivity. This is a prime example of nanotechnology in action. We move forward from one Shabbat to the following Friday, bringing it to the present moment in time. We are in essence closing the gap, the space between now and the coming week, until the next Shabbat. What happens when we close the space? We put an end to time. No time, no space. No space, no chaos.

We are here to change. What happens in the afternoon? The sun begins to set because negativity is awakened. The sun goes away to make room for the moon to take over. With this prayer, we convert that—we are converting the power of the sun and the moon. There is always an unseen force behind everything. Nothing is ever the way we see it.

For example, look at your hand. It cannot move without a force telling it to move. Nor can the Earth move without the force of the sun telling it to move. We are converting that force of negativity, which is attempting to inject itself, bringing instead the moon to be in control, and in doing so, we maintain the positive energy of the Shabbat. This is deeper than nanotechnology—this is dealing with transforming consciousness.

Einstein had an idea about closing the gap of time and space but he did not have access to nanotechnology. The kabbalists understood this many, many years ago, and Rav Ashlag has brought us the understanding found in his works titled: Study of the Ten Luminous Emanations.

For 2,500 years, the Zohar has understood nanotechnology. Heart attacks are not a result of what was originally thought—cholesterol. Do we even know how many billions of dollars were spent on research? Is there anyone with a heart condition and not on Lipitor? This is the biggest seller for Pfizer. Is Lipitor really helping? Why do I ask that? Because now medical science is telling us that heart attacks are caused by inflammation. Other conditions, such as rheumatoid arthritis, are also caused by inflammation. Inflammation is expansion, adding space. Every disease is ultimately caused by inflammation or space. With nanotechnology we are eliminating that space. Science is looking for robots, vehicles that can transfer energy from one place to another. The Hebrew letters are our robots. With the power of the mind we can do anything.

Controlling Natural Disasters

It is strange that Korach should have been so antagonistic, so ungrateful for all he had received. He was the wealthiest Israelite. What did he want? Was he envious of Moses? Was this portion named after him to give him honor? Three thousand years later, we still refer to Korach—he is not forgotten. Although he became the wealthiest of all the Israelites, for whatever reason, Korach did not receive notoriety. What did Korach desire? Why was he disruptive? Why did he bring about this rebellion? As if the Israelites did not have enough problems, along came Korach.

According to the kabbalists, Moses knew exactly where the fault line was. Today, we cannot even determine exactly where a fault line might be. The Zohar says that from this portion we learn how to control natural disasters—the power rests with the people, if they have the right technology.

The Zohar is clear on how Korach and his entire congregation of 250 people were swallowed up by an earthquake. They were swallowed up so completely that where the earthquake took place was imperceptible. One would think knowing an earthquake was an absolute possibility, Korach would have remained quiet. Why create a disruption especially when there were so many people outside of the nation of Israel determined to put stumbling blocks all along the path of the Israelites? If Korach was not so foolish, he would have left it to others. He would not have become the kind of person people might look upon and say: "With all the money he had, and with all the glory he had, he still was not satisfied. He had fame, fortune, family. What more was he looking for?" What was the one thing that bothered him?

Obviously, something did bother him otherwise he would not have gone to such extremes as to oppose Moses, who was his first cousin. Yet as we have come to learn family does not necessarily mean there is a good relationship, in fact, in families we can sometimes find the reverse. Moses tried his best to avoid confrontation with his cousin. The Zohar goes on to explain, in a very lengthy discourse, what troubled Korach and why he was not correct in his actions.

Being the wealthiest man, certainly amongst the Israelites, or even taking it one step further, the wealthiest person in the whole world, Korach lost sight of how he arrived at his stature. What made him the wealthiest person amongst the Israelites? What the Bible wants to teach us is that, while amassing wealth is an admirable feat, there is a price to being provided with all the material things that exist in this world, and that price could be getting carried away in believing that we must be someone special to have acquired such fame, such wealth, such glory.

The Bible wants to teach us that we can fall. There are no guarantees. The fact that you are the wealthiest person in the world does not mean that ego does not take over. Ego does not die with the acquisition of wealth—as we have learned here.

Although, from his statement, it might appear that Korach was envious of his cousin, Moses. He was not. The Zohar believes otherwise. He was still a man. He was part of the community but he was missing something, and he thought this something was leadership of the tribe of the Levites.

What the Bible and the Zohar want to teach us is that with the acquisition of wealth comes responsibility. According to the Zohar, there are grave dangers that come with wealth. What we learn in Kabbalah is that you have to share, you have to recognize your community and help others wherever you can. Korach did not get that message.

Swallowed Up By the Earth

Korach came to Moses, and to paraphrase, said: "Your sister is the leader of the women, and also a prophetess. Your brother is High Priest, and you are the spiritual leader. I want to be the High Priest! Who said your family deserve to be the leaders?" Then the earth opened its mouth and swallowed them up. Why is the word "swallow" used?

There is another place we know of where the word "swallow" is used, which is at Mount Sinai, where it was said: "Death will be swallowed up for all time." Mount Sinai was the only instance when the Israelites had control for forty days and nullified Satan. Korach caused form to be equated with the earth, that is, the Desire to Receive for Oneself Alone, which is why he was returned to the earth.

Korach's uprising was for his own sake, so that he could receive honor. He wanted to be a Priest because he wanted to have influence but since his wish derived only from his Desire to Receive for Himself, the earth swallowed him up. This is why there are things in the world that can overcome the power of the earth, like the tree and the spring.

We listen to the reading of the Torah on Shabbat not to fulfill some sort of religious obligation but because these weekly readings empower us to control chaos. This is why the portion of Korach mostly occurs during the month of Tammuz, the astrological month of Cancer, when it is possible to control doubt, disease, relationships infiltrated by chaos, and confusion. The word cancer in Hebrew is *sartan* סרטן, and when you separate the syllables into *sar tan* סר טן it means "averting confusion and chaos."

This portion describes how the earth opened up, and that an earthquake was right next to Moses. On one parcel of the land there was no earthquake, and right next to it there was an earthquake. Furthermore, the houses of those who brought the incense were destroyed, while the house of someone right next door, who did not offer incense, remained intact; the earthquake took place only at a specific site. When one purchases an insurance policy, acts of God are not covered. However, there is no such thing as an act of God—and, furthermore, many of God's actions are hidden. Also in finances, not everyone has a hard time in a downturn of the economy. Some people are making money. Everything that happened was due to negative behavior.

It is written, "The earth opened its mouth and swallowed them and their houses," and this is followed by, "and a fire broke out from God and consumed the two hundred and fifty men who had offered incense." It would seem that these events should have happened in the opposite order, first there should have been a fire, and then the earth should have opened its mouth. The reason for this sequence of events is to teach us that the root of the negativity occurred the moment these people opened their mouths. On this physical plane, we never see the cause. The consciousness of the 250 people who sided with Korach was negative and the moment they opened their mouths, the earth opened its mouth in response.

Korach was very rich but he wanted honor, and therefore he lost everything. A person should always pray the prayer of a poor man because we are all poor. Even if we have everything, it can all disappear in one moment. There are tools for getting rid of chaos right here in this portion.

There are 95 verses in the portion of Korach, and 95 is the numerical value of Daniel the Prophet. We know that the code for Daniel is ך.ת.ה, and when these letters are rearranged they form one of the 72 Names of God—ת.ה.כ, which has the power to break down and transform negativity. The name Daniel is composed of two names, *Din* (Gevurah; Judgment) and *El* (Chesed; Mercy), meaning that within his name and in this portion there is the power to sweeten judgments.

One should never make an attempt to acquire what someone else has. However to acquire at no one else's expense is acceptable. What happened in this section was that Aaron's sacrifice was accepted, and 600,000 Israelites witnessed the spectacle as an earthquake swallowed up only Korach and his followers and no one else. A massive earthquake affected only one area, stopping in its path, when it reached Moses and the Israelites.

The Lightforce of God and Human Dignity

Kabbalah teaches us that God is compassionate and that we should love God. But how can you love something you have never seen? Can you love a child you have never seen? Rav Ashlag teaches that it is impossible to grasp God but that one can comprehend the Lightforce of God. We all experience energies, even though they are immaterial, not tangibly represented in the physical world. We all experience gut feelings. The Lightforce of God is something like electricity—it can be beneficial or disastrous, depending on how we use the energy. The same applies to any force, such as atomic energy, which can be put to a productive purpose or a destructive one—it is up to us. We can use the Zohar to connect to the Lightforce of God and remove chaos from our lives. We can use the energy of the Lightforce of God for positive or negative purposes.

The earthquake in this portion was not a natural disaster. It was the result of chaos. Man creates disasters because of the inhumane way we treat each other. We cannot avoid the chaos we may meet throughout the week if we do not hear the reading of the Torah on Shabbat. Even after the incident of the golden calf we still have the unique opportunity every Shabbat to make a connection and thereby remove chaos. We have the ability to control events. This power was taken away from us because of certain negative actions but now, with this reading, it is restored. Only certain people were killed in the earthquake; it did not affect those who treated others with human dignity. This is a natural law: if you treat others badly it results in chaos.

After this great miracle, the people complained to Moses; you can see many examples of this throughout the Bible. They said, "Why did you kill these people?" But neither Moses nor God killed those people, intolerance did.

Where did the word "nazi" originate? The first time this Hebrew word is used is in the Bible. The Hebrew word *Nun, Alef, Tzadik, Yud* נאצי is used by God to describe those intolerant, insensitive individuals. People seem to have lost the idea of human dignity. The Bible teaches us that there is no good reason to treat others with anything less than human dignity. The Kabbalah Centre maintains that we need to treat everyone this way.

How can we have an understanding of what really took place between Korach, Moses and Aaron? Korach and 250 followers decided to rise up against Moses and Aaron, and accused them of nepotism. Korach challenged Moses because he appointed his brother Aaron as the High Priest, and yet both of them originated in the tribe of Levi and, while Korach was also a Levite, he was left on the sidelines without any honors bestowed upon him. This seems to be the essence of his argument.

The Zohar raises several questions concerning this incident because, according to the Zohar, the literal translation of what transpired is meaningless. Of what interest is it that there was a quarrel among the Israelites in the wilderness some 3,400 years ago? Are we of a different breed, with no arguments among us? Only by reading the Zohar can we achieve a greater awareness of the very same essence that we are discussing here, and raise ourselves to another level of consciousness. Why not take advantage of the material and tools that have been placed before us?

Right and Left Columns

What was really happening with Korach? Why did he rebel? Was Korach a stupid man? The Zohar says, "No." In fact, it describes him as very wealthy, implying his wealth also made him intelligent and capable. He was certainly a respected man in the community, if only because he was extremely wealthy. What then did he want? Furthermore, was he unjustified when he claimed that Moses was unfair in his actions of taking all the power and glory for his immediate family? Was what Korach said so terrible that it warranted an earthquake to come and swallow up 250 people? This was not even a case of rebellion. Korach simply felt that he was entitled to as much as anyone else in the tribe of Levi. Why did he have to suffer this kind of dishonor, and the great misfortune of being swallowed up alive?

What is the essence of Aaron? The Zohar says that Aaron was born a Levite and was considered to be the Chariot of the Sefira of Hod, and Hod represents Left Column, the aspect of negativity in the Lower Triad of the Magen David (Shield of David). The Zohar further says that Aaron was also of the Right Column. How did Aaron become Right Column? When was he given the energy of Right Column?

In this same Zohar section it is discussed that Moses' mother Jochebed saw that "Moses was good." The Zohar asks if this is indeed what the Bible wants to say. What kind of mother would she be if she had said her child was not good? Why does the Bible consider that this kind of exclamation is something of importance? The Zohar says that Jochebed was a prophetess and she could rise above the illusionary reality; she knew the essence of Moses' incarnation, and she saw that he was an incarnation of Abel. Within every individual there is good and bad, and Jochebed saw that Moses was incarnated from the "good" part of Abel. While there was a Desire to Receive on the part of Moses since he did return to the world, nevertheless it was dominated by the positive aspect of sharing and therefore had no dominion.

Korach, on the other hand, says the Zohar, was an incarnation of Cain. So what really took place with Korach? Why was he swallowed up? His complaint seems justifiable—perhaps he should have been entitled to the priesthood. Why should Moses, while it was with the blessing of the Lord, appoint Aaron as the High Priest? Aaron stemmed from the Left Column, as did Korach.

Yet the Zohar says Aaron was Right Column. The Talmud and most of the commentaries on the Bible say that Aaron was an individual who constantly strove to make peace; whether it was between man and wife, two friends or two individuals, peace was his objective. When an individual stems from the positive aspect, which is Chesed, as Aaron did, meaning to create completeness, a wholeness within the universe—because this was his objective—through his effort to achieve peace he was making a connection to the Sefira of Abraham, the aspect of sharing. Therefore, Aaron elevated himself to the Upper Triad, and connected to the Sefira of Chesed and was appointed as High Priest.

If this is the case, what was the problem with Korach? What was his internal motivating thought? The Zohar says it was that he wanted the priesthood. Did his sin lie in his questioning of Moses' dispensation of political offices to members of his own family? Says the Zohar, "Of course not. The question was very valid." Korach was not disputing the fact that Aaron had achieved the level of consciousness of Chesed, the first Sefira of the Seven Sefirot; he was asking why the Priesthood, which indicates blessings, healing, and being a channel for positive energy could not also be channeled through the Left Column, the negative column. In fact, if we are to observe any system of energy on a physical level, it is the negative quality that draws the energy, not the positive one. In a lightbulb, the energy is first drawn through the negative pole but ultimately, energy is dispensed through the positive pole.

Understandably Korach was asking why the Levites, who are in essence the negative aspects of Israel, should not be the channels for drawing down this powerful energy. Although this seems to be a logical question, the Zohar says he was punished because he wanted to change the principles of the universe. Korach asked why there had to be two aspects and why there could not be just one, where everything flows from the negative aspect. It was because of this that the earth opened up and swallowed him. According to the Zohar, we have to delve deeper into the significance of what Korach was attempting here.

For those of us who have at least learned some of the elemental rules of Kabbalah, we know why the world was created. It was created only because of a simple concept called Bread of Shame. In other words, the focal point of Creation, even in the *Ein Sof* (Endless World) originated for only one reason: The Creator wished to share, and He created a Vessel to receive. There was no such thing as Right Column, Left Column or Central Column in the Endless World. There was a Lord who wished to share, yet without a recipient the Lord could not have achieved this aspect of sharing, so the receiver, the aspect of negativity, was created. This was the reason for Creation. However, because of the Bread of Shame, Three Columns came into existence.

This was the concept that Korach was making an attempt to undo. We are now moving away from the idea that this particular section is discussing politics. The Zohar says that Korach spoke *lashon hara* (evil speech) when he accused Moses of taking everything for himself. He could have merely asked about his own concerns: "Why not me?" rather than ask about Moses and speak *lashon hara*.

At this point, again, we must recall that Moses had achieved a level referred to as Da'at, which means a connection between the Sefirot of the Magen David (Chesed, Gevurah, Tiferet, Netzach, Hod, Yesod, and Malchut) and what is referred to as the storehouse of energy—the Upper Three Sefirot: Keter, Chochmah and Binah.

Moses was the chariot for this raw, naked energy. He represented the aspect that things would no longer be as they were in the *Ein Sof* (which was only the aspects of sharing and receiving). With Moses another concept came into existence, a third column. Things were no longer simple as they were in the *Ein Sof*—sharing and receiving. Moses represented the aspect of restriction. Moses represented the essence of why we come to this world, which is to alleviate and remove Bread of Shame. There is no other reason.

Korach, who was also a wise man, understood that the only way he could accomplish his purpose was to undo the Three Column System. He was making an attempt to lead the Israelites into believing that there was nothing more important in this world than receiving. After all, did the Creator not originally intend for the souls of the world to be established as Vessels for capturing energy? Korach's attempt was not only to mislead the nation of Israel but to have them revert back to what the Egyptians believed and practiced. · We have already discussed the power of the Egyptians and the purpose of the Pyramids—in essence, that this world is established on receiving. That we are here to take—there is no other reason for existence.

Korach wanted to accomplish the very same thing that the Pharaoh and the Egyptians aspired to: that this world not work on the principle of an atom, containing three essences but rather only one, the Desire to Receive for Oneself Alone. In other words, Korach did not question the ability of Aaron to be a channel for positive energy. He wanted to know why this world should be based on the principle that all energy ever to become manifested must work through restriction, and then come down through a positive channel. Why not let it come straight through the negative channel, as it is in the *Ein Sof*.

Both the Zohar and Rav Isaac Luria (the Ari) tell us that Korach was an incarnation of Cain, an aspect of negative energy. The Bible states that when God was presented with the two sacrifices of Cain and Abel, Abel brought wool, a sharing energy, while Cain brought linen, a receiving energy—and that God favored Abel. Why? Because God's internal essence is one of sharing and this was in direct conflict with what Cain was presenting—the negative aspect of drawing to oneself alone.

As in the incarnation of Cain, Korach did not want to recognize his proclivity—which, in essence, was his *tikkun*—to overcome that aspect of negativity. He refused to recognize this and therefore he was swallowed up. Could there not have been another form of punishment? These 250 people rebelled but they did not drag down the nation of Israel with them, as the spies did in the previous portion of Shlach Lecha. The spies suffered no consequence other than that they would never enter the land of Israel, yet they created total havoc.

Korach, together with his 250 followers, had a logical disagreement, yet look at the judgment wrought upon Korach by God. The reason for this was because he intended to change the essence of the universe, removing from existence the aspect of the Desire to Receive for the Sake of Sharing, therefore he was swallowed up—removed from existence. The earth is symbolic of gravitation, which draws to itself. The earth swallowed him up because this was the aspect he shared with the earth.

Why is it said that Korach is still screaming? Because perhaps now he realizes he was wrong, and that the reason for our being in this world is the Desire to Receive for the Sake of Sharing, not just for the Sake of Receiving—and this was his *tikkun*.

Protective Shield

Scholars struggle with the idea that Moses pleaded with God not to destroy the entire nation—and God agreed. This dialogue between Moses and God does not make much sense. The Zohar says what we are discussing is not a conversation with God, who has to be corrected by a mortal human being but rather when we discuss punishment it is not God who punishes. We know from the study of Kabbalah that God does not have a single negative characteristic. Where then do we get the idea that God would destroy an entire nation?

What we learn here is that there is a Lightforce out there, and that the Lightforce of God is given to the people and can be directed as they wish, just as an electrical current can be channeled into a refrigerator, air-conditioner, a city or anything else. When the Lightforce of God is being channeled in a negative fashion, the consequences will appear in a negative way, and it can destroy. It is not within the essence of God to destroy. The Lightforce of God that is channeled into our universe brings people energy that can be used in a multitude of ways. What is this idea of destroying an entire nation because of the actions of a few? The answer is in the Zohar. In several places the Zohar asks if all the people in this world are evil. Obviously not. Yet some people are, and because of the actions of these few, the negative energy they have brought prevails throughout the universe to such an extent that we can consider the entire environment hostile.

The Zohar says that when Satan had been given free reign over the entire world, Rav Shimon, who could see the Angel of Death, would tell his students not to linger outside, not literally, but meaning there is nothing that anyone could do to prevent a catastrophe. For instance today innocent children are being afflicted with leukemia in unprecedented numbers—never before have we seen the numbers of people being afflicted with diseases like cancer.

Are all the evil people to be blamed? God directs the show but He does not cause negativity, God channels energy and cannot interfere, despite the fact that the world is engulfed in devastation. This does not mean that the few who are innocent should not have an opportunity to isolate themselves from the destruction that is getting worse and worse. We know we should be in a position to shield ourselves from the chaos that visits mankind every century.

By virtue of Moses and Aaron, something miraculous happened, but it was not a miracle—just as the Splitting of the Red Sea was not a miracle; those who used the technology of the 72 Names could pass through the water. In a similar fashion, what happened here was that an earthquake swallowed up the congregation of Korach. This, too, is concealed. The misinterpretation, which has persisted 3400 years, is that God came down and created an earthquake to swallow up those people, which seems planned because it did not affect anyone else. From this incident we learn a very basic truth: God does not consist of negative energy. When we speak of "acts of God" like hurricanes or earthquakes or people being corroded by radioactive waste—these are not acts of God.

Was the Torah given before or after the story of Korach? The significance is not the timeline, it is that this portion is not about the story of Korach but rather it is the configuration of these words that contain a protective shield against such events as earthquakes. We, in the Center, have witnessed how the wisdom of Kabbalah and the simple presence of the Zohar can prevent and remove earthquakes. We need to be aware we are not just reading a story; there is a shield of protection that we receive from the Zohar, and this is the power we can achieve today to sustain ourselves. The

Torah is the Tree of Life, and when we hold onto it we connect to the Tree of Life.

During the time of the holocaust, there were more Torah Scrolls than exist today. We were told that God knows what he is doing, and we accepted this. Most people will not accept what we are discussing, they believe that we cannot connect to the power that eliminates earthquakes from the reading of the Torah. We are not talking about missiles or bombs, we are talking about a parchment with words and letters. The reason we come to listen to the reading of Korach is because we want to tap into and receive the power to sustain ourselves; we want to be protected against all the dangers lurking in the shadows around us.

We need to know that we will be tested, even after connecting with this reading. We might fall into devastation and then wonder where the energy of the reading has gone. This is where many of us may fail, so we must recognize that what we are experiencing is just an interference to see if we can be distracted from our elevated consciousness.

You receive a report from the doctor that someone has cancer—impossible, you say, I was just at the reading of Korach! You will say the report is wrong, even though it just came from the laboratory. This is how we separate the men from the boys. We do not believe that if an earthquake comes we will be protected from being "swallowed up." Yet if we do not appreciate what we have here, then Satan will be calling tomorrow. The only way to keep the energy we capture from this reading is if we have the consciousness that we are protected from all chaos. This is what we have the Torah for—only Korach and his followers perished, everyone else was saved from the earthquake.

Envy

In this portion we see the contagious disease called envy. What is envy? When you are envious you want something that is not yours. You look at your neighbor and see the profit he has gained, all the good things he has, and you want them. But you want them without putting in the effort, without the process. As a result, you lose what you have as well as what you envied and wanted to possess. This causes sadness, and you feel depressed.

The entire disease of cancer is caused by sadness and envy. Envious people suffer because they are blocked in themselves and do not consider going through the process necessary to obtain what they want. Everyone must go through something to obtain what they want. Nothing is free.

The lesson of this portion is in the opening and closing passages. This portion is about an earthquake, and we are given the capability of preventing such disasters. Obviously, if we tell ourselves we cannot, then it will not happen. Nevertheless we have to understand that, with God's help, if we can direct the universe, this is what will happen.

There are people who say about us and this work, "Don't believe them, they can't stop any earthquakes," and it is those same people who are not giving the Light a chance to enter. They are instilling doubt in people who could be making a difference. If we do not succeed in our efforts, God forbid, then there will be total judgment, God forbid. This is the work and power of Satan in preventing what is beneficent from happening.

The earthquake that swallowed up Korach and his assembly was something supernatural. Moses forewarned them by saying, "And if God has created any creation," which is code for us to understand that this is something new the Creator is doing. The Bible says that an earthquake happened to only 250 people and that Moses was close by yet unharmed. This was the power of the miracle because there was a separation between good and bad. It was not that everyone around was killed indiscriminately, as in an ordinary earthquake.

There are 95 verses in the portion of Korach, which, as we discussed previously, is connected to the name Daniel. The sages could have chosen to divide the weekly portions differently resulting in different numbers of verses. However, the reason they structured the portions the way they did is because each portion gives us what we need for that cosmic time period. The energy force that is revealed in and from this portion is fitting for the word Daniel. Daniel was present at the time of Purim, and together with Mordechai, they brought us the knowledge of the Zohar before the physical Zohar was even revealed. What is the power of Daniel? When the Jews overcame Achashverosh, who reigned in 127 countries, their success did not involve conquering each and every country. When we control the head we rule over everything.

In the month of Cancer (Tammuz), the letters of the Tetragrammaton are reversed to form, *Hei*, *Vav*, *Hei*, and *Yud* ה.ו.ה.י, which is an acronym for a verse found in the Story of Esther: Haman said, "And all of this means nothing to me (וכל] זה איננו שׂוה לי)." In opposition to him, we have Daniel and Mordechai paired with the knowledge of the Zohar for removing negative energy and introducing the energy of Daniel to form a reign of goodness.

Korach was like a cancer in the midst of the nation of Israel. This was the reason for the earthquake; it was to separate 250 people who embodied the nation's cancer, who had no spark of goodness at all in them, only evil. Nonetheless, the Israelites once again complained, accusing Moses of killing Korach's congregation.

In spite of everything they had seen and the phenomenon of the discriminate earthquake, the Israelites again started to disbelieve. This was the same problem regarding Mordechai. At the end of the Story of Esther it is written, "…for *most* of his brethren." It does not say, "…for *all* of his brethren." Even then not everyone went along with him. Those who did go along with Mordechai and Daniel, however, achieved control over evil.

The main problem with Korach was that he felt entitled to everything, and he also wanted to rule. It was not because he wanted to make things better for the children of Israel but simply because he wanted to be in charge in place of Moses. His assembly consisted of 250 people, a very small part of the Israelites. He saw that he did not have many followers and, in contrast, Moses was a good leader for the people; they had a well of water near them at all times. Manna came down for them from Heaven. In seeing that the Israelites were not following Moses, Korach told them, "Come with me and you will be better off."

Similarly, with political leaders, what do they do when they see themselves out of favor with public opinion? They say that you will be better off with me than you would be with the others. This is not how the Light works, though. The Light wants what is good for everyone. Korach did not want what was good for the world. Korach did not come to improve the situation of the Israelites. He simply wanted to be the one at the top because if he really cared about the Israelites, and he did not approve of Moses' leadership, he would have proposed someone more suitable than himself. From this we learn that Korach felt he wanted what someone else had that he was lacking. This was the energy motivating him, not the energy of helping, not the energy of making things better.

Moses knew there would be an earthquake, so he tried to extricate Datan and Aviram so they would not die with Korach. What was their reply? They said, "Even if you promise that despite those giants in the Land of Israel we will still be able to go up to Israel, we will not go with you." They did not care about anything except what happened to themselves. They did not change their position towards external circumstances. These are the people Moses had to work with.

Charity Saves from Death

Concerning the concept of "charity saves from death," if someone is sick in bed and about to die and he gives charity to a truly poor man, this is "charity saves from death." What is a truly poor person? As we know, there are people who collected charity and, when they died, they left behind huge sums of money. How can this be? Such people did not benefit from the money they accumulated, so they are the ones who are truly poor. They never felt worthy of the money they possessed. A truly poor person is not someone who does not have enough to eat because that would not be "charity saves from death." This is the "I deserve it" problem many people have.

Bamidbar 17:1 And the Lord spoke to Moses, saying: 2 "Speak unto Elazar, the son of Aaron the priest, that he take up the fire-pans out of the burning and you scatter the fire yonder; for they have become holy; 3 even the fire-pans of these men who have sinned at the cost of their lives, and let them be made beaten plates for a covering of the altar, for they have become holy, because they were offered before the Lord, so that they may be a sign to the children of Israel." 4 And Elazar the priest took the brazen fire-pans, which they that were burnt had offered; and they beat them out for a covering of the altar, 5 to be a memorial to the children of Israel, to the end that no common man, that is not of the seed of Aaron, draw near to burn incense before the Lord; that he fare not as Korach, and as his company; as the Lord spoke to him by the hand of Moses. 6 But on the morrow all the congregation of the children of Israel complained against Moses and against Aaron, saying: "You have killed the people of the Lord." 7 And it came to pass, when the congregation was assembled against Moses and against Aaron, that they looked toward the Tent of Meeting; and, behold, the cloud covered it, and the glory of the Lord appeared. 8 And Moses and Aaron came to the front of the Tent of Meeting. 9 And the Lord spoke to Moses, saying: 10 "Get you up from among this congregation, that I may consume them in a moment." And they fell upon their faces.

11 And Moses said to Aaron: "Take your fire-pan, and put fire in it from off the altar, and lay incense thereon, and carry it quickly to the congregation, and make atonement for them; for there is wrath gone out from the Lord: the plague has begun." 12 And Aaron took as Moses spoke, and ran into the midst of the assembly; and, behold, the plague had begun among the people; and he put on the incense, and made atonement for the people. 13 And he stood between the dead and the living; and the plague was stopped. 14 Now they that died by the plague were fourteen thousand and seven hundred, besides them that died about the matter of Korach. 15 And Aaron returned to Moses to the door of the Tent of Meeting, and the plague was stopped 16 And the Lord spoke to Moses, saying: 17 "Speak to the children of Israel, and take rods, from each prince according to their fathers' houses, twelve rods; you shall write every man's name upon his rod. 18 And you shall write Aaron's name upon the rod of Levi, for there shall be one rod for the head of their fathers' houses. 19 And you shall lay them up in the Tent of Meeting before the testimony, where I meet with you.

The Complaints of the Israelites

Clearly the Israelites had short memories because after they saw the earth open its mouth and swallow Korach and his assembly, they blamed Moses. They claimed Moses killed the people of God. This reaction is scarcely believable. The assembly of Korach died and the earthquake stopped. Did that not make an impression? It was not that God wanted to get rid of them, rather it was their negative attitude that brought about the earthquake. These people were the very cause of why they should not have been among the living. This section on Korach provides us with a protective shield, however without the help of the Zohar bringing this knowledge into our consciousness we could not tap into its power.

This whole portion is referred to by the name, Korach, and usually portions do not have the names of individuals. Even Moses does not have a portion named after him, yet this disreputable person has a section of his own. This is because Korach is not only a name but a metaphor for the enemy we have the option to create a protection shield against and destroy. This portion is structured so we will see that unless we maintain our consciousness and awareness we will lose our connection as did some Israelites. Immediately after the earthquake, a plague broke out and 14,700 people died in a second. The message of the Bible is that Moses, with the tools of Kabbalah, stopped death right then, and there was no more death. This was the real miracle. The people died in one minute and then in two minutes no one dies.

The portion of Korach is the first spiritual vaccine, and is combined with the treatment of the next four weekly readings, which also contain other vaccines to protect against negativity; all are instruments for our cleansing in preparation for the healing energy of Pinchas.

The Power of Illusion

How could the Israelites blame Moses? Let us remember that we are discussing the Generation of Knowledge (*Dor De'a*), which is the Hebrew expression for the most advanced people in levels of consciousness and intelligence that ever existed. When we live in the physical reality level, it is like two people witnessing the same event and seeing the opposite of what the other saw, and we wonder how this is possible. This is the power of illusion. We, with prideful egos, refuse to accept the possibility that we can succumb to illusion. The Bible is merely demonstrating that the illusion, which is actually referred to as the Satan, has a very strong sway over people.

Here the Bible wants to say that, despite the fact that it happened only the day before, many of the Israelites were under an illusion that Moses was the culprit and therefore responsible, in their consciousness they actually saw the action of Moses as destroying Korach's congregation. These were people who could understand things from a higher level of consciousness. They understood the power of Moses, and the connection of his status, yet they could not prevent this kind of short-circuit. The Bible says that on Mount Sinai these same people saw voices. How does one see voices? Dogs hear on a frequency that humans cannot. A dog can hear something three blocks away, and the average person cannot. These people were able to see at this level, and yet they saw Moses actually being the cause of all that occurred.

The Middle of the Book of Numbers in Verse

Bamidbar 17:19 marks half the number of verses in the book. Half implies the Central Median. "Place it in the Tent of Meeting in front of the Testimony, and I shall encounter you there (*shama*)." The book's halfway point is at the word *shama* "there" שׁמה, which contains the same letters as Moshe משׁה, the power of Moses to combat negativity and also Mem-Hei- Shin מ.ה.שׁ, the 72 Name of God for receiving the power of healing.

20 And it shall come to pass, that the man whom I shall choose, his rod shall bud; and I will rid Myself of the complaints of the children of Israel, which they complain against you." 21 And Moses spoke to the children of Israel; and all their princes gave him rods, one for each prince, according to their fathers' houses, twelve rods; and the rod of Aaron was among their rods. 22 And Moses laid up the rods before the Lord in the Tent of the Testimony. 23 And it came to pass on the next day, Moses went into the Tent of the Testimony; and, behold, the rod of Aaron for the house of Levi was budded, and put forth buds, and bloomed blossoms, and bore ripe almonds. 24 And Moses brought out all the rods from before the Lord to all the children of Israel; and they looked, and every man took his rod. 25 And the Lord said to Moses: "Put back the rod of Aaron before the testimony, to be kept there, for a token against the rebellious children; that there may be made an end of their complaints against Me, that they die not." 26 So Moses did; as the Lord commanded him, so did he. 27 And the children of Israel spoke to Moses, saying: "Behold, we perish, we are undone, we are all undone. 28 Whoever comes near, that comes near to the Tabernacle of the Lord, is to die; shall we utterly perish?"

The Prevention of Negativity

In Bamidbar 17:20, the word *vehashikoti* וְהֲשִׁכּוֹתִי "and I will silence" is similar to the time of Purim, when the Jews discovered the Light and it is written, "…and the king's anger was hushed/quieted (שָׁכְכָה)." This signifies the power to avert the force of chaos.

We must do the Ana Beko'ach prayer daily to prevent negativity from entering our lives. Of all the prayers this is the most important. Rav Shimon writes in Tikunei haZohar that it is even more important than reading Zohar, which brings you understanding and connects you to the power of Ana Beko'ach.

Bamidbar 18:1 And the Lord said to Aaron: "You and your sons and all your fathers' house shall bear the iniquity of the sanctuary with you; and you and your sons with you shall bear the iniquity of your priesthood. 2 And your brethren also—the tribe of Levi, the tribe of your father—bring you near with you, that they may be joined to you, and minister to you, you and your sons with you being before the Tent of the Testimony. 3 And they shall keep your charge, and the charge of all the Tent; only they shall not come near to the holy furniture and to the altar, that they die not, neither they, nor you. 4 And they shall be joined to you, and keep the charge of the Tent of Meeting, whatever the service of the Tent may be; but a common man shall not draw near to you. 5 And you shall keep the charge of the holy things, and the charge of the altar, that there is no more anger upon the children of Israel. 6 Behold, I have taken your brethren, the Levites, from among the children of Israel; for you they are given as a gift to the Lord, to do the service of the Tent of Meeting. 7 And you and your sons with you shall keep your priesthood in everything that pertains to the altar, and to that within the veil; and you shall serve; I give you the priesthood as a service of gift; and the common man that draws near shall be put to death.' 8 And the Lord spoke to Aaron: "Behold, I have given you the charge of My heave offerings; even of all the hallowed things of the children of Israel to you have I given them for a consecrated portion, and to your sons, as a due for ever. 9 This shall be yours of the most holy things, reserved from the fire: every offering of theirs, every grain offering of theirs, and every sin-offering of theirs, and every guilt-offering of theirs, which they may render to Me, shall be most holy for you and for your sons. 10 In a most holy place shall you eat thereof; every male may eat thereof; it shall be holy to thee. 11 And this is yours: the heave-offering of their gift, even all the wave offerings of the children of Israel; I have given them to you, and to your sons and to your daughters with you, as a due for ever; everyone that is clean in your house may eat thereof. 12 All the best of the oil, and all the best of the wine, and of the corn, the first part of them which they give to the Lord, to you I have given them. 13 The first-ripe fruits of all that is in their land, which they bring to the Lord, shall be yours; every one that is clean in your house may eat thereof. 14 Every devoted thing in Israel shall be yours. 15 Everything that opens the womb, of all flesh which they offer to the Lord, both of man and beast, shall be yours; nevertheless the first-born of man you shall surely redeem, and the first-ling of unclean beasts shall you redeem. 16 And from a month old shall you redeem them, and their redemption-money shall be according to your evaluation, five shekels of silver, after the shekel of the Sanctuary—the same is twenty gerahs. 17 But the firstling of an ox, or the firstling of a sheep, or the firstling of a goat, you shall not redeem; they are holy: you shall dash their blood against the altar, and shall make their fat smoke for an offering made by fire, for a sweet savor to the Lord. 18 And the flesh of them shall be yours, as the wave-breast and as the right thigh, it shall be yours. 19 All the heave offerings of the holy things, which the children of Israel offer to the Lord, I have given you, and your sons and your daughters with you, as a due forever; it is an everlasting covenant of salt before the Lord to you and to your seed with you." 20 And the Lord said to Aaron: "You shall have no inheritance in their land, nor shall you have any portion among them; I am your portion and your inheritance among the children of Israel. 21 And to the children of Levi, behold, I have given all the tithe in Israel for an inheritance, in return for their service they serve of the Tent of Meeting. 22 And hereafter the children of Israel shall not come near the Tent of Meeting, lest they bear sin, and die. 23 But the Levites alone shall do the service of the Tent of Meeting, and they shall bear their iniquity; it shall be a statute for ever throughout your generations, and among the children of Israel they shall have no inheritance. 24 For the tithe of the children of Israel, which they set apart as a gift to the Lord, I have given to the Levites for an inheritance; therefore I have said to them: 'Among the children of Israel they shall have no inheritance.'" 25 And the Lord spoke to Moses, saying: 26 "Moreover you shall speak to the Levites, and say to them: When you the tithe take of the children of Israel which I have given you from them for your inheritance, then you shall set apart of it a gift for the Lord, a tithe of the tithe. 27 And the gift which you set apart shall be reckoned to you, as though it were the corn of the threshing-floor, and as the fullness of the wine-press. 28 So you also shall set apart a gift to the Lord of all your tithes, which you receive of the children of Israel; and thereof you shall give the gift which is set apart to the Lord, to Aaron, the priest. 29 Out of all that is given you, you shall set apart all of that which is due to the Lord, of all the best of it, even the hallowed part of out of it. 30 Therefore you shall say to them: When you set apart the best from it, then it shall be counted to the Levites as the produce of the threshing-floor, and as the produce of the wine-press. 31 And you may eat it in every place, you and your households; for it is your reward in return for your service in the Tent of Meeting. 32 And you shall bear no sin by reason of it, seeing that you have set apart from it the best of it; and you shall not profane the holy things of the children of Israel, lest you die."

Conclusion

Korach was a relative of Aaron, Miriam, and Moses. He was a powerful man, and as a result was able to gather 250 people to confront Moses. These were very reputable, credible people; the Bible goes to great lengths to show us who these people were. They assembled and essentially said to Moses: "Do you think you are holy? We are all holy, God is within all of us, so why do you consider yourself above us?"

God told Moses to separate the entire nation, to move them away from the 250 people who were with Korach or else they would be swallowed up. As promised, the earth opened up and swallowed Korach's people, and from this incident emerged a plague and many people died. What does scripture want to teach us here? Why did Moses not share the honor that was bestowed upon the leaders of the priestly family? Here we learn what the Zohar brings us: All people die because of evil eye; cancer, heart attacks, accidents, all the different categories of the way people die are not the cause. The one cause of death is the evil eye.

The first evil eye, strangely enough, occurs in Beresheet. The Zohar explains that death came about because the snake was envious of Adam and jealous because he could not take Eve as his wife. Remember this was a snake that could stand up and speak. The Zohar goes on to say that the evil eye is so destructive because it does not always mean we wish our enemy evil, which is only one aspect. The reason evil eye is so harsh—and I am not only talking about just for the perpetrator—is because it is very destructive. Whenever we think, even without realizing it, that someone has something we should have, this too is evil eye.

To wish ill upon another is not the only methodology of evil, there are others. The single event of the serpent in the Garden of Eden was so severe because, as the Zohar explains, when someone steals, they at least benefit. But when someone has the evil eye—and this could be, for example, when one family member has what another does not, the individual is energetically drained for what they have.

This is the power of the evil eye. It is like a laser beam focusing in on something, it is so strong it can cause a fire. It brings the force of Chochmah on that level. This is why it is so destructive, and a person can even die under certain circumstances.

What did Korach want? A little recognition? Under the circumstances, was that so bad? With the evil eye, there is an opening and someone is able to drain the energy of the other person, yet the perpetrator does not receive that energy. With a relative, does one want to see the other lose? Not necessarily, they just want the same blessings.

We cannot look around ourselves and want what someone else has. It is only by comparison that we consider we lack this or that. The Zohar states that the evil eye is so damaging that, not only did Korach not get what he sought, he lost all that he had. Most misfortune, one way or another, has to do with our eye. With this portion we can at least receive this immunization. The portion of Korach is here to teach us this so that we do not fall into the trap of the serpent, so we do not look outside instead of within, and we prepare our Vessel to receive everything from our own efforts. Preparing our Vessel is far more difficult than we think and it can only come by working through our difficulties.

We need to be aware that thinking our lack can be fulfilled by looking at what someone else has is Satan's primary weapon. It is so subtle, it takes a long time to even develop the acuity to be aware of it. The thing you desire may not be part of your paradigm in life. When something does not come to us, it is because we have not built up our Vessel to receive it. We must remember that if we are missing something we want or lack, it is not because someone else has taken something away from us. The Zohar says that Korach wanted the benefits Moses had, even when Moses would have been willing to give them away.

The Zohar speaks about the idea of why, when, and how earthquakes occur. But leaving that for a moment, what is discussed here is the phenomenon of how the earthquake was confined to just to those 250 people. Although the entire congregation of the children of Israel was also present, no one was affected except Korach and his assembly, indicating that, according to the Bible, it is possible to contain earthquakes. Some scientists suggest that animals can hear and can sense seismic activities that precede earthquakes. But, by and large, when an earthquake strikes, God forbid, it comes without warning. Modern science does not yet possess the answer as to how we can prevent or confine earthquakes.

This particular portion of Korach should be scanned each week to help protect us from natural disasters. This is one of the surest methods by which we can, if not contain an earthquake, at least become a survivor, and most probably protect our immediate environment.

I gave a lecture some time ago on earthquakes and their full ramifications, as well as how it fits in so clearly with what is written in the Zohar. I, for one, certainly do not subscribe to the idea that it is God's intention to punish us because if you look at the development of civilization, it has always been under the influence of some kind of natural disaster, whether it be a tsunami, earthquake, tornado or forest fire.

Therefore, keeping in mind that what is necessary in the prevention or confinement of earthquakes is, initially a realization that we have caused the earthquake in the first place and, secondly that those who might have been involved in the cause of an earthquake have, nevertheless, at any given time had the opportunity to remove themselves from this cause and effect because it is not a decree of God to punish people. On the contrary, the earthquake follows the rule of this universe, which is cause and effect.

If we have infused negativity within this confine, let us say the coast of California, there must be a reason. To assume that because there are faults along this line, earthquakes occur here more often than in any other area, is incorrect. The first question we must ask is: Why are there more fault lines here than elsewhere? The Zohar says it is because mankind has not yet learned the idea of unity, of *Shalom*, and thus there are disagreements, separation, and fragmentation.

The only solution for this situation is if everyone begins to realize that by and of themselves there should be diversity and difference. It is about inter-connectedness, just as in the positive and negative poles of a lightbulb, opposing forces must be brought together for the Light to shine.

As mentioned previously, the Continents of the world are divided into seven distinct parts, and the world rests on seven major tectonic plates, which the Zohar explains are the seven Sefirot. The reason there are seven is because each one represents a specific Sefira, another form of energy. Earthquakes do not appear only in California, they occur throughout the world because there are fault lines everywhere.

Then we have to raise the question: Why are certain people drawn to an area where there are fault lines? The San Andreas Fault, which runs through Los Angeles down into Palm Springs, is no secret, and yet people find it difficult to leave, despite the assurance from researchers that the major quake is looming.

How do they know this cataclysm will soon be here? On what basis? There is so much speculation about whether or not it will occur. Nevertheless why do people still inhabit this region? Is it sheer folly to ignore scientific evidence? We are talking about our own lives. Why would we take the chance? The answer is that people are drawn to this area. The Zohar and Rav Isaac Luria (the Ari) explain that as reincarnated individuals, we find the proper location where our *tikkun* can be accomplished.

Most of us think that those who were not born in Europe during World War II—and did not suffer the consequences of a concentration camp—were lucky, while those who were born in that place and time were unlucky. This is, again, a conclusion people come to. We have to assume that some were just lucky in being born elsewhere. From a kabbalistic point of view, the idea of lucky and unlucky simply does not apply. The idea of luck suggests that this world was established in a haphazard manner and is beyond our control, indicating that there are no laws that specifically apply to this universe. The Zohar, of course, is not of that opinion. The Zohar says the reason evil originates in such a manner in a certain area, and not elsewhere, is again primarily due to mankind's negative activity in that specific area.

This portion would have us believe that the saying "divide and conquer" comes from the Israelites. We read it right here in Korach; this is what he was trying to do. He was upset that Moses had appointed his brother, Aaron, to be the High Priest. He wanted the position to flatter his ego not to help the nation of Israel. This is why Korach was not remembered for anything else. Korach's argument was that Moses should give to everyone the opportunity to participate in the glory of leadership. Moses answered that the only way we can find out who should be the High Priest is to prepare an offering and see what is accepted by God. We know what happened as a result—Korach and his followers were swallowed up by the earth. If we do not contribute and make this world better than how we found it, our life is not worth a thing, and the punishment is that no one will remember our name.

We always have to remind ourselves why we listen to the Torah reading on Shabbat. It is certainly not to hear the historical sequence of events that took place in the wilderness some 3,400 years ago. It is so we can connect during the Torah reading and overcome the Korach, this selfish energy within ourselves.

Some people think that because they share, it makes them righteous but it is not true. We have to be so careful not to commit any negative actions because the entire residue of all our negativity will have to be removed at some point. We want to take every measure possible to avoid adding to the chaos, since any negative action creates a further impediment to the removal of chaos from this world. Therefore, Korach is us and if we want to prevent evil, we must not behave like him.

God told Moses to separate from those people because He was going to destroy them. The earth opened up its mouth just where the assembly of Korach was standing, and everyone else remained untouched. From this it is obvious that we can prevent earthquakes or we can cause them. Earthquakes are not acts of God but rather a result of human negativity.

There are only 95 verses in this portion, and the number 95 refers to Daniel the prophet. The Book of Daniel is almost in its entirety written in Aramaic, providing us with the ultimate redemption from chaos and transformation from the Tree of Knowledge to the Tree of Life. We study Kabbalah and listen to the reading of the Torah on Shabbat to eliminate the causes of chaos in our own lives. When we think of earthquakes, we also have a hard time imagining any possible preventive measures. The problem is that we tend to cling to our ego and to people who have chaos in their lives. It is very common that we speak one way, act another, and feel yet another way; and the excuse is that everyone does it. If we do something negative how often do we justify it by saying that everyone does it?

It is important to know the inner meaning of what we are reading. It is next to impossible for us to remove chaos from our lives, which is why we come to learn the wisdom of Kabbalah, attend Shabbat, and scan the Zohar for support. It is imperative to allow the energy to flow and to comprehend what is truly going on. We do not sit in the Kabbalah Centre War Rooms because it is required but because it is the way to remove chaos from our lives.

The reason the Centre does not involve itself in politics is that, while we may personally have an opinion, the Centre, as a body, cannot participate in separation. As we know, in quantum physics everything is interrelated, the universe is one, a whole. We have to think of everything as one unified whole. Korach was into separation. He was against Creation itself because Creation is one. When you separate yourself, you disconnect. We must think that way always. We are all one. We are all part of the same whole.

The portion of Korach is connected to the idea of earthquakes. An earthquake is when the land is divided into two, it kills one person on one side and a foot away another person is saved. What a marvel. The portion of Korach gives us the ability to prevent earthquakes and all other natural disasters. Moses had the ability to prevent natural disasters from creating chaos. We have the power to control the physical reality. One key is the power of certainty. Some people have certainty they cannot control the physical reality; we have the certainty we can.

This portion contains the idea that anytime we come upon something that requires us to act, we should do it with all the strength we have. This does not mean physical strength. King Solomon was so wise and said: "Everything that comes to your hand, do it with all your strength." What is wisdom? How do we arrive at it with all our strength? People usually do not do things with all their power. In the case of an earthquake, this can be stopped by making the correct connections and having the correct consciousness. How? With our minds. We are born with an instinct for self-preservation. Is it for ourselves or for the other people of the world who have not had the merit to come to Kabbalah? The Zohar asks: "Who is truly wise?" It answers that those who are concerned about doing for others are wise.

About the Centres

Kabbalah is the deepest and most hidden meaning of the Torah or Bible. Through the ultimate knowledge and mystical practices of Kabbalah, one can reach the highest spiritual levels attainable. Although many people rely on belief, faith, and dogmas in pursuing the meaning of life, kabbalists seek a spiritual connection with the Creator and the forces of the Creator, so that the strange becomes familiar, and faith becomes knowledge.

Throughout history, those who knew and practiced the Kabbalah were extremely careful in their dissemination of the knowledge because they knew the masses of mankind had not yet prepared for the ultimate truth of existence. Today, kabbalists know that it is not only proper but necessary to make the Kabbalah available to all who seek it.

The Research Centre of Kabbalah is an independent, non-profit institute founded in Israel in 1922. The Centre provides research, information, and assistance to those who seek the insights of Kabbalah. The Centre offers public lectures, classes, seminars, and excursions to mystical sites at branches in Israel and in the United States. Branches have been opened in Mexico, Montreal, Toronto, Paris, Hong Kong, and Taiwan.

Our courses and materials deal with the Zoharic understanding of each weekly portion of the Torah. Every facet of life is covered and other dimensions, hithertofore unknown, provide a deeper connection to a superior reality. Three important beginner courses cover such aspects as: Time, Space and Motion; Reincarnation, Marriage, Divorce; Kabbalistic Meditation; Limitation of the Five Senses; Illusion-Reality; Four Phases; Male and Female, Death, Sleep, Dreams; Food; and Shabbat.

Thousands of people have benefited from the Centre's activities, and the Centre's publishing of kabbalistic material continues to be the most comprehensive of its kind in the world, including translations in English, Hebrew, Russian, German, Portuguese, French, Spanish, Farsi (Persian).

Kabbalah can provide one with the true meaning of their being and the knowledge necessary for their ultimate benefit. It can show one spirituality that is beyond belief. The Research Centre of Kabbalah will continue to make available the Kabbalah to all those who seek it.

— Rav Berg, 1984

About The Zohar

The Zohar, the basic source of the Kabbalah, was authored two thousand years ago by Rabbi Shimon bar Yochai while hiding from the Romans in a cave in Peki'in for 13 years. It was later brought to light by Rabbi Moses de Leon in Spain, and further revealed through the Safed Kabbalists and the Lurianic system of Kabbalah.

The programs of the Research Centre of Kabbalah have been established to provide opportunities for learning, teaching, research, and demonstration of specialized knowledge drawn from the ageless wisdom of the Zohar and the Jewish sages. Long kept from the masses, today this knowledge of the Zohar and Kabbalah should be shared by all who seek to understand the deeper meaning of this spiritual heritage, and a deeper and more profound meaning of life. Modern science is only beginning to discover what our sages veiled in symbolism. This knowledge is of a very practical nature and can be applied daily for the betterment of our lives and of humankind.

Darkness cannot prevail in the presence of Light. Even a darkened room must respond to the lighting of a candle. As we share this moment together we are beginning to witness, and indeed some of us are already participating in, a people's revolution of enlightenment. The darkened clouds of strife and conflict will make their presence felt only as long as the Eternal Light remains concealed.

The Zohar now remains an ultimate, if not the only, solution to infusing the cosmos with the revealed Lightforce of the Creator. The Zohar is not a book about religion. Rather, the Zohar is concerned with the relationship between the unseen forces of the cosmos, the Lightforce, and the impact on humanity.

The Zohar promises that with the ushering in of the Age of Aquarius, the cosmos will become readily accessible to human understanding. It states that in the days of the Messiah "there will no longer be the necessity for one to request of his neighbor, teach me wisdom." (Zohar, Naso 9:65) "One day, they will no longer teach every man his neighbor and every man his brother, saying know the Lord. For they shall all know Me, from the youngest to the oldest of them." (Jeremiah 31:34)

We can, and must, regain dominion of our lives and environment. To achieve this objective, the Zohar provides us with an opportunity to transcend the crushing weight of universal negativity.

The daily perusing of the Zohar, without any attempt at translation or understanding will fill our consciousness with the Light, improving our well-being, and influencing all in our environment toward positive attitudes. Even the scanning of the Zohar by those unfamiliar with the Hebrew *Alef Bet* will accomplish the same result.

The connection that we establish through scanning the Zohar is one of unity with the Light of the Creator. The letters, even if we do not consciously know Hebrew or Aramaic, are the channels through which the connection is made and can be likened to dialing the right telephone number or typing in the right codes to run a computer program. The connection is established at the metaphysical level of our being and radiates into our physical plane of existence. But first there is the prerequisite of metaphysical "fixing." We have to consciously, through positive thought and actions, permit the immense power of the Zohar to radiate love, harmony, and peace into our lives for us to share with all humanity and the universe.

As we enter the years ahead, the Zohar will continue to be a people's book, striking a sympathetic chord in the hearts and minds of those who long for peace, truth, and relief from suffering. In the face of crises and catastrophe, the Zohar has the ability to resolve agonizing human afflictions by restoring each individual's relationship with the Lightforce of the Creator.

— Rav Berg, 1984

Kabbalah Centre Books

72 Names of God, The: Technology for the Soul
72 Names of God for Kids, The: A Treasury of Timeless Wisdom
72 Names of God Meditation Book, The
And You Shall Choose Life: An Essay on Kabbalah, the Purpose of Life, and
    Our True Spiritual Work
AstrologiK: Kabbalistic Astrology Guide for Children
Becoming Like God: Kabbalah and Our Ultimate Destiny
Beloved of My Soul: Letters of Our Master and Teacher Rav Yehuda Tzvi Brandwein
    to His Beloved Student Kabbalist Rav Berg
Consciousness and the Cosmos (previously Star Connection)
Days of Connection: A Guide to Kabbalah's Holidays and New Moons
Days of Power Part 1
Days of Power Part 2
Dialing God: Daily Connection Book
Education of a Kabbalist
Energy of the Hebrew Letters, The (previously Power of the Aleph Beth Vols.
    1 and 2)
Fear is Not an Option
Finding the Light Through the Darkness: Inspirational Lessons Rooted in the
    Bible and the Zohar
God Wears Lipstick: Kabbalah for Women
Holy Grail, The: A Manifesto on the Zohar
If You Don't Like Your Life, Change It!: Using Kabbalah to Rewrite the Movie of
    Your Life
Immortality: The Inevitability of Eternal Life
Kabbalah Connection, The: Preparing the Soul For Pesach
Kabbalah for the Layman
Kabbalah Method, The: The Bridge Between Science and the Soul, Physics and
    Fulfillment, Quantum and the Creator
Kabbalah on the Sabbath: Elevating Our Soul to the Light
Kabbalah: The Power To Change Everything
Kabbalistic Astrology: And the Meaning of Our Lives
Kabbalistic Bible: Genesis
Kabbalistic Bible: Exodus
Kabbalistic Bible: Leviticus
Kabbalistic Bible: Numbers
Kabbalistic Bible: Deuteronomy
Light of Wisdom: On Wisdom, Life, and Eternity
Miracles, Mysteries, and Prayer Volume 1
Miracles, Mysteries, and Prayer Volume 2
Nano: Technology of Mind over Matter

Navigating The Universe: A Roadmap for Understanding the Cosmic Influences that Shape Our Lives (previously Time Zones)

On World Peace: Two Essays by the Holy Kabbalist Rav Yehuda Ashlag

Path to the Light: Decoding the Bible with Kabbalah: Book of Beresheet Volume 1

Path to the Light: Decoding the Bible with Kabbalah: Book of Beresheet Volume 2

Path to the Light: Decoding the Bible with Kabbalah: Book of Beresheet Volume 3

Path to the Light: Decoding the Bible with Kabbalah: Book of Beresheet Volume 4

Path to the Light: Decoding the Bible with Kabbalah: Book of Shemot Volume 5

Path to the Light: Decoding the Bible with Kabbalah: Book of Shemot Volume 6

Prayer of the Kabbalist, The: The 42-Letter Name of God

Power of Kabbalah, The: 13 Principles to Overcome Challenges and Achieve Fulfillment

Rebooting: Defeating Depression with the Power of Kabbalah

Rethink Love: 3 Steps to Being the One, Attracting the One, and Becoming One

Satan: An Autobiography

Secret, The: Unlocking the Source of Joy & Fulfillment

Secrets of the Bible: Teachings from Kabbalistic Masters

Secrets of the Zohar: Stories and Meditations to Awaken the Heart

Simple Light: Wisdom from a Woman's Heart

Shabbat Connections

Taming Chaos: Harnessing the Secret Codes of the Universe to Make Sense of Our Lives

Thought of Creation, The: On the Individual, Humanity, and Their Ultimate Perfection

To Be Continued: Reincarnation & the Purpose of Our Lives

To the Power of One

True Prosperity: How to Have Everything

Two Unlikely People to Change the World: A Memoir by Karen Berg

Vokabbalahry: Words of Wisdom for Kids to Live By

Way Of The Kabbalist, The: A User's Guide to Technology for the Soul

Well of Life: Kabbalistic Wisdom from a Depth of Knowledge

Wheels of a Soul: Kabbalah and Reincarnation

Wisdom of Truth, The: 12 Essays by the Holy Kabbalist Rav Yehuda Ashlag

Zohar, The

BOOKS AVAILABLE AT
WWW.KABBALAH.COM/STORE
AND KABBALAH CENTRES AROUND THE WORLD

With an immense amount of gratitude for
the Rav and Karen

May this book be a blessing by shining Light to all corners of the world
inspiring all souls to treat each other as they would themselves
and encircling the planet in pure love and abundance.